Real Life
Real Death

I didn't mind the doctors not working on him. I had done my best. They were just being realistic. Maybe, just maybe, with a little luck, they could save his friend.

If this had been the movies we would have saved the patient, but this was real. Most of the really tough cases end with death. You spend a lot of time on losing causes. You don't usually worry about it—it's part of the job. Once in a great while you make a difference and save a life. It doesn't happen often, but when it does there's nothing like it.

I didn't know anything about them. Just two young black males, probably drunk or high, who went too fast on the highway. I would never even bother to ask about the one ejected from the car, whether he lived or died.

I had done my job, used my skills, won a race, and had my adrenaline fix for the night. It was enough.

PARAMEDIC

THE TRUE STORY OF A
NEW YORK PARAMEDIC'S
BATTLES WITH LIFE AND DEATH

BY PAUL D. SHAPIRO
WITH MARY B. SHAPIRO

BANTAM BOOKS
New York · Toronto · London · Sydney · Auckland

PARAMEDIC

A Bantam Nonfiction Book / December 1991

ISBN 0-553-29383-4

Published simultaneously in the United States and Canada

PRINTED IN THE UNITED STATES OF AMERICA

RAD   0 9 8 7 6 5 4 3 2 1

This book is dedicated to my partners,
who made the job worth doing. Thanks.

This book would not have been written without Ed and Suzy's misguided encouragement. Or without Joan and Theron Raines' very real support. And we'd like to thank our editor, Tom Dyja.

PARAMEDIC

INTRODUCTION

We were parked on Forty-sixth Street and Broadway. It was three-thirty A.M. on an achingly slow night. The city was dead quiet, and my partner, a fairly new medic, was half dozing in the passenger seat. I was hoping for some action, listening carefully to the radios, ready to jump on any good calls.

A basic life support ambulance was assigned to a report of a motor vehicle accident on the West Side Highway by Eighty-sixth Street. The medic unit that covered that area had a reputation, depending on who was on duty, for never volunteering for calls. It wasn't unusual for me to jump on a good call in the middle of their area, but an MVA didn't sound juicy enough for me to go out of my way.

Then the call was upgraded to a possible overturn, off the highway. That could be interesting. I switched off the FM station I had on for background music and

changed frequencies on the police radio. I tapped my
partner awake and told him about the job.

"Thirteen Willie," I called into the Emergency
Medical Service radio, identifying my unit, "do you
need medics on the West Side Highway job?"

The Emergency Medical technician at the scene
responded through the static, his voice cracking: "Uh,
we've got one patient trapped and pinned inside the
car, in critical condition, and another ejected from the
car, also in critical condition. *Medics would be nice.*"

"Thirteen Willie on the way!" I announced, flipping on the lights and siren and starting toward the
highway.

Then another voice came on the radio. "Sixteen
X-ray, we're on the highway heading south. We'll take
that job."

"Those fuckers! They're trying to steal our call!" I
shouted. I tossed the EMS radio to my partner and
floored the accelerator. Only a few moments earlier I
had heard Sixteen X-ray inform the dispatcher they
were just coming out of Metropolitan Hospital. They
might have held their signal—departed earlier from
the hospital without informing the dispatcher that
they were available again—but I suspected they were
lying, claiming to be closer to the scene to steal the
call from us. I pushed the diesel engine as hard as it
would go. Traffic was nonexistent and we flew through
the city.

My partner shouted into the radio, over the wail of
the siren, "Thirteen Willie, we're already on the
highway heading north." He was lying. "We'll be
there before X-ray." We grinned wildly at each other,
glad that we were on the same wavelength. There are
some medics out there who aren't trauma junkies, and

they're not much fun to work with. This guy was still a rookie, but he had a good attitude.

The challenge had been made; the race was on. No way were we going to let X-ray steal our call, even if it really wasn't ours. It sounded like there would be enough work for all of us, but the first medic unit there would have scene command, could choose which patient they wanted, would have the most fun. Yes, fun. You don't get calls this serious every day, and you get awfully sick of sitting around waiting for them.

By the time the dispatcher acknowledged our transmission I was approaching the on-ramp to the highway. Twenty-fourth Precinct cops on the scene were squawking messages over the police radio to the Emergency Service officers, who were also responding. The Highway Patrol was notified, as they are in all cases when a crash may result in death.

I saw the crash from a distance. There were already several emergency vehicles there—a few police cars, including an Emergency Services vehicle, and the basic life support ambulance—all with flashing lights. I could see Sixteen X-ray coming south on the highway. They were, technically, closer to the scene, but I knew we had them beat. The crash had occurred on the northbound side; X-ray had to go several blocks farther south to the Seventy-ninth Street Boat Basin circle to turn around. My partner and I crowed and waved as we sped past them at Eighty-second Street.

A small victory, but we loved it. The joy was quickly pushed aside, though, to be relived and appreciated later. Right now, we had a job to do. I did a quick survey of the situation as Sixteen X-ray pulled up. The young black male who had been thrown from the vehicle was in serious condition, not likely to survive. We helped the Sixteen X-ray crew and the EMTs get this guy immobilized and into the antishock pants while the cops worked on cutting the car open. Sixteen X-ray headed to St. Luke's Hospital with their patient; we waited helplessly for ours to be liberated.

His body was twisted like a pretzel and he was literally bent in half, upside down with his head thrust between his legs. He had massive internal injuries. The smashed pieces of metal and steel that used to be his car had compressed around him like a folded-up accordion. He was pushed up against what might have been the rear roof support, but it was dark and hard to tell exactly what was what. Parts of the car had been sheared away from the frame when the car slammed against the tree. He was going to die. If we got him out of the car, he'd die on us; if not, he'd die in the car. If, by some miracle, he actually made it to the hospital "alive," he'd die there.

I got close enough to look at his face, and was amazed to find him conscious. His eyes were open. He was trying to talk, but he couldn't produce any recognizable words. For a chaotic situation like this it was surprisingly quiet, almost surreal, like watching a horror movie with the sound off.

When enough of the twisted wreckage had been cut away, we could finally remove the victim by pulling him out on the long backboard we had placed under him. I was holding onto his head, trying to protect his neck from further damage. Unfolding the patient's body, although necessary to protect his spine and control his airway, allowed his internal injuries to bleed uncontrollably. He took a breath, then had a small seizure and died.

We inserted a small airway into his mouth to help us breathe for him, started CPR, and applied anti-shock trousers. We completed the immobilization and moved him to our backup's bus—no reason to get ours all messed up. My partner took our ambulance and went ahead to clear our way to the hospital.

Blood began to ooze from the patient's mouth and nose. It didn't spurt or flow; just sort of bubbled up. As we pulled out I attempted to start an intravenous line, though it was probably futile. The few hundred cc's of fluid I could possibly infuse in the five minutes to the hospital would be a drop in the bucket compared to the thousands of cc's of blood that this man had lost internally. My first two attempts were unsuccessful. I thought for a second about not trying for a third, but I went on. The IV needles that had not found veins were dangling from his left arm as I searched for a site on his right. My third stick found a suitable vein, and the IV fluid began to flow into his lifeless body. With every chest compression more blood, and now vomitus, came out of his mouth. Effective suctioning was difficult in the moving vehicle, and a great quantity of his insides were soon on the outside—some on us, but most of it making the floor of the ambulance a slippery mess.

The EMT with me in the back of the bus shook his head. "This guy's dead, don't you think?"

"Yeah, I think so," I said, and continued to work.

Trauma teams were standing by at St. Luke's Hospital and hustled us into trauma slot 1. Our patient's driving companion was in slot 2. As I was reporting our patient's condition prior to extrication and what had happened since, the hospital staff took over CPR and moved him to their stretcher. When I finished, the head surgeon had a brief conference with his staff and decided not to initiate further resuscitation. Their efforts would better serve the patient who was still alive in slot 2.

Our patient was declared dead—no surprise to us. We knew it before his body did, when he was still in the car. In those few minutes, his heart was beating, his lungs still attempting to move air in and out, but it was just a matter of time.

I didn't mind the doctors not working on him. I had done my best. They were just being realistic. Maybe, just maybe, with a little luck, they could save his friend.

If this had been the movies, we would have saved the patient, but this was real. Most of the really tough cases end with death. You spend a lot of time on losing causes. You don't usually worry about it—it's part of the job. Once in a great while you make a difference and save a life. It doesn't happen often, but when it does, there's nothing like it.

I didn't know anything about them. Just two young black males, probably drunk or high, who went too fast on the highway. I would never even bother to ask about the one ejected from the car, whether he lived or died.

I had done my job, used my skills, won a race, and had my adrenaline fix for the night. It was enough.

CHAPTER 1

People always ask how and why I became a paramedic, it not being a common ambition for an upper-middle-class white kid in New York City. My parents blame it on the *Policeman Paul* book I had as a kid or on my watching too many episodes of *Emergency!* But I don't think there's any one reason. It either gets into your blood or it doesn't. As a kid, I never dreamed of being a paramedic. I got sucked into it as a college student. My parents hoped I'd grow out of it, but here I am, pushing thirty and still hooked.

I had no interest in emergency medicine until I finished my first year of college and worked as a security officer in Saltaire, a sleepy summer community on Fire Island where my family has a house. It seemed like a good way to pick up a few bucks while spending the summer at the beach. It wasn't a very serious job—no gun, no sticks, no mace or handcuffs. Just a uniform, a radio, a flashlight, and a summons book to write tickets for offenses such as incorrect garbage disposal or bicycle riding after dark. Basically, you were just supposed to stay awake and call for help if anything happened.

I was "on dock watch," which required me to spend hours on end doing nothing but literally watching the dock, bored out of my mind, when a call came over the radio.

"Saltaire Two to all Saltaire units: Has anybody seen Susie Block?" It was a small enough community that you knew almost everybody by name, even the kids you hardly ever talked to.

"Negative," I replied. "I haven't seen her." The other security officer answered the same way.

"The family reported her missing. She was expected home from a party a few hours ago."

I knew from my own experience that teenagers went to a particular stretch of beach to party because it was outside the village's jurisdiction and the Suffolk County police have better things to do than worry about minors drinking or smoking pot. Another pseudocop and I found the girl there with another fourteen-year-old. They had drunk themselves into unconsciousness, were barely breathing, and beginning to choke on their own vomit. I was terrified. I had had some basic first aid training in high school and a cardiopulmonary resuscitation (CPR) class, but I didn't have a clue about what to do.

This wasn't supposed to happen. This was supposed to be a joke of a job in a staid summer place where nothing much ever went on. I wasn't a real cop, for God's sake. I was a photographer! I had a darkroom at home; I was photo editor of my high school yearbook; I was studying photography at the University of Michigan Art School . . . What the hell did I know about saving lives?

I radioed for help as we turned the girls over. I seemed to remember from somewhere that their mouths should be cleaned out to let them breathe, so we did that. And then we waited and waited and waited.

It took about six minutes for the ambulance to arrive, but it felt like hours. For them, this was a simple case. They knew what to do and they did it quickly. I decided right then and there to get some training. I never wanted to feel so helpless again.

The following summer, I went back to the Saltaire security job, but instead of spending my free time on the beach or at the ball field, I would head back into New York City to attend a class to become an Emergency Medical Technician (EMT). Every Monday and Wednesday night, all summer long, I went to City College on 135th Street to learn the Basic Life Support (BLS) skills: CPR, splinting, bleeding control, oxygen administration, delivering babies, etc. Instead of working five steady night tours for Saltaire security, I would do a double shift Sunday night and Monday morning. I'd get off at two P.M., race home, change and catch the two-ten boat off the island, hop on the Long Island Railroad, run home, have a bite to eat, and drive up to Harlem for the class.

It was hectic. I started to wonder how much I could learn this way. By the end of Monday's session, I was toast. All I did Tuesday was sleep. It was a real pain in the ass, but it was probably good training for some of the weird schedules I'd end up working later on when I would bounce around from one shift to another.

The two instructors, Dick and Don, were great, but they were wasted on much of the class. Out of thirty students, only four or five of us were competent. A half dozen who seemed to have trouble reading flunked out, and a dozen more could have been flunked. We spent most of the time going over and over the same basic stuff, trying to hammer it into some of the thicker skulls. Still, I loved it all.

I also joined the Saltaire Volunteer Fire Department that summer, which meant that I had hardly any time to myself. Every Sunday morning for two months I sat through the basic fire fighter class. The Suffolk County Fire Academy sent out an instructor each week. I was very interested in the material, but the presentation was pretty dry. Ropes and ladders; extinguishers and hoses; pumps and hydraulics; salvage and overhaul; search and rescue; self-contained breathing apparatus.

I quickly got tired of talking about hypothetical fires. By the time we took the final exam, I was itching for some real hands-on experience, something to make the summer worthwhile. I got more than I had bargained for in the final phase of the training.

"Now remember," the instructor, one of the deputy chiefs at the Yaphank Fire Academy, told us, "the fire will be lit in the other room. It will get hot. Really start to cook. You'll see the smoke hit the ceiling and begin banking down the walls."

Most of us first-timers to the training center shifted nervously from boot to boot. We had all completed the fire class taught out of the book. I had scored well on the exam. But now I was standing inside the Class A building, a concrete and cinder block structure, and these pyromaniac instructors were lighting a huge fire in a room adjacent to us. The instructor's assistant was putting a torch to scores of two-by-four boards and skids coated in gasoline.

I double- and triple-checked my equipment: boots all the way up, turn-out coat buttoned and snapped, helmet fitting snugly, gloves. Okay. It was starting to get hot. Really hot.

"Remember to get low," reminded the instructor, who was still standing upright. His old helmet was caked with soot and ash. The leather had even started to buckle and crack apart. Only half of the word Deputy was still visible.

The fire was fully involved now, and the smoke was getting thick. Beneath my glasses, my eyes were starting to water, and I couldn't see the ceiling anymore, but the red glow of the flames illuminated the rest of the room. The smoke was banking down, getting lower and lower, starting to push us closer and closer to the floor.

Soon I was on my knees and still trying to get lower. The only breathable air was on the ground. All the people in the room were hugging the floor. Even our instructor was getting close to the ground.

"Everyone listen up!" the instructor demanded. "Everyone take one of your gloves off and *slowly* raise your hand over your head." I did as I was told, but I couldn't raise my hand more than a foot or two. The heat was too intense.

The reassuring voice of the deputy chief filled the room. "If you stand up it will really ruin your day."

He wasn't kidding. I thought of the ramifications: severe burns, massive internal injuries, respiratory failure, instant death. I thought I'd stay right there, prone on the floor, thank you very much.

"Okay," the instructor's voice rang out, "now I'll show you what happens if someone should accidentally attack this fire from the wrong direction."

Bad news. In a structure fire such as this one, you would always attack the fire and push it away from the rescuers inside the building. He was going to demonstrate what happens when a hose line hits the fire with water, pushing the extremely hot smoke and steam over us.

"Okay, Bob. Hit it," he shouted.

The room was suddenly dark and hot. I couldn't see. I couldn't breathe. My eyes burned and I felt the mucus running out of my nose.

One of the escape doors to the building opened up and we started to crawl toward it. I don't know how I found it. I couldn't see or think. I just moved.

As I lay on my back outside the building, looking skyward, gasping for fresh air, I seriously wondered what the hell I was doing. Why was I here? I was a goddamn art student! This was not my idea of a fun time. Or was it? I wasn't sure. For as terrible as that first experience was, I think I loved it. I got up and followed the class back inside the building time after time. Once you got used to being in a fire situation, you had to learn how to put the damn thing out.

This was a kick, but I never thought about being a professional fire fighter. I was still more excited by the fire department's rescue squad; that I also enjoyed fighting the fires was just an added bonus. I started going out on rescue calls with the squad. I would watch the experienced EMTs evaluating patients or performing skills I was learning in class, and it would all click together—"So that's what they were talking about. Okay, I can do that."

At the end of EMT school I was required to spend sixteen hours observing in an emergency room. I chose two midnight shifts at Metropolitan Hospital, First Avenue and East Ninety-eighth Street, a wild place. I was pretty nervous when I arrived with my stethoscope, penlight, and EMT scissors.

The staff claimed that it was a relatively slow two nights, but not for me. I got to do CPR, watched a lot of suturing, took hundreds of blood pressures. By the second night I started to do triage work. I sat at a desk and people told me what was wrong with them. I wrote the chief complaint down, took their vital signs, and then usually told them to sit down and wait. I had been instructed to get one of the nurses if the patient said he or she was having chest pain, difficulty breathing, or had been shot or stabbed. Almost everything else could wait a few minutes.

My parents seemed amused by this newfound interest of mine, but I think they were also impressed by how seriously I was taking it, how hard I was working for it, and how well I was doing at it. I had never been a model student. Now I had found something that really motivated me, that made studying seem fun. Still, my folks were a bit uneasy as to where it might lead me.

At first I thought it had to be a typo. Right there, in the course catalogue under "Psychology": Project Outreach, two credits, volunteer in the U. of M. emergency room. Simple. Show up for a lecture and discussion section two hours a week, write one paper, hang out in the E.R., and pick up some easy credit. It seemed too good to be true.

The classroom part of the course was a snap. Some of the lectures included talks about death and dying, the effects of a terminal illness on a family, people's reactions to stress. I thought most of it was bullshit, and even giving it the benefit of the doubt, it was still pretty far removed from the job to be done: I would be running errands, not discussing abstract theories of death. But to get credit for the course, all I had to do was sit, stay awake, look wise, and nod occasionally. I could do that.

The instructors put a lot of stress on empathy training so we could talk the "right" way to someone. This wasn't just an abstract concept to them; it was a skill you had to learn and actively practice. The theory behind empathy training is to keep the conversation focused at all times on the person you're speaking to, not on yourself. Instead of adding new ideas to the conversation, you paraphrase what he says to show that you're listening and that you understand. This will encourage him to keep talking, to open up and deal with his feelings. Instead of answering questions or giving advice, you try to help the person discover his own answer, his true feelings. I thought this was ludicrous, the very height of bullshit, but the instructors assured me that I would need this skill to deal with patients or with family members waiting anxiously while their loved ones were in the treatment areas.

My first night in the E.R. was relatively slow. I spent most of it getting to know the hospital, taking blood samples to the various labs, and wheeling a few patients to X-ray. A rather large man was pacing in the waiting area. I walked over to him and asked him if there was anything I could do.

"Why don't you tell me what the hell is taking them so long?" he asked angrily. "Why don't they tell me what's going on?"

I was calm and collected. I had my empathy training. I looked him right in the eye and said, "I can see you're very concerned." I knew it was an absurd thing to say.

"Of course I'm very concerned, you idiot," he snapped. "Did you actually go to school to learn that bullshit?"

I nodded.

"Well, forget it," he advised me. "No one likes it. We want answers, not observations."

He was right. I never did the empathy routine again. I answer questions when I can, and apologize when I can't. There are people who specialize in psychiatry and psychology—maybe they can use empathy techniques effectively. It didn't work for me.

I worked Thursday nights from six to ten P.M. For the most part, I rolled patients around and took blood samples from the E.R. to the labs. After a while the staff let me do little things for patient care—just enough to make me feel like I wasn't simply watching from the sidelines; things like assisting in the cast room, hooking up EKG monitors, occasionally doing CPR.

Project Outreach had a number of other medical assignments: a hospice team, a children's floor, and the V.A. hospital. All of the programs met for the same lecture, but then we broke up for individual discussion sections. The students volunteering in the other places got to know the same patients week to week and developed interesting relationships with them, but for me, the emergency room was the place to be. I wasn't interested in the patients as people. I had no desire to get to know them. Their conditions were what fascinated me, and in the E.R. I got to see some pretty wild conditions.

U. of M. Hospital is a trauma center with a helicopter and the best of everything. It's also the only hospital I've seen where the E.R. was on the fourth floor, since the building was built into the side of a small mountain. One night following a meal break, I was wandering around downstairs when two guys came running toward me, one doubled over in pain and bleeding quite heavily from his face. The non-injured one was holding a towel over his friend's face.

"Where's the emergency room?" he demanded. They had entered the hospital by the wrong doors and had gotten completely lost. I told them to follow me, and I went over to look a little more closely at the injured man.

"What happened to him?" I asked as we headed through the hallways, a trail of blood growing behind us.

The friend answered, "We were just fooling around, you know, like, roughhousing. Bobby and me get pretty rough, and he threw me against the wall and I threw him, but Bobby slipped and his face hit the wall." The bleeding man let out a yell.

"It was a hook," he bellowed.

"A hook?"

"Yeah, sort of," the friend said. "You know, the things you hang your jacket up on. A coat hook. Screws into the wall. Like a sideways J. Little J underneath it." He showed me with his free hand.

"His face hit the hook and it, uh, sort of caught his nose on it."

"It ripped my fuckin' nose off!" Bobby said in a surprisingly nasal tone, spitting blood out from his mouth.

"Do you still have it? You still have it?" he asked his friend.

"Yeah, Bobby, I got it. I promise."

"What? What do you have?" I asked as we reached the E.R.

"His nose." From his pocket he pulled a clump of flesh covered in blood and ripped tissue and lint. "I still have it." He held it up for the rest of the emergency room to see.

"Amputated nose here!" I broadcast excitedly as we burst through the doors. No one looked up. They had seen weirder things. After what seemed like an eternity, one of the nurses spoke without glancing up from what she was doing.

"Okay. Put him in that bed over there." She gestured with her pen. "There'll be someone over in a minute."

I followed this guy's case for hours. The surgeons had a field day sewing his nose back on. I was amazed that they were able to get all the pocket lint off it.

As soon as I started working in the hospital, I became fascinated with trauma. It wasn't the physical trauma that attracted me—I'm not some ghoul who just wants to look at ugly wounds—it was the process of dealing with the trauma, the urgency of the treatment, the split-second decisions, the way cops, fire fighters, medics, doctors, and nurses suddenly snapped into life and worked as a team. In those few

minutes everyone was more alive, even if the patient
were to die despite their efforts.

I had plenty of chances to see this, and I never got
tired of it. There was a never-ending flow of people to
the E.R.: serious injuries, shootings, stabbings, accidents, all of it. Sometimes I'd latch onto one case and
follow it from arrival to admittance upstairs or dis-
charge. Half the time I'd stay past my allotted hours.
A few times I felt a bit faint, although I never
admitted it at the time. I'd tell the doctor or nurse, "I
have to check if there are any bloods that need to be
taken to the lab. Back in a second." I'd wander out for
a minute, catch a breath of air, feel better, and head
right back in. If there weren't any bloods that needed
running, of course.

Back in New York for summer break again, I wore
my hospital greens constantly and talked about nothing but the E.R., both of which sparked my mother's
persistent and misguided hope that I would decide to
become a doctor. No such luck. I still firmly believed
that I would be a photographer and use my medical
skills on the side.

I was wearing my greens one day as I worked on
the car outside. I heard a crash and ran to the corner.
Two cars had collided on Fifth Avenue and Seven-
teenth Street. One guy had busted the windshield
with his head and was slumped over the steering
wheel. He was in rather good shape considering the
circumstances, alert and even chatty. I climbed into
the backseat and held his head steady until the
ambulance came. A cop arrived on the scene. He
asked me if I was a medical student, and I got to watch
him turn green as I said no, that I was a photography

student. I added a moment later that I was also an EMT, to reassure him.

I was scheduled to return to my Saltaire security job in July and August, but U. of M. gets out in early May and I had time to kill. I decided to try for a paying EMT job. I opened the Yellow Pages and looked up private ambulance companies. I didn't know anything about the different services, so I used my usual method of decision-making—ease! Medical Transportation Ambulance was the closest company to my parent's apartment, so I just walked over one Monday morning and asked for a job. After a ten-minute interview and a few forms to fill out, I was told I started the next day. It turned out that they had been trying to hire people without any luck. I think the guys in charge were happy to see a clean-cut, English-speaking college student applying.

It wasn't exactly what I had dreamed of. The life-and-death emergencies were few and far between. Most of the calls were taking little old ladies home from the hospital or delivering people to and from their clinic appointments. Medical Transport Ambulance's most lucrative contract was with one of the local hospital's chemical dependency units. Drug addicts were locked into a special ward across the street from the hospital. Most of these folks still needed occasional treatment for various things. Since they couldn't be allowed to walk across the street and down the block, the hospital needed to call an ambulance for their transportation.

I was partnered with a slightly crazy guy named Pablo. We got along all right, which was important since no one else would talk to me. Everyone else thought I was a narc.

A week or so before I started work there, one of the patients in the locked ward had overdosed and died while behind the locked doors. How did he get the drugs? Who had access to the patients? The ambulance guys were prime suspects. They came and went unquestioned. They had access to the patients in the back of the ambulance. Anything could have happened.

Then I showed up: a young, clean-cut white guy who supposedly spoke no Spanish (I still don't) and who had never worked as an EMT before. Definitely narc material.

I didn't really care what they thought. I knew I was only going to be there for a few months. I knew there were a lot of abuses going on within the company, thefts and cheating, EMTs doing odd jobs while supposedly working for MTA, but they left me and Pablo alone.

Once in a while I got to do something medically worthwhile, usually when I got flagged down for some sort of emergency on the street. Just driving around the city you'd find yourself in the middle of a motor vehicle accident or you'd see someone collapsed on the street. Someone would already have called 911, but they'd see the ambulance and call us over. The bosses at MTA bitched about us stopping to help. They didn't like to give freebies, and we'd be unavailable during that time for the money call or the contract assignment. A number of times they'd try to explain how easy it was "not to see" the street job.

"You're healthy young guys," they said. "The next time you see something on the north side of the avenue, look over to the south side and check out the girl with the big tits. Nobody will be able to say otherwise. You just didn't see the accident. You were looking the other way." I didn't like the attitude and never took the advice. My last few weeks there, when I knew I was leaving anyway, I let myself get flagged down for calls left, right, and sideways.

I had already given MTA my two weeks' notice when I tried to squeeze the ambulance underneath the awning of a nursing home in the Bronx. Technically speaking, I did fit it under the awning. I just didn't manage to get the lights and siren and part of the roof under there with the rest of the bus. It was a horrible sound, part screech and part crunch. Silly me. I honestly thought I could fit under there.

Strangely enough, none of my employers have ever done anything to teach me how to drive an ambulance. They just put me in this four-ton vehicle without any formal training and sent me out to bounce off cars or run people over. All they asked for was a class-four chauffeur's license, which anyone can get if he's got fifteen dollars and a lot of time to spend in the lines at the Manhattan Department of Motor Vehicles.

City Emergency Medical Services (EMS) employees (not EMTs and medics employed directly by private companies and hospitals) are required to take a defensive driving course known as EVOC— Emergency Vehicle Operators Course. They go to a deserted area and drive old, beat-up ambulances forward and backward and around pylons. It's supposed to make them safer drivers, but I don't think it works. They seem to get in just as many accidents as the rest of us.

Normally, a rookie doesn't drive too much, but he has to start eventually. Hopefully his partner, who's been doing it for a while, will say "No! Stop! Don't run through that red light; you don't have your lights on." Or tell him that he has to change frequencies of the siren when he goes through an intersection. You learn from experience, supposedly. But just two days after I practically turned the ambulance into a convertible, I got into another accident.

It really wasn't my fault. I was driving near the end of our shift and had just dropped off a coworker on the lower East Side. I was completely stopped, waiting to turn onto Allen Street when I saw the car barreling down on us. Neither my partner nor I said anything, but we both felt the horror of anticipation. The guy broadsided us but good. The ambulance was physically lifted off the ground and bounced down the block. Amazingly, neither of us was hurt. The driver of the other car, who had probably been drinking, was wearing his seat belt and walked away from the accident.

The damage to the brand new ambulance was extensive. The impact point was right at the frame level, sending cracks around the whole frame besides caving in the entire passenger side. I was demoted to Ambulette driver for my last two days there, picking up wheelchair-bound patients in a rusty, busted-up, beaten-down old hunk of junk. The bosses at MTA didn't seem to mind much when I left.

The final blow to my photography career came in my senior year. Required to complete a senior project, I proposed an independent-study photo essay on the Ann Arbor Fire Department. Unfortunately, I needed permission from both the university and the city of Ann Arbor, two institutions notable for their talent for wrapping things securely in red tape.

Anticipating an easier time from the art school, I approached them first with written proposals, drafts, concept charts, all that crap. Then I went face-to-face with my advisor, a very cool guy, and lied. I said I already had permission from the fire department. He figured that if the F.D. was willing to let me ride along, so was he. Bingo.

The same logic applied when I sat down with the chief of the fire department and told him that I had already been approved by the university to receive credit for the independent study. But for him I changed my tactics a little. I got a haircut, changed into a suit and tie, and wore real shoes, not sneakers—I did own a pair, I just had to look for them. I made an appointment with his secretary and was actually on time.

I tried to sound very confident. I was, after all, a member of a volunteer fire department—which, I did *not* tell him, only handles a handful of calls a year. I was a New York State–certified Emergency Medical Technician with street experience—maybe a dozen calls, tops.

I had actually gone back to the Fire Academy in Yaphank that summer with the new batch of trainees from my volunteer department. I wasn't required to go again, but I wanted to see if it would get easier with practice. It did. This time, in addition to "normal" fires, we practiced on oil-pit fires. The instructors filled a huge pit with gasoline and heating oil and lit it up. Once it really got cooking, we had to extinguish it. At least two hose lines are required to even attempt this safely, and you better work together or there are going to be serious injuries. The heat was severe and the wind shifts were a challenge, but we did it, so I didn't feel like I was stretching the truth too far when I told the chief of my experience.

He was very concerned about the direction of the photo essay and about violating patient confidentiality. Obviously, he didn't want me to do anything that would reflect badly on his department—I think he had visions of exploitative, ugly photos of victims grimacing in pain while the fire fighter looked unconcerned. He didn't seem to worry much about *me* getting hurt. I signed a million releases. If I fell off the truck, got run over, was involved in an accident, if anything or everything happened to me, no one but myself would be responsible. He agreed to a one-time trial shot one day the following week. For a twelve-hour period, seven A.M. to seven P.M., I would be assigned to Rescue Truck 1. The number was just for show; there was only one rescue truck in the department.

The Ann Arbor Fire Department had a number of outposts, most with two vehicles—a pumper and a ladder truck. The main station had the batallion chief's car, two pumpers, a ladder truck, and the Rescue Squad. Rescue 1 was a multipurpose vehicle. In a fire situation, it responded like a ladder truck, doing search and rescue, and ventilation. In building collapses or motor vehicle accidents, it acted as a heavy rescue unit with the jaws of life, hydraulics tools, and extrication equipment. When available, they also responded to reports of medical emergencies within the confines of the city. Each member of the Rescue Squad was an EMT, and one of them was a nationally registered paramedic.

The three platoons in the Ann Arbor Fire Department worked twenty-four hour shifts, one day on and two days off, with extra days off mixed in. I selected, at random, a Tuesday with B platoon. They were a great group of people and made me very welcome. Most were hams and enjoyed having their pictures taken. The few who didn't, I didn't shoot.

My trial day was memorable for the *lack* of calls. No one could remember the last time it had been so quiet. It figured. Even now, whenever I have an observer or friend out on the ambulance and I really want to impress them, we always get a slow day.

A few smoke detectors went off in a hotel, but there was no fire, not even any smoke, just malfunctions. Two motor vehicle accidents without injuries. One sick lady who passed out on the street. I spent most of the day wandering around and clicking pictures of trucks, radios, hoses, ladders, and other assorted boring fixed objects. By dinnertime I had met most of the fire fighters in the platoon, including the one female fire fighter in the department who had just joined the year before. They apologized for not being able to give me more to shoot. The dinner was the most exciting part of the day. Each platoon is responsible for their own meals, and B platoon had some excellent chefs, including one who had gone to a culinary school before becoming a fire fighter.

Before I left that day, I stopped a few of the guys and took their portraits. Nothing fancy, just a simple shot of them against a wall or truck. I thanked them all as I headed out the door. Most wished me well and hoped that I'd come back sometime and see some real action. Unfortunately, that still depended on their chief. I needed to get that permission. I was already committed. What could I tell my senior advisor? "Sorry, I lied"? No, I don't think so.

I spent two days developing the film and printing the pictures. The following Monday, B platoon day, I went back into the tie and shoes. I stopped off and said hello to the guys before heading up to the chief's office. I spread extra copies of my pictures on the pool table and they started going over them.

"Can I get a copy of this? Can you blow that one up? Shouldn't there be police numbers across this person's mug shot?"

The chief asked me how the day had gone, what I took pictures of, what the crew thought, if there had been any problems.

I tried to sound as professional as possible. My essay, assuming he let me continue, would be focused on the men (and one woman) who were prepared to respond twenty-four hours a day. I wasn't as concerned with the actual blood and guts as I was with the guys sitting around the table, cleaning up, restocking, training.

He told me to wait in his office for a few minutes, and I held my breath. I hoped he would look at the pleasant, uncontroversial pictures I had spread out downstairs. When he returned he informed me that I had gotten good reviews and was welcome to ride with B platoon for the remainder of the semester, twelve hours at a time, just as long as I signed the releases before every shift.

I tried to "work" once a week. It took me a while to feel comfortable with the professionals. They fell automatically into routines that I hadn't figured out yet. A couple of times I didn't even bring the camera. I just rode along and watched them work.

I got so caught up in this project that I dropped a couple of classes at the university to have extra time with the fire fighters. This meant that I would have to stay in school for an extra semester to make up the credits, but I was enjoying the first senior year so much that I didn't mind sticking around for another one. My mother was terrified that I would graduate from college and join the fire department. My roommate didn't help matters much. Occasionally when Mom called and I wasn't home, my roommate would say, "I don't know where he is. Oh, wait a minute. I hear sirens. He might be coming this way."

Once in a while when they were short-handed, I got a chance to fetch something or assist in a minor way. After a few weeks I felt I had learned a tremendous amount. I began to feel secure and competent. And I gained a few pounds. While the other two platoons had burgers, we had incredible lasagna. Instead of Kentucky Fried chicken, we once had cornish hens. I had made an excellent choice of platoon.

There was something strangely relaxing about being there, partly because I had no responsibilities. Whatever the mayhem, I didn't have to take care of it. There was also a sense of peacefulness in the routine, the community, the freedom between calls. In the mornings, everyone signed in, checked out their personal equipment and trucks, and except for a few simple scut-work assignments like doing inventory or copying over paperwork, they were free to do whatever they wanted. A lot slept, some read or watched movies on the VCR, two or three of the guys baked cookies or muffins.

At least once a week a school class would come by for a tour. Each little kid would get a chance to sit in the driver's seat of one of the trucks. Everyone got to put on a helmet. Of course, they all wanted to see someone slide down the pole. The main station was a three-story building with a three-story pole. The tour guide, usually one of the lieutenants or captains, wasn't going to run up the stairs and slide down the pole. He had underlings for that. He'd call out someone's name, and whoever it was would run up three flights and then slide down. The kids would cheer and clap and call for him to do it again. The captain would agree and the underling would go again. And again. When the kids finally seemed to have enough, the officer would give the kids a big, *"How about one more time?"* and the kids would applaud and beg for one more slide down.

I didn't usually slide down the pole. I learned how, but I never got very good at it. I was much too slow. If there was a call and I slid before any of the guys, I'd have footprints on my scalp when I reached the apparatus floor, so I usually took the stairs.

Completing the essay was a drag. It had to be done or I wouldn't get credit for the time spent, but I didn't really enjoy taking the pictures. I could watch the rescue, even give a hand, but it didn't seem fair to take photos of the sick or injured in their own homes. On the street everything was supposed to be fair game—you can't invade someone's privacy when they're "in public view"—but I still felt bad closing in on people who had been hit by cars and were in pain and embarrassed. I was supposed to be an artist, not a ghoul. I didn't mind shooting the fire fighters, who were aware of my presence and ignored me, but it upset me to capture on film patients in pain or people watching their house burn.

I had always thought that I'd end up as a photo-journalist. I knew from my reaction that I never could. What I really enjoyed was riding with the squad, treating patients, helping people. It was more fun and much more rewarding.

The people I dealt with in Ann Arbor impressed me greatly. Everyone was professional, but the Rescue Squad personnel were awesome. Fire fighting was worthwhile and exciting, but I was mostly drawn by the medical emergencies.

Before I knew it, I was hooked. Like many medics and professional rescuers, I had become a trauma junkie. The rush of adrenaline when racing to a confirmed "good" call, the excitement on the scene, the feeling of power when making split-second, life-and-death decisions, the feeling of pride and satisfaction from saving someone's life—these things make the job worthwhile. They make it possible for you to endure the boredom between calls, the hassle of writing incident reports, the occasional "emotional hangover," and all the other bullshit that goes with the job.

I graduated from Michigan with a Bachelor of Fine Arts, but I have never used my photography skills professionally. My walls are covered with my pictures, except for some gory ones taken on the job. Those are in a separate album, only for rare intrepid viewers.

CHAPTER 2

I returned to New York after the December graduation and immediately started looking for a job as an
EMT. I was in a real hurry because I wanted to enroll
in the paramedic course at Beekman Hospital, and
they only accepted people employed as EMTs. The
pretests for the course were just a few days away. If I
missed it, I'd have to wait for the course at St.
Vincent's, but that might be as long as six months—
way too long for me.

First, I called New York City's Emergency Medical Service, but I found out that working directly for
EMS was out of the question because they have their
own intake classes ("the EMS Academy"), and they
weren't being offered again for a couple of months.
Also, with EMS there would be no guarantee of
getting a good shift. There would be no point in

working as an EMT if the hours made it impossible for me to take the medic course anyway.

I called the "Voluntary Hospitals"—non-city-owned hospitals that run their own ambulance departments, subcontracted to EMS to work the 911 system—but they all wanted previous 911 experience, and all I had was volunteer work and in-hospital experience.

Everyone I talked to suggested that I try a private ambulance service. MTA might have given me another job if I could face the thought of actually going back there, but I had moved out of my parents' place into an apartment of my own, so they no longer fit my criterion of being the closest to where I was living. Once again I got out the phone book, found the closest ambulance service, and within a couple of hours had a job as an EMT with the Empire State Ambulance Company.

About a dozen EMTs worked for Empire State, which shared a big garage off Twenty-sixth Street with an armored car company. Most of the EMTs worked only two shifts a week, one for twenty-four hours, the other for sixteen. Since the work was easy and the call volume very low, there was always time for them to sleep on the job. Normally I wouldn't mind a schedule like that, but because I would be taking the medic course I had to work more traditional hours, Monday through Friday eight A.M. to four P.M.

Empire State was one of the few private ambulance companies in New York City that had corporate contracts at that time. Many voluntary hospitals are now developing their own private services in addition to their 911 call-receiving ambulances, such as Roosevelt Hospital's FastCare service. Private services, with clients who call the hospital directly for an ambulance, bring prestige and pride to a hospital as well as additional funds. The hospital charges the clients a subscription fee, and when the service is used, the patient also gets a bill. Many corporations have switched to these new hospital-based services. Empire State eventually went out of business, but I figured it was probably due as much to mismanagement as to the competition. Their business was mostly taken over by Roosevelt and New York Hospital.

Most of the clients of the private service were corporations that wanted their people to go to a "nice" hospital if they got sick or hurt. The patients were clean, upper-class businessmen and women, suffering from standard illnesses or injuries. Many of the calls were in the companies' medical offices and were simple transport operations. If they called 911, their people would be brought to the nearest emergency room, which they might not want. A lot of our clients were in midtown Manhattan, which meant they'd probably be taken to St. Clare's or Bellevue. Exxon and Time/Life don't want their executives going there. They think Bellevue is a zoo and consider themselves above it. St. Clare's is a small, poor hospital that has recently become one of the leading AIDS treatment centers. Mr. Hoity-Toit doesn't want to be taken there.

My view of the emergency rooms was less superficial, and the conclusions I came to were strikingly different. I soon decided that Bellevue was a damn good emergency room. It was certainly a zoo, a real madhouse, chaos in motion. So what? In an emergency, Bellevue was and is one of the best places in the city to be. And if it isn't an emergency, you shouldn't be in an emergency room. St. Clare's had some good doctors in its emergency rooms and intensive care units. Depending on who was on duty, the care might be better than at some "nicer" hospitals.

Of course, if a private client had a life-and-death emergency, the patient was taken to a trauma center or the nearest emergency room anyway. It was written into the contract that patient care couldn't be compromised. So the clients sometimes ended up at St. Clare's or Bellevue or St. Vincent's anyway. Once they were stabilized and "safe," they could arrange transfers to whatever facility they wanted.

But true emergencies were rare. Most of the EMTs slept or read on the job. Two EMTs there were dating each other and would occasionally park the ambulance under the Fifty-ninth Street Bridge to make out. It was a good job for a lazy EMT, but a lousy one for a trauma junkie.

I don't want to sound too critical of private ambulance services. Some older or burned-out medics prefer this kind of work because it's not as weird and uncontrolled as it is working 911 on the streets; the adrenaline level isn't there. When I became a full-time medic at Roosevelt, I saw that their private FastCare service has added extra employees to the hospital and improved the quality of our equipment. We can't send old, broken-down ambulances to these corporate sites, so we have some of the newest and best equipment in the city. But personally, I'd like to see the FastCare ambulance out there responding to 911 calls. The system is overloaded and desperately in need of additional crews, while most of the day a fully stocked paramedic ambulance waits at Roosevelt Hospital for one of the seventy-five or so big money corporations to call. It's important to keep that unit available, I know. If we sent it out on 911 calls, it might not be available when one of our clients called. We'd lose our clients, and the service would go down the drain. I understand this, but it still galls me to see the ambulance just sitting.

Although the work at Empire State was mostly boring and had nothing to do with what I would later see working the 911 system, there was still an occasional hint that working in New York City would be bizarre and unforgettable.

My company had a contract with the famous Trump Tower on Fifth Avenue. We got a call there, situation unknown. The caller was hysterical and couldn't give much information. When we arrived, there were already several police cars, a fire truck, and two NYC ambulances on the scene.

Some guy, about thirty-five years old, had decided that the Trump Tower would be a perfect place to commit suicide. The Tower is a beautiful building, all marble and shiny chrome, with several stories of shops, walkways, and an indoor waterfall that rushes into a pool in the underground atrium café.

This fellow, for whatever reason, climbed to the top floor of the inside shopping center, walked over to the ledge and, without saying a word to anyone, jumped.

Now picture this: you're eating your sandwich, drinking your cup of coffee, discussing whatever people who can afford to eat there discuss, watching the water roll down the wall. The café is full and there's a long line of people waiting to get in. Suddenly, Mr. Considerate splashes down in the pool.

His head hits the marble embankment and explodes. The police and ambulance crews arrive and try to cover the body and all the parts that have leaked out. Bits and pieces of the body are floating around in the pool.

Do you scream? Faint? Get sick? Leave immediately without paying the bill? Ask for the food to go?

Not one person did any of the above. They continued with their meals and their conversations as if nothing had happened. There was still a line to get in. Maybe they were all in shock. Maybe if you're spending that much for lunch, you're going to sit there and eat it no matter what. I don't know, but I no longer believe that people are all the same under the skin. New Yorkers are different. I grew up in this city, but it wasn't until I started working as a medic here that I was sure of it.

The pretest for the New York Infirmary/Beekman Downtown Hospital Paramedic Program consisted of simple English, basic math, and a basic EMT test. I did well enough to be called in for a follow-up interview. The Education coordinator asked rather predictable questions: Why do you want to be a paramedic? Where do you see yourself in ten years? Why do you think you'd be a good medic?

Dr. Diane Sixsmith, the medical director of Beekman's Emergency Department, also presented me with the obligatory moral dilemma: What would I do if my partner, who was also a friend, needed some of the narcotics we carried? If, say, his grandmother had cancer and was in pain. We carry morphine. It wouldn't be difficult to take a little, claim that we broke a vial—which does happen occasionally—and sign out another. He could siphon out a few milligrams, put it in another syringe, then break the empty one, hand it in, get another and walk away with the morphine in a syringe in his pocket. I *never* knew of anyone actually doing this, but anyone who works out there knows lots of ways it can be done.

I gave the standard answer, of course. I looked her right in the eye and said I would not allow it and would even turn in my partner if it came to that. I wouldn't take the rap for a federal offense. Besides, I said, if Grandma has cancer, my partner should have no problem getting a doctor somewhere to write a script for whatever pain meds she needed.

It was the correct answer, at least as far as they were concerned. I think I meant it at the time. If someone were to ask me the same question now, I wouldn't be nearly so sure. I think I'd talk with my partner first, maybe talk with some other people too, people I respect and trust. I'm amused now to think about how confident I was, how righteous. Everything seemed so simple to me then, so cut and dried.

But it was the answer they wanted. I was in the class, as long as I could come up with the $2100 tuition, not counting the enrollment fees, books, equipment, transportation, and all the extras that pop up. Nowadays, the class is up to almost four thousand bucks.

The first night, March first, started with a wine and cheese party for introductions and information in the second-floor Radiology conference room, a tiny, cramped space we would come to know all too well. The fourteen other students in the class seemed like a nice, heterogeneous combination of people. Some were EMS EMTs, some already worked as EMTs for the hospitals. I hit it off right away with three guys from volunteer departments in New Jersey. They were as enthusiastic about the class as I was, but an older guy named Lenny, who was about forty, bald, short and smart, seemed even more psyched about it than we were. There was only one woman in the class, Georgia, a nurse who had decided to become a paramedic. For the first time, I was surrounded by people who not only understood my passion for trauma, but shared it. Nobody thought I was weird for wanting to be a paramedic. We all had the same goal.

The real classes, three nights a week, began the next week with anatomy and physiology; pretty dull stuff, especially for "hot shot" EMTs who want to be paramedics. We wanted to move straight to IVs, EKGs, medications, intubations, life-saving hero stuff, but for the next few months we were stuck with books. Lots of big, thick books. It was more reading and work than I had ever done in college, or ever before, for anything.

Our teacher, Dr. Paul Zweil, Ph.D., made it bearable with his humor and directness. A thin, balding man, he was full of energy and almost never sat down. The classes were taught in the same Radiology conference room. It had horrible fluorescent lights, and the radiologists always forgot we were there. They'd come barging in and out, holding onto films that needed evaluating.

Dr. Zweil had answers for almost everything, but Lenny occasionally managed to stump him.

"Only God or Mickey Mouse knows for sure," the doc would say, shrugging his shoulders. When someone looked skeptical, he would add with mock reproach, "I only lie to my wife."

The two responses became themes of our class. After a while Dr. Zweil would start abbreviating: "God or Mickey Mouse," "Only to my wife," or even just, "Mickey." We always knew what he meant.

To remain in the class an average of 80 was required. There was a test about every two weeks, not counting quizzes, and every one counted. One student flunked out after anatomy and physiology, about two months into the class. We didn't mind losing him in particular—he had become rather obnoxious—but his failure reminded us that this was for real.

Our senior instructor was explaining how to prepare mentally for a call while still on route to the scene. There are certain questions you have to ask yourself: What will you need when you get there? What are the problems going to be? What about hospital availability? etc.

"You are on route to a confirmed Man Shot on West 105th Street," he started, to give us an example. Then he paused. "Or to a Cow Down, for those of you from New Jersey."

The Jersey guys—Steve Moffett, Tom Clappi and Paul Browning—took a good amount of teasing, especially about lousy Jersey drivers and living in the boonies.

Every class, the instructor would finish up at ten P.M. with the traditional, "If there isn't anything else . . ." We were all exhausted after working a full day and attending class, but without fail Lenny's hand would shoot up. He was always the last person to shut up. I liked the guy, but I wished he would chill out a bit. He would fight for an extra half point, even though it really didn't matter. The competition wasn't that important.

The first of many rotations, supervised hands-on experience in real situations, started at the New York City Medical Examiner's Office. The rotations were almost always conducted during the daytime, before the evening classes, which frequently conflicted with my work schedule. I had to call in sick, take vacation time, personal days, and work extra shifts to make up for them.

Except for a few funerals and a few dead elderly people, I had never really been exposed to death. My father, who had been a police reporter for years and had watched a few autopsies, gave me one piece of advice—always keep a piece of chewing gum or a mint in your mouth. The air in a morgue is altered to such a degree by the smell of formaldehyde and the feeling of death permeating the atmosphere that you physically start to taste it. The mints take care of that.

It only took about twenty minutes for me to start feeling comfortable there. The doctors and technicians really seemed to enjoy their work, and seemed unaffected by all the death surrounding them.

There is nothing sacred about a morgue. Naked bodies are splayed like pieces of meat on hard, cold aluminum tables, which are built like sinks so that when the bodily fluids leak out, they don't run down the body or off the table.

Six bodies were prepared when we arrived bright and early with our white lab coats on. Our morgue preceptor greeted us and told us to split into teams and pick a body. I almost passed out when the pathologist doing the postmortem cut into the dead guy. I think it was because there was no blood. A few days of death had drained the blood from the chest. When the doc made the first incision, from shoulder to navel, and there was no blood, I got a bit weak-kneed for a second.

It's a rude procedure. I wouldn't want to think of any of my relatives or friends on that table/sink. I know they'd be dead and wouldn't feel it or know about it, but still. After the breastplate is completely removed from the body, individual organs are removed, weighed, examined. Then all the body parts are simply dumped back into the body without rhyme or reason. Plop. The chest is sewn back on the body with thread almost thick enough to be used as shoe laces. The head is opened with a saw, the brain removed and examined. Sometimes hay is put inside the head to restore it to its proper shape. The skin is pulled down over the face to gain access to the skull. The thought of someone doing that to my dead body is almost worse than the thought of dying.

We were only there for a day, but after that one day I could understand why medical students spend months doing this. Books are good, but nothing beats hands-on practice. The pathologists let us get our feet wet, and, best of all, we couldn't hurt the patient.

After a hearty Italian lunch, we couldn't wait to get back to the morgue to go to the Morgue Museum, a great collection of extremely weird things. My imagination was struck by cross sections of the throat of a man who tried to swallow an entire steak. It got caught and the guy choked to death. The museum preserved the throat for all posterity, with the steak still in place. There was a mummified head, various body parts in exotic positions, insides out and outsides in. I strongly recommend the museum if you ever get the chance. I don't think it's open to the public, so you might have to make an appointment.

We spent hundreds of hours on rotations. My least favorite was the phlebotomy rounds (blood-letting), partly because I had to wake up at four-thirty A.M. to get to the hospital on time. Also, I had limited experience sticking people with needles, and now I was waking someone up, saying "Wake up, Mr. Abernathy, I'm going to draw some blood"—*not* telling him that I was a medic student and was probably going to miss a few times first. I felt sorry for the little old people who had been there too long and whose veins weren't so good.

My favorite rotation was the operating room. If the patients had known who was in there, I seriously doubt they'd have consented to their surgeries. I would arrive at about seven A.M., check in with the head nurse, go into the locker room and change into the blue scrub suits. There I'd be in a surgical scrub suit, face mask, plastic booties, with a stethescope around my neck. Who would know that I wasn't a surgeon? It was here that we practiced endotracheal intubation. In class we had done it on an anatomically correct intubation head—Fred the Head—but now it was time for the real thing. People undergoing major surgery were moved onto an operating room table, strapped down and doped up as the surgeons, the assistants, the anesthesiologist, the scrub nurses, my preceptor, and I stood by. Once the patient was "under," the surgeon was in charge, but until then . . . he was mine.

My preceptor would administer various medications to get the patient ready for intubation. This involves paralyzing the patient to make him stop breathing. I would use the AMBU bag to breathe for him. When I was ready, the preceptor would remove the AMBU bag and I'd slip the laryngoscope into the patient's mouth, hoping to see the trachea and to pass the tube into the lungs. The first few times I did this, my hand shook and I wasn't very successful. With time, I got better. Soon, I was running from O.R. to O.R., doing as much intubation as possible, and sometimes watching a procedure from start to finish. Some of the surgeons were not very friendly. They resented being delayed the extra few minutes to put up with a student, and not even a medical student at that. But some were great and went out of their way to explain their operations to us.

The first time I saw a surgical incision, I reacted as I had at the morgue. This time there was lots of blood. I was accustomed to seeing blood from injuries, but I had never seen blood inflicted by medical personnel. I knew it was appropriate, but I still had that momentary feeling in my knees and thought that it was suddenly too warm in there.

By the last day of my O.R. rotation, I was feeling pretty confident. Good thing, too. A patient decided at the last minute that she didn't want the operation she needed. She had consented to it earlier, signed the papers, understood the need for it; but when she got on the table and looked around, she was very scared. She had been premedicated, but not enough. If she hadn't been strapped down, she would have leaped off the table.

"I am revoking my consent. I am refusing the surgery," she stated clearly but not at all calmly.

There was a quick conference in the O.R. suite as doctors, nurses, and administrators tried to convince her. She continued to squawk. They brought down her private medical doctor and had him plead with her to consent. She had huge ovarian tumors that had to come out. Finally, after nearly thirty minutes of yelling, she nodded her head and said okay. The anesthesiologist quickly blasted her with enough night-night stuff to knock all of us out. Now all sorts of interested people were in the room waiting for the surgery to start, and there I was, holding on to my laryngoscope, waiting to tube this lady. Intimidating. I took a deep breath and did it perfectly. Whew. A half hour later I was watching the operation when an older man walked into the room and asked the gas passer if "the student" had passed the tube.

"Yes, he did. A very nice job," he replied. The older man, who turned out to be a big cheese in anesthesiology, said, "Too bad he didn't take out a vocal cord. That might have shut her up for a while." A word to the wise: in a teaching institution, find out exactly who is going to be working on you. According to the Patient's Bill of Rights, you have the right to know the identity of anyone associated with your care. As hypocritical as it may sound, I would not want a student working on me. I might allow it, I might let myself get talked into it, but I would at least want to be aware of it. Don't be shy about asking.

The most intimidating of our many lecturers was a doctor who sat on NYC's Medical Advisory Committee, which decides on the protocols the paramedics have to follow. A soft-spoken man who seemed to punctuate every word, he scared the hell out of our entire class. He was one of the few people who called on us at random, without waiting for someone to raise his hand. He taught Fluids and Electrolytes; a difficult chapter to begin with, and this guy wearing a bow tie every night didn't make it easier. I remember when he called on me for the first time. He was giving a scenario and asked me what IV fluid I would administer to the patient.

"D5W TKO with a small-gauge angiocath," I replied.

The doctor looked around the room and asked, "Are there any other answers?" I looked for the nearest rock to crawl under. Then he cleared his throat and continued: "Good. That was absolutely correct."

He commanded absolute respect. If he asked me how much is one plus one and I answered "Two," he could make me feel sure I was wrong just by looking around and asking for another answer.

As my class progressed, we moved into Respiratory and Cardiology, losing a student in each section and reducing the class to twelve students. All my friends—the Jersey guys, Lenny and Georgia—made the cut.

School doesn't prepare students for much of what's out there. When you're new, almost everything seems out of your control. An EMT who already has a few years of street experience enrolls in a paramedic program and spends close to a year in school. After some six hundred hours of classroom work and rotations in the emergency room, operating room, intensive care units, psychiatric E.R., labor and delivery rooms, and the morgue, he starts his field training by riding as the third man on a paramedic bus. The veteran medics will ask him to interpret the EKG strip before they decide what it is, and give him other opportunities to get his feet wet without any real pressure.

Riding with these medics was incredibly exciting. It was everything I'd wanted; I knew I'd made the right choice. I was amazed by all the things they could actually do on the street. I'd been studying it in books, practicing it in nice, clean hospitals but these guys could do all these complicated procedures in the worst conditions, in the dark, in the dirt, in a hurry. And they did it all without any fuss, as a matter of course.

Twenty years ago ambulances were strictly "you fall, we haul" operations. They provided no care whatsoever, and a lot of people out there don't realize how much progress has been made since then. Medics are definitely no longer just "ambulance drivers."

At some point the powers that be realized that an enormous number of patients were dying on route to the hospital. It is a fact that if a victim of multiple trauma or severe medical illness does not get *prompt* medical attention, he or she will die. Time is essential. Someone figured out that if the ambulance crew had some basic medical knowledge, they might be able to increase the survival rates. Slowly, standards evolved requiring that ambulance people know CPR, basic bleeding control, splinting, and oxygen therapy. During the Korean War, medics were empowered to start intravenous lines, administer medications, and suture. A lot of medical people realized that nondoctors had the ability to diagnose and intervene in emergencies, providing advanced life support. Thus was the modern paramedic born.

With just a few years of training, a lay person can be transformed into an excellent provider of emergency care. The modern paramedic, in addition to basic emergency training, can establish IV lines, perform endotracheal intubation, interpret electrocardiograms, administer a multitude of medications and insert chest tubes.

I made my share of dumb mistakes when I was the third man. During my training runs I blew IVs, botched medical histories, forgot the basics and the advanced stuff, stammered on the radio. I was lucky to do most of my training under two medics who had at least fifteen years of medic experience between them. They both had impressive skills and knowledge.

Although one of the veteran medics still had considerable enthusiasm for the job, the other was well on the way to being burned out. I tried to think of the enthusiastic one as a role model and the other one as a warning. If I wasn't careful, that could be me in five years. I would see it happen to other medics who started out as gung-ho as I did. I must have been doing something right because the one with the bad attitude, who never said anything nice about anybody, used to tell me that I was the only student in my class that he tolerated.

I didn't even realize just how crispy that medic was until I did an ambulance rotation at another hospital. We picked up a patient and the medics got on the EMS radio to say they were "10-82 to Cabrini Hospital."

"Doesn't that mean that you're *at* the hospital?" I asked.

"Nah," the medic not driving explained. "Ten-82

means you're on route to the hospital with a patient. Ten-81 means you're at the hospital."

I was stunned. I had never even heard of a 10-81. On my other ambulance rotations, every time we pulled into the hospital, one of the medics I was training under called on the EMS radio, "Eleven Victor, 10-82 to such-and-such a hospital." It hadn't occurred to me to question it, but I saw now that those medics had been cheating, holding their signals. They would tell the dispatcher they were on route to the hospital when they had actually already arrived there. The dispatcher would then give them a certain amount of time to get to the hospital, to give their report, restock, do the paperwork, etc. That gave the unit ten or twenty minutes to goof off.

As I came closer to completing the paramedic course, I became more impatient with my humdrum EMT job. As punishment for shooting off my mouth to my boss one day, I was assigned to work the transfer bus for a week. Empire ran four ambulances, three of which responded to "emergency" calls from corporate sites and one that just did transfers. Bellevue doesn't have sophisticated radiation treatments and has to transfer patients who need certain types of radiation therapy or tests to New York University Hospital. It's just around the corner, but because they're in-patients and some of them have IVs, they go by ambulance. I almost quit rather than subject myself to this mind-dead task, but I wasn't a real medic yet and I still needed the money to complete the course.

On my first day of transfers I went to a room to pick up the patient, and zap! Love at first sight. She was young and beautiful, with Oriental features but a darker complexion and a full, wide mouth. I double-checked the transfer request form.

"Uh, Miss Kitagawa?" I said tentatively. "Your ride over to NYU is here."

"You weren't supposed to bring a wheelchair," she said, sliding out of bed. "I have my own." Dressed in nice street clothes, long black hair brushed over one shoulder, she looked more like an executive in a Marriott Hotel suite than a patient in Bellevue.

"Sorry, I don't know anything about that," I said as I glanced at my forms. "It doesn't make any difference."

"As long as we take my chair." She was adamant.

"I think we have to take mine," I said, taken aback by her demand. "I'm responsible for this one and I can't really leave it lying around."

"Well, this is *my* chair and I don't want *it* lying around while I'm gone. It took way too much trouble to get it, and I don't want it disappearing."

"We'll just leave it in your room. I'm sure it will be here when you return."

"This is Bellevue," she said simply. "Do you really think it'll be here?"

She did have a point, but I was responsible for Empire State's chair. I would have convinced, cajoled and/or bullied any other patient into submission, but not this woman. I was already too far gone. I just wanted to see the worry leave her face, to see her smile.

"What if we take my chair"—I looked around the room—"and we hide yours?"

"Hmm . . ." She seemed suspicious, but interested. "What do you have in mind?"

"What if we fold yours up, slide it behind the bed and cover it up with an extra sheet?"

"Show me." I did as I had suggested. The folded wheelchair fit flush against the wall and, when covered with a sheet, was almost invisible.

"Well?" I asked.

"Let's roll," she said cheerfully, hopping into my chair. She smiled then, a wide, friendly grin. I'd have done much more than hide a wheelchair to see that.

Helping her into the ambulance, chatting with her on the way to NYU, I just kept thinking, This is a great girl, I have got to get to know her. But what could I do? It was an awkward way to meet; I'd feel uneasy about hitting on someone in an ambulance. Some ghoulish guys might consider this a great way to meet women: they have to talk to you, they're vulnerable, they have to tell you their names and addresses. You ask all sorts of intimate questions, including asking indirectly if they're involved with anybody. If a woman gives the name and number of a boyfriend or husband to contact in case of an emergency, you know she's off-limits. If she gives her father's name, she's probably not married.

It doesn't usually happen that way, however. Not too many EMTs or medics make dates with people they meet on the bus. You're there for a job; to take care of them, not to hit on them. Plus, the woman isn't exactly at her best. There might be some flirtation in minor injury cases. If a girl falls down and breaks her wrist, she's in pain, but it's not serious and she may still look good. If, however, she's just been run over by a truck, it's hard to tell if she has a good personality or if she would normally be beautiful.

I didn't ask for a date. I didn't ask unnecessarily personal questions, however desperately I wanted to know all about her. After her session at NYU, when we got back to her room at Bellevue, I checked to make sure that our trick had worked. The wheelchair was still there. Thank God. She probably would never have forgiven me if it was gone. As it was, I had earned another big smile. I was happy.

I was even happier the next day when I saw another transfer request for Ms. Kitagawa. This time she greeted me as an old friend. We had graduated to first names: hers was Jo-Ann, or Jo. She told me a bit about herself. She was from Hawaii and had traveled widely. She was in New York for tests, but it was taking forever. She didn't know anybody and she was bored stiff.

When I showed up for Jo's third transfer that week, I was carrying a stack of books I thought she'd enjoy. Big smile. I was pretty sure now that the attraction was mutual, but I still felt self-conscious. The fact that EMTs and medics don't pick women up on the job is not always due to their self-restraint. For some reason, women don't go crazy over men on ambulances. The profession seems to lack sex appeal. It may have something to do with the crazy hours you work, the low pay you get, and the gory stories you come home with. Maybe the uniforms just aren't snazzy enough.

Whatever the reason, I had trouble getting up the nerve to ask for a real date, although I knew she'd be getting out of the hospital soon. As it turned out, I didn't have to. When Jo was discharged, she came over to my apartment to return the books and stayed. It was that simple. I had no reservations about her moving in—I wanted to spend all my time with her.

It was a fluke, and it thwarted the intention of my employers to punish me, but I had found love on the ambulance. Unfortunately, Jo-Ann's tests were positive for cancer, so the fairy tale didn't end happily ever after, and I now try to avoid meeting people that way. Metastatic paraganglioma is a rare, painful, and deadly disease. Only a handful of people in the United States have it. You can't find it in a normal dictionary, and when I looked it up in a medical dictionary, I found that it was "a chromaffin tumor with neoplasms appearing in parts of the body remote from the seat of the primary tumor." That didn't help much. I had never heard of it, but it was about to control my life for a couple of years.

When I had paid my debt to society, Empire State took me off the transfer bus and assigned me a day of Soap Opera Standby. Occasionally one of the soap operas that was filmed in New York City would need an ambulance for a scene and would call Empire State. As a private company, Empire didn't care who they were renting the ambulance to or why, but they wouldn't rent the bus without the crew thrown in.

This soap was filming a scene in which one of the regulars was going to be struck in the head with a tree, perhaps because his contract had expired. The "paramedics" would save his life and put him in the ambulance.

I already had a healthy contempt for glamorized Hollywood portrayals of our profession. I wasn't a medic yet, but even I could see how glaring the errors are in all of these productions. It infuriated me to see TV "heros" do CPR for five seconds, then stop resuscitation, saying, "He's gone." This is not only inaccurate, but would probably get the medics fired, if not sued.

My partner for that day and I were ushered out of the way. For a few hours we sat just off the set, watching them film and strike sets. When they were finally setting up for the tree scene, one of the actors came over to us. She was wearing a white lab coat and an ID tag that identified her as Doctor Something. She was clutching her stethoscope in her hands, obviously very agitated about something.

"Are you two here because of the ambulance?" she asked.

"Yes," I said. "We're the Emergency Medical Technicians."

"Oh good," she exhaled. "Who told you to wear your stethoscope that way?"

I looked at my partner. "What?"

"Over your neck that way. Sort of across your shoulders. Did the director tell you to do it that way?"

I suddenly realized what she meant. "I'm sorry. I always wear it that way," I told her. "I'm real. We're not with the show. That's our ambulance."

"Oh! You're not the paramedics for the show?"

I assured her that we weren't, but she would have figured it out on her own a minute later when the two actors in question appeared. They were incredibly beautiful, both over six feet tall, clean-cut with short-cropped hair. They were right off the pages of *GQ*, manicured nails and all.

After they filmed the poor guy getting clobbered by a tree trunk which was somehow uprooted, they needed to get him into the back of the ambulance and make it look somewhat realistic. The director called us over and asked for advice.

I thought we should get paid extra, or at least get technical advisor credit, but then again they didn't use anything we told them. The cervical collar interfered with the lighting. The oxygen mask covered too much of his face. The two "medics" couldn't seem to get a grasp on the long board.

Eventually they settled on a scoop stretcher and a bandage around his head, but not covering his eyes. And for the pièce de résistance, they didn't want to use the ambulance stretcher. After strapping this guy to the metal scoop, they just slid him on the floor of the ambulance and left him there by himself as both medics got into the front of the ambulance and drove away, lights and siren. I guess I'm glad my name wasn't on that.

My parents weren't happy about my relationship with Jo. A Japanese woman dying of cancer wasn't exactly what they had in mind for me. We spent a few weekends with them that summer out at the beach, which only aggravated the situation because we insisted on sharing a room. My folks, throwbacks to an earlier, sadder era, still thought that unmarried people should not share the same room. Jo handled the situation with incredible poise and tact, which only increased my admiration of her.

Jo needed to use a wheelchair for prolonged trips but could get around the house pretty well with crutches or a cane. We primarily kept night hours, going for long walks at strange times. Fire Island is incredibly beautiful when it's dark and eerie. The trees and bushes make intricate patterns and shadows on the boardwalks. The lights reflect off the water. It was worth braving the strained atmosphere in the house during the day to have the peaceful nights to ourselves.

I introduced Jo-Ann to almost everyone, but especially the members of my volunteer fire department. God forbid something should happen to her there, I wanted everyone to know that she was family. I made sure that she met the medical director of our department, Dr. Robert Furey. "Dr. Bob," as the kids refer to him, is a surgeon in the city who doubles as our community's doctor. I didn't want any problem if Jo needed medication on short notice. I had some excellent resources available to me, and I would be a fool if I didn't at least have them on standby.

My last day at Empire State Ambulance was a memorable one. I had gotten pretty disgusted working there and was ready to quit. It was early December. I still had three weeks to go in the medic course, but I wanted to spend more time with Jo, and I really couldn't stand much more of this job. The business had changed hands, and the new owners must have believed in voodoo maintenance. You'd report a problem with the alternator on Friday, the bus would be put in the back of the garage, Monday you'd pull it out from the exact same spot and be told, "All better! Ready to go." You'd be certain that they hadn't fixed it, but what could you say? By the end of the shift, it would be dead.

Morale was horrible. I was one of the few people still there from when I was hired less than a year previously. I was almost through with medic school; we only had a week or so to go before the state exams.

That day I was working in one of the worst vehicles, and was amazed that it had lasted as long as it had. I was breaking in a new guy who had never worked as an EMT before. The assignment was a simple one: take a very stable lady from New York Hospital up to a rehab center in Westchester. Piece of cake.

The patient was a fifty-year-old female with chronic lung disease. She had low-flow oxygen on her at all times. The new guy was in the back and I was driving. As I headed up York Avenue toward the East River Drive, I came to a stop at a red light. My siren was not on and we were not in a hurry. As the light turned green I stepped on the accelerator and nothing happened.

I didn't worry. It wasn't the first time we'd stalled. I tried to restart the thing. Nothing. No sounds whatsoever. I tried to radio to the base to advise them that the bus had broken down. Nothing. Our only radio was powered from the ambulance.

I was about to get out of the bus to find a phone when I smelled something. I looked out the window and saw smoke pouring out from under the hood. Worse still, flames were coming from under the dashboard inside the ambulance. I screamed a warning and jumped into the back of the bus. I grabbed the fire extinguisher from the wall and pulled the pin. The patient was screaming, "What's happening? What's happening?" My partner was too freaked to answer.

I shouted that everything was okay as I began spraying the fire extinguisher into the front of the ambulance. When I thought most of the flames on the inside of the ambulance were out, I kicked open the back doors and pulled my partner out. We had to get our patient out of the vehicle. She was still on the stretcher, still on oxygen, and still screaming. We yanked her out of the back and into the fresh air, the traffic, and into the middle of a blinding thunderstorm which chose that very moment to burst.

The only building where we might have sought shelter was the upper East Side ASPCA, but I couldn't see rolling our patient in there. We got out of traffic and more or less out of the rain by huddling up against a tree, which wasn't too smart considering the thunder. I ran down the block and found a phone. I called the dispatcher and yelled for another ambulance forthwith. It arrived surprisingly fast.

The dispatcher asked if there were any other ambulances back in the garage that I could switch into and finish the tour. I started laughing. Not only didn't I care if there were any other buses, but I was quitting. I never wanted to get into another Empire State ambulance again as long as I lived.

The graduation party for my medic class could have doubled for a Christmas party since it fell only a few days short. Lenny had taken the top honors, despite all of our attempts to edge him out. Steve Moffett and I were a close second and third. At the party, we finally got to meet the infamous Mrs. Zweil. She seemed quite nice, and denied that her husband ever lied to her, but I refused to be convinced. Dr. Zweil's teachings would stick with me. I still believe that Mickey Mouse has the answers but won't tell us, and I only lie to my mother.

CHAPTER 3

I was lucky. St. Luke's/Roosevelt hired me right out of medic school as a per diem, meaning that they called me whenever they needed a shift filled and I got paid by the shift, as opposed to having a regular schedule and a regular salary and benefits. Normally they required a year of medic experience, but I pushed hard for it, and my boss, Dan Mathisen, probably figured I wouldn't go away, so he took a chance on me.

Actually, I really wanted to work for St. Vincent's Hospital, partly because of my tradition of choosing the closest working place, but also because Jo-Ann now belonged to the Vinny's hospice program. I thought it would be more convenient for both of us to keep it all in the family. They were less flexible, though, about the one-year-experience requirement.

Steve Moffett and Tom Clappi both got medic jobs at Beekman, and Lenny went to work for EMS.

Cabrini Hospital downtown hired Georgia instead of me, but I think I got the best deal in Rosy anyway.

Once upon a time, St. Luke's, on 113th Street, and Roosevelt Hospital, on Fifty-eighth Street, were independent institutions. They merged to become one large hospital center on the two sites. Although the two hospitals still have very distinct personalities, they work as one corporate entity. The ambulance department for St. Luke's/Roosevelt primarily functions out of the Roosevelt site. When I started, there were about twenty EMTs and medics working fulltime for the Pre-Hospital Care department, and at least as many working on a per diem basis.

Before they actually let me out on the streets, I had to have a meeting with the Medical Director and a complete physical exam. I don't know which was worse. The Medical Director was the same doctor who had intimidated the hell out of me during my training. He approved me for the position, but I was still terrified of him. I respected him immensely but hoped I wouldn't run into him often.

The physical was a disaster. First, they locked me in a soundproof room and forced me to identify various bings and clangs. This proved that I had a slight left ear hearing deficit. Then, to get back from the hearing lab to the employee health services office before it closed, I had to run down eight flights of stairs and through the building. Surprise! I now had slightly high blood pressure and a previously undetected, but not serious, heart murmur. Finally, they tested my vision, only to find that my sight had somewhat deteriorated and I needed a new prescription for my glasses. I had walked into the hospital thinking I was in perfect health. I walked out thinking I was in worse shape than Jo-Ann.

I already knew some of the EMTs and medics at Rosy from my ambulance rotations there. I got a beeper and made sure I was available for any shift they wanted me to work at any time with any partner. I was raring to go.

My introduction to the 911 system was unpleasant, though probably fairly typical: my first day as a paramedic, we only handled a few calls, but not one person was alive.

I was working with Sean Faughnan, a veteran medic, on Twelve Young. Sean was a great person to work with as a rookie because you learned exactly the way things should be done. A classic obsessive-compulsive, Sean did everything strictly by the book. I knew all the protocols by heart, but he even had the punctuation memorized. If a protocol said to administer Y five minutes after X, Sean would count the seconds.

Sean introduced me to about forty people, many of whom I'd be seeing around for years to come, even if we didn't exactly become close personal friends. It was all a big blur; no one made a particular impression on me, and I'm sure I didn't make any impression on them. Because the turnover is high on the streets and in the E.R.s, there are always new people coming on the job.

Sean took one look at the first patient, a look at his watch, and said, "The time is now . . ." Then he picked up his radio and called EMS.

"Twelve Young, we've got a 10-83NR," he said, and we were finished with the call.

Ten-83 (DOA, dead on arrival) is one of EMS's

most commonly used codes. Paramedics never have to ferry corpses about, so we use the NR code (DOA, not removed). Many medics have their own favorite way of expressing it. I was surprised at first to hear dead people being referred to as "10-83 Nancy Reagan" or "10-83 Noodle Roni."

When we arrived at one of the DOAs, the cops told us that this was "a good one." The guy died lying on his side with his arm sticking out over the bed. Rigor mortis set in and his arm froze in that position. A woman who claimed to be his secretary discovered him the next morning and rolled him onto his back, which left his arm sticking straight up into the air. It looked a bit funny like that, but even funnier when the police officer grabbed the arm and shoved. The whole body tipped over and sprung back, the arm swaying like one of those inflatable punching clown dolls.

There we were, playing with a corpse and having fun. I felt a bit uncomfortable about that at the time, but Sean assured me that the feeling wouldn't last, and now, hundreds of dead people later, I know he was right. You can't get all serious, he explained. If you get wrapped up in the death or the moment of pain, you could never go out there and treat someone else. Each call has to be a separate issue; no overlapping. Imagine if someone called 911 because his spouse was having a heart attack, and the medics walked in teary-eyed because they just saw a six-year-old die in a car crash. You have to be able to devote a hundred percent to each call. Theoretically, at least.

A large part of the job is "pronouncing." A medical authority has to legally pronounce somebody dead. Nobody with less medical training than an EMT can do it. The police can't. If the corpse is decapitated, disemboweled, blue and stiffer than hell, the cops still have to call EMS in to pronounce. The morgue or the funeral home cannot collect the body until the legal pronouncement has been made. You don't have to know how, why, or when the person died or who he is. You just document, legally, that on this day, at this time, this person was declared dead by a qualified medical authority.

It isn't always so obvious, and it isn't always tragic. The job affects your sense of humor. I've seen dead bodies in just about every conceivable position, and I'm sorry, but some of them were just plain funny. I saw one old lady who died sitting up, with one arm resting on a table. I sat next to her, and when the cops arrived it took them about ten minutes to realize she wasn't alive. I once arrived at a call to find the cops talking to a dead guy who still had a cigarette in his mouth that the cops had lit for him.

There are varying states of death. It doesn't always look the same or smell the same or inspire the same kind of reaction. There's obvious death, such as decapitation, or when rigor mortis is present, or when there's significant dependent lividity. Lividity occurs when the heart hasn't been pumping, so the blood that normally stays in the blood vessels and organs starts to leak out into the lower parts of the body's tissues. If you come upon a patient in cardiac arrest who has dependent lividity, there's no sense in trying to save him. He's been dead too long. If he's in cardiac arrest but doesn't have significant lividity or rigor, you have to start CPR and attempt resuscitation. These are guidelines, but there are exceptions and freak cases. Sometimes, deciding that there's nothing more that can be done and that resuscitation should not be attempted is a tough call.

− I got used to corpses very quickly. Starting that first day, I saw them in cars, in bars, crammed under the bathroom sink, in closets, behind beds, in bathtubs, in the Hudson River. The hanging bodies were and still are the worst. The whole face is distorted, and if the eyes have stayed open, they seem to follow you around the room, staring at you as the body slowly swings around.

The TV shows never deal with this aspect of the job—the DOAs, the pronouncing—although it is a major part of what you do, along with the paperwork, the boredom, and the mess that are also miraculously absent from the lives of television medics.

After a few days working 911, it was strange to realize that for me to have an exciting day at work, someone had to get run over by a bus, jump out a window, get shot, or have an equally life-threatening medical emergency. On any given eight-hour shift at the hospital, the paramedic ambulance will respond to up to twelve calls. I was a prime example of the White Knight syndrome—of wanting to save the day, itching for exciting calls. I was on a perpetual adrenaline high.

I probably looked like a typical rookie, loaded down with all my equipment. One sign of a rookie is how much stuff he's got on his belt. You have to wear one to carry the radio, scissors, tourniquets, lights, or any other accessories you want with you. Normally, the more experience a medic has, the less stuff he carries. You just don't need it all. I've had a red reflex hammer on my belt for six years, and I've only used it a handful of times. I only keep it there for variety in color. I don't have many red things.

I'd come home after every shift I worked and babble a bit about what I'd done. Jo-Ann probably wasn't very interested, but she let me ramble on, with a tolerant, amused, "boys will be boys" attitude.

At the end of my second week on the job, I sat down in the ambulance crew room with a handful of scrap paper and a mile of EKG paper, all ready to write up my first cardiac arrest kill report.

The ambulance call report is a legal document that has to be filled out on every call. Theoretically, every report is sacred. In reality, no one really pays attention to them unless the call involves unusual events, patients who refuse medical attention, or death.

In this case, we had worked up a cardiac arrest and then decided to pronounce him on the scene. To explain the call to a nonmedic, I would say, "In consultation with the medical control physician, we elected to discontinue the resuscitation efforts and declare the patient dead." To a medic, I would simply say, "A kill."

The kill came at the end of the eight A.M. to four P.M. tour. We wouldn't be going out on any other calls, so we went back to the hospital to restock and do the paperwork. I was writing the call up as my partner put the ambulance back together. The four-to-twelve crew came staggering in. Each one felt he had to look over my shoulder and give me a hard time.

"Your first kill?"

"Plant him there?"

And so on.

But Jim O'Kelly was the roughest on me.

"You don't honestly think you're going to hand in that report, do you?" O'Kelly was one of the more scholarly medics at the hospital. He always knew the answers to everything and made sure that everyone knew that he knew.

"What's wrong with it?" I demanded.

"Lots. The down time isn't clear. Is that total down time, down time to CPR, or down time to ALS? Which?"

I rewrote the entire thing. He wandered back to take a look at it.

"Nope . . . Nope . . . You forgot to label the EKG strips. You got times on these?" He tossed it back to me.

I rewrote the whole thing again. Jim took another look.

"Better. But you forgot to document what he was doing prior to the arrest."

"Why didn't you tell me this before I started rewriting it again?" I asked, getting pretty fed up.

"It isn't my job to write your reports. Do you want to just write it or write it correctly?"

After the third or fourth rewrite I came close to getting it right. I was about to stick the ambulance call report into the envelope and go home when Mike Gebhardt popped in and demanded to take a look. Gebhardt was a veteran medic who was so thin and pale that he looked more like a patient than a medic. By this time I figured Gebhardt and O'Kelly were in cahoots. I fully expected Mike to find all sorts of faults and tell me to rewrite it again. He held it up and started reading.

"Uh-huh, uh-huh," he said. "Did O'Kelly help you with this?"

"Sort of. He gave me some suggestions."

He chuckled. "How many rewrites?"

"Too many."

"I subscribe to the 'brevity is best' rule," he said. "What would *you* have written?"

He thought for a second before saying, "We arrived. Gave him some drugs. It didn't help. He died. We left."

I respected both of the medics, but I decided to find my own middle ground on this one. Jim, Mike, and Sean busted my chops a lot at first, but they taught me well and I enjoyed their company. I made a lot of mistakes, but never the same one twice. When I rode with them, I knew that Twelve Young—now Fourteen Young—had a certain reputation to uphold, and they were very serious about it.

Medics have rotating schedules, to make sure all the shifts are covered. Most work every other weekend and have days off in the middle of the week to make up for it. You might be two days on, one day off, three days on, one day off, two days on, a weekend off. . . . That's considered normal and regular. As a per diem, taking whatever shifts I could get, my schedule was even more erratic. I could never remember when I would be working without checking my pocket calendar. But I had no trouble remembering the first afternoon shift I was scheduled to work with Gebhardt. Only two months earlier, I had ridden with Mike as a student, the third man on his bus, and I really enjoyed it. I was looking forward to working with him now as his partner, though not yet his equal.

Partners generally take turns driving, switching roles halfway through the shift unless something unusual comes up and one partner clearly has more experience in that field. If a male and female medic are working together, they may quickly switch roles for sensitive gender-specific calls. A rape victim may be uncomfortable dealing with a male medic and would feel better about having a woman ride with her. If a guy got hit in the nuts with a baseball bat, the male medic might take the call.

The medic driving is responsible for cleaning the ambulance after a call. This can be more disgusting than the call itself. There are two essential pieces of equipment in back to minimize the damage: emesis basins (more commonly known as barf bags) and a suction unit. If a patient says he's feeling nauseous, the medic in the back usually warns his partner, "Hey, he feels sick. I wouldn't hit too many bumps if I were you." The ride is never too smooth anyway. New York City is full of potholes, and the suspension on an ambulance is not great. The bus makes all sorts of bouncy squeegee noises as it moves.

If you screw your partner by messing up the bus while he's driving, he'll do the same to you. Better to keep it clean. On a very nasty call, I'm very likely to transport the patient in the backup BLS crew's ambulance. I try to use their suction, their AMBU bag, their MAST (Medical Anti-Shock Trousers) pants. . . . Let them clean up the mess afterward.

In addition to driving and cleaning the bus, the driver is responsible for restocking whatever is used and doing routine stuff for patient care. The medic not driving, who rides in back with the patient, does most of the talking, gets the patient's history, makes most of the medical decisions and does all the paperwork.

I was the one driving when the EMS dispatchers

assigned us to a Jumper Down at 436 West Fifty-second Street.

"That's right next door to St. Clare's," Mike said. As we approached and looked at the street numbers, I had a funny feeling.

"Shit, that's not next door to Clare's," Mike said, "It is Clare's!" Just what I thought.

I called EMS back on the radio to confirm that this call was coming from inside the hospital. I had been told to expect the unexpected on this job, that anything could happen, but this seemed ridiculous. The police were arriving and seemed as befuddled as I was.

Oddly enough, Mike explained, paramedics are sometimes called for emergencies inside hospitals. If someone has a heart attack in a specialized hospital such as the New York Eye and Ear Hospital, the staff there is ill equipped to handle it. Occasionally someone will fall or get hit by a car in front of the specialized hospital. Good samaritans will see the hospital sign and drag the victim inside. The last thing Eye and Ear could possible deal with is a multiple trauma from a car crash. They call 911. The medics treat the patient and transport him to a hospital with a proper emergency room.

In this case a terminally ill cancer patient had apparently decided that she didn't want to live anymore. She climbed out her fifth-floor hospital room window and jumped into an air shaft. She was discovered much later by a maintenance man who called the emergency room. They called 911. I'm still not sure why. They might not have had the people to spare. In all fairness to them, the E.R. doctors and nurses have little or no training in extricating people from air shafts, but in this case there was nothing to do but pronounce anyway.

"If you touch the radio, I'll break your hand."

It wasn't a joke. I had been warned about Ted Dunn.* With all the rotating schedules, medics trading shifts, getting injured, banging in sick, taking personal days, marriage days, death-in-the-family days . . . everyone in the department ends up occasionally working with everyone else in the department. It's important to find partners you work well with, whose company you enjoy, but it's also important to be flexible enough to work with just about anybody. Ted wasn't known for his flexibility. He probably wouldn't really have broken my hand, but I wasn't sure I wanted to risk it. He wasn't a tough-looking guy, just a tall, thin white guy with a handle-bar mustache, but he had a real don't-fuck-with-me attitude.

"You might be some hotshot new medic," he continued, "but you're working with me tonight."

"Okay," I said quietly.

"I have some reading to do. And I don't want to run around the city doing bullshit."

"No problem," I said, resigned to a horrible shift. Dunn was in his late thirties; he had been a medic for years and would probably be in the department for years to come. I didn't want to get on his bad side.

"Here," he said, thrusting two radios into my hands. "You can carry the hospital radio and the police

---

*Unlike the others I write about, Ted Dunn isn't a real person. He is, however, a composite of some of the burned-out medics I have worked with.

one. But don't turn the P.D. on. If they want us, they'll tell EMS and they'll call us."

Yes, this was going to be a long eight hours, maybe one of the longest nights I'd ever spent. We went out to the ambulance. Normally the two partners check out the bus together, one checking on the supplies inside the bus and the other checking the outside compartments. Ted climbed into the driver's seat and slammed the door shut.

"Do you want to check the outside things?" I asked him hopefully as I began opening the drug box.

"You check what you want," he replied coldly. "I don't plan on using any of that stuff." Oh, wonderful.

It was my first shift on that particular bus, vehicle 1764, so I checked everything out pretty carefully. When I was finished I went to climb in front, but my door was locked. Ted didn't bother opening it. He already had his books open and his head down. I unlocked the door and tossed my knapsack onto the floor.

BBBLLLLOOOONNNNNKKKKKKKKKK!! The sound was explosive.

"What the *fuck*?" Ted screamed at me, suddenly jolted upright. "Why don't you fuckin' look what you do?!"

Just my luck, this vehicle had an alternate air horn on the passenger side of the cab right on the floor, right under my knapsack. How many times can you apologize? I must have set a record because I hit that stupid button at least a half a dozen more times that night.

"Hey, Ted, they're calling for another bus on Broadway and Eighty-third, for an MVA. Want to go?"
"No."

"We'll probably get called for it anyway." I tried to sound reasonable.

"If they call us, we'll go. If not, we'll stay right here." I was almost pleased with his answer. At least it was more than one syllable. And at least he was willing to respond if we got called. I hadn't been sure up to then.

At about five A.M. Ted decided to take a nap on the stretcher in the back. How had he let himself get so burned out? The guy was black toast; completely crisp. Doing Advanced Life Support is hard work, a lot harder than Basic Life Support, so Ted refused to use his ALS skills except in situations where he had absolutely no choice. I couldn't understand it. Why was he still a medic when he obviously hated every minute of it? Why didn't the department fire him? His skills were excellent but it had to be clear to the supervisors that he was using them as little as possible.

I stretched out. BBBLLLOOONNNNKKKK!!

"I'm sorry. I'm sorry. I'm sorry."

"Asshole!"

"I said I was sorry."

"Asshole!"

I prayed I'd never have to work with this jerk again. I'd rather go hungry.

"How did your shift with Ted go?" one of the senior medics asked me.

"Miserably," I said. "How come he doesn't get fired if he's always like that?"

"Are *you* willing to write him up?"

"No," I admitted.

"We've got a good union," the medic told me. "No

EMT or medic can be fired without an incredible amount of documentation, which is almost impossible to obtain. No one wants to write up a coworker, and the boss can't follow someone around to get proof because the union will accuse him of selective prosecution and harassment. If someone gets fired without adequate proof, the union will get him reinstated with back pay and back benefits, and then he's really untouchable."

"Yeah, well, it sucks," I said. "He shouldn't be on the streets."

"Oh, he's not that bad," the veteran medic said, almost cheerfully. "I've seen worse."

Like the police and fire departments, EMS uses "10-codes" such as the famous 10-4 to show that a message has been received and understood. It's a whole new language that has to be more than just memorized—it has to become second nature. The codes probably do save time. It's easier to say "Fourteen Young, it's a 10-90, we're 98," than to say "This is Fourteen Young, there was no patient found, we're now available for another call." There is, however, no apparent logic to the code system. If you're 10-82, you're on route to the hospital with a patient. A 10-81, which you might expect to come before a 10-82, means that you're already at the hospital. You're 10-63, on route to a call, until you get to the scene, at which point you become 10-88.

The radios can get pretty complicated. Between the police radio, which is almost constantly squawking, the EMS radio, the hospital radio, and the AM/FM stereo, the ambulance can be a noisy place. Not to mention the background noises in this city and the bus's own sirens when they're going. You do get used to it, but it's always tricky to work the radios properly. When the sirens are on it's hard to hear anything else, including necessary follow-up information about the call.

The call sign is crucial. You have to be able to hear it over the EMS radio as soon as you're needed. Most medics work the same bus regularly and get so used to it that they can snooze between calls and wake up automatically as soon as EMS calls their number. One of the partners always stays awake, of course.

Just as I was getting used to operating the radio and responding automatically to the calls for Twelve Young, EMS changed all the call signs and really screwed me up. Medic units begin with a letter toward the end of the alphabet—Union, Victor, etc. BLS units, manned by EMTs, begin with letters toward the beginning of the alphabet—Adam, Boy, Charlie, David, etc. Manhattan used to be divided into three sections: anything below Thirty-fourth Street was 11; between Thirty-fourth and Ninety-sixth was 12; anything above Ninety-sixth was 13. Simple, until the call volume became far too high for only three regions and EMS split the borough into nine areas. As a result, Roosevelt's Twelve Young became Fourteen Young, St. Clare's' Twelve Willie became Thirteen Willie, St. Vincent's Eleven X-ray became Twelve X-ray, and so forth. No one could remember their call signs.

I'd be sitting in my bus, which I still thought of as Twelve Young, hear EMS calling Fourteen Young, and wonder why those jerks didn't respond. EMS would repeat the call several times until the dispatcher would get fed up and say "Roosevelt Hospital medic unit Fourteen Young, you used to be Twelve Young," and I'd realize it was for us. Or I'd hear a call for Twelve Young and respond without thinking. When the dispatcher gave us a call intended for the lower East Side unit from Cabrini Hospital for a job on the Bowery, miles out of our area, I'd realize I had goofed. I'd have to call back and say, "Oh, sorry, I forgot. We're not Twelve Young anymore."

Every now and then there'd be a glitch in the EMS radio system and the dispatcher would have to instruct all units to turn off the radios simultaneously, count to ten, and turn them on again. Once, a ditzy dispatcher told everyone to "Turn off your radios. We'll tell you when to turn them back on." Everyone complied gleefully and went off for a very long lunch.

Too much blame is put on the dispatchers. They have a very hard job. I would go crazy trying to juggle a couple dozen units with a hundred calls coming up on the dispatch screen every hour. Unfortunately, judging from the calls we get, some of the dispatchers do seem to lose some marbles. They have been known to send downtown crews to Harlem, Harlem crews to Greenwich Village, and East and West Side units to the wrong side of the park when units are available in each of those areas. They have lost crews and left them sitting idle for hours while calls came in for their area. But as I said, it's a bitch of a job.

Several years ago I was in Coldwater, Michigan, with an old college girlfriend. We were driving around town when I heard a siren far off in the distance. Denise slowed down and pulled off the side of the road, as did the cars in front of us and behind us, to allow the sheriff car to go by. I was dumbfounded. I had never seen this happen before—it was just like in the books. Even if New York drivers wanted to do this—and they don't—there's just no place for them to go.

Driving in midtown or downtown Manhattan is a joke. Beekman Hospital units have to deal with Wall Street traffic. St. Vincent's has Greenwich Village. St. Clare's has the worst problems of all. Their area not only includes Times Square, but also runs into the Lincoln Tunnel and Penn Station traffic, not to mention the West Side Highway, which is always wall-to-wall cars. Don't even bother trying to call Thirteen Willie on a Friday afternoon. All the sirens and lights in the world won't help them get to the call quickly.

A veteran medic, my partner for the day, was driving the bus when we got a call for a cardiac arrest. The traffic was awful, and as we inched downtown a taxi stayed right in front of us and refused to let us pass as he looked for a fare. He was bugging the hell out of us. It's very frustrating to be stuck in traffic, trying to respond to a confirmed call with your lights flashing, siren blaring. The police or the BLS unit is calling for medics, and you can only sit there and fume.

When there's traffic, there's traffic, and there's nothing you can do about it, but it's even more frustrating to be held up unnecessarily by bad drivers like this guy. New York is full of lousy drivers. Most of them are from New Jersey, but some are merely guilty of what EMS people call "DWO" for "Driving While Oriental." Racist, I know, but even Oriental EMS people use the phrase. I can't explain why there are so many lousy Oriental drivers, but the phenomenon is common knowledge. This particular case was one of New York's famous taxi drivers. They've gained their reputation by doing eighty miles an hour in city traffic, weaving in and out of lanes without looking. Not this guy. He was only typical in his attitude that he was the only car on the road that mattered. He wasn't going anywhere and he wasn't letting us go anywhere either.

My partner took charge. When the taxi came to a full stop to let someone walk over and get in, we rammed him. I couldn't believe it. The taxi lurched forward about five feet. The cabby still refused to pull over. Since we still couldn't get around him, my partner backed up and, as we tried to pass him on the left, we bashed in his left rear taillight. I thought we should stop, but my partner, who really seemed to be enjoying himself, said no.

The cabby followed us to our call. As we went through lights, he ran them right behind us, honking his horn and screaming at us so loudly he drowned out our siren. I thought we were going to have real trouble. After all, we had left the scene of an accident; an accident we had caused. We probably could have gotten away with hitting him the first time given the circumstances, but backing up and hitting him again would be hard to explain. I had worked so hard to get this job, and I was sure that this would get me fired already.

In the end, nothing happened. Maybe the cabby didn't have his papers in order and reconsidered his position when he saw the army of police officers at the scene of our cardiac arrest. I still expected him to lodge a complaint with Roosevelt, but weeks went by without trouble. Ambulance 1765—"the old Enterprise," as we lovingly called it—was so banged up to begin with that nobody even noticed a new dent.

I personally hate responding to motor vehicle accidents. If the call comes in as "car vs. truck," "overturned vehicle," or "car off the highway," then it's probably a good call, with people who really need help. But if the dispatcher just says "MVA," then it's sure to be a Mickey Mouse fender bender with lots of whiny people saying, "Oh, I think my neck hurts." They've all got what's known in the trade as Allstate-itis. Nobody is truly injured, but one out of a million might be, so we always have to take it seriously. It involves a lot of work: full cervical immobilization and lots of documentation for the insurance companies.

I was assigned to work a shift with Mike Roth, and I was more than a little apprehensive about it. The guy was a legend in the department, but no one would really point him out as a role model. A veteran medic, he was forty-nine, balding, pushing 300 pounds, and he seemed to think everything was funny. Everyone said he was a good medic and seemed to like him, but they also rolled their eyes back whenever they said his name. He teased every-one unmercifully and made the crudest jokes imagin-able. You could never get a straight answer from him. As it turned out, this shift was extremely and unpleas-antly memorable, but it wasn't Mike's fault at all.

Mike and I had an observer riding with us, a new E.R. nurse who was supposed to see medics in action and get to know the procedures for ambulance crews. All new E.R. nurses come out for a shift or two, and new E.R. attending physicians come out from time to time. E.R. personnel need to see what goes on out on the streets. Maybe medics won't start an IV on a patient because the crowd is unruly or because there are no lights. There is a world of difference between providing care in a nice, safe, deodorized, well-lit emergency room and doing it in the streets. Since the doctors are the ones who establish the protocols for EMTs and paramedics, it's good for those doctors to see the conditions the medics work in. All this observing supposedly builds a stronger working relationship. This nurse wasn't really approaching the experience with an open mind, however. She obviously didn't think she would learn anything by riding with us, and she made it clear how she felt.

A call came in for a suspicious smell. Mike and I grimaced at each other. I had already learned what that meant. Bodies are often not discovered until they start to smell. Someone calls the cops, and the cops call EMS.

EMS Call-Receiving Officers (CROs) aren't allowed to classify a call as a DOA because the victim is not officially dead until a qualified medical person says so, no matter how obvious it may seem. The call comes in as an "unconscious" or a "cardiac arrest." Someone will call 911 and say, "There's a really weird smell coming from this apartment, and we haven't seen the lady who lives there for two days." That call also comes in as a cardiac arrest. Two units, a BLS bus and a medic bus, hurry to the scene to stand outside a locked door for twenty-five or thirty minutes until the cops can get it open for you to pronounce.

Death doesn't look pretty, but believe me, it smells a lot worse. Everybody in EMS knows what a DOA smells like, but no one can really describe it. All you have to say to an EMT or a paramedic is that the body had that terrible DOA smell and everyone knows what you're talking about. The worse the decomposition, the stronger the scent. Medics categorize DOAs as fresh, ripe, or very ripe.

This smell was coming from one of those single-room-occupancy hotels, which never smell too good to begin with. As soon as we got off the elevator—by some miracle it was working—we could pronounce just by virtue of the stench.

"Oh boy, is this guy ever dead," Mike said. I facetiously made the sign of the cross without saying anything. As we approached the room, it became harder and harder to breathe. The cops were outside the room with handkerchiefs over their faces.

"The door's locked. The super's coming up with the keys," one of the cops told us. There are no ventilation systems in those places. The windows either don't open or are nailed or painted shut. The air was still and every breath was heavy. This was obviously a very ripe DOA. In a nicer place the neighbors would have called a few days earlier, but nobody much cares in these places. All EMS crews dread getting called to them. Any medic could tell you all the names and addresses of the SROs in his area. They've got long, dark corridors, thirty or forty cell-like rooms per floor, one bathroom for the whole floor, and they're roach and rat-infested.

Luckily the super came quickly. We could hear the lock opening and closing, but the door would not open. We tried to force it by kicking and pounding it, but it wouldn't budge.

The police called for the Emergency Services Unit (ESU), who handle anything unusual or dangerous. These guys are great. When a civilian needs emergency help he calls the police. When the police need emergency help they call the ESU. Two ESU guys showed up with a sledgehammer. Crude but effective.

We were right behind the ESU officer when he took a mighty swing and broke the door down. A rush of stagnant, decomposing, maggot-infested air burst out of the room and choked us all. Two regular cops, two ESU cops, two paramedics, and one new nurse almost killed each other as we lunged down the hallway to get away.

The son of a bitch inside had not been content with just killing himself—he had turned his room into an airtight crypt by nailing his door shut and epoxying around the door and window areas. Normally the smells get out through the door airspaces or out the window. In this case the smells had to go through the walls and ceilings and floors before anyone called. This guy had been dead, overdosed on pills, for weeks.

I was glad the nurse had been along for the ride. It was the sort of experience she would never have inside the hospital. The only DOAs they get there are fresh ones that don't stink yet. Since she seemed determined not to enjoy her time in the ambulance, she might as well suffer as much as possible.

I finished the paperwork downstairs in the lobby, pitying the poor cop who had to babysit the stiff until the morgue guys came to remove it. I did get my nerve up to look at the body after the mass exodus. I held my breath, ran as fast as I could down the corridor, and took a guess at the suicide's age and skin color and fled. How can I describe that smell? It was like ten-day-old rancid meat mixed with two-week-old sour milk and rotten eggs, all fermented into a stew and shoved up my nose. No, it was worse than that.

• • •

My imagination ran wild when Gebhardt and I were called in mid-April to the scene of a high-rise fire in midtown Manhattan. I pictured lots of victims, injured, burned, or suffering from smoke inhalation. I'd already dealt with burn victims, mostly from fires, although there were also the occasional "stupid" burns. You still see people who open up the radiator when their car overheats to add fluid to it, and of course the stuff is high pressure and goes up in their faces. They're in a lot of pain, but you just want to berate them for being such morons.

I visualized the call in my mind the way we had been taught in medic school. I asked myself what I expected to find, what the problems could be, where I would take the victims. I imagined victims with seventy-five to eighty percent total body burns, grisly third-degree burns, the skin charred and leathery, sloughing from the body, pus oozing from open sores, everything red, purple, and black, smelling of burnt hair.

I'd have to transport the victims extremely carefully, I reminded myself, wrapping them completely up in burn sheets and putting dressing on them. They'd be in a shitload of pain, and there would be nothing I could do about it except be as cautious as I could not to add to it on route to the burn center.

Where would I take the patients? St. Vincent's used to be a burn center and is still very good with burns. Harlem Hospital qualifies as a burn center, but I think N.Y. Hospital/Cornell Medical Center is the best. If I had a severe burn case, I'd take it to Cornell.

I had it all set up in my mind, but it didn't quite happen that way. We arrived and they handed us a very stable patient, a fire fighter who had gotten too much smoke. We gave him oxygen and took him to Bellevue.

Believe it or not, this won me my first award; a Manhattan Borough Command commendation "for conduct above and beyond the call of duty." Doesn't that sound impressive, even heroic? I couldn't believe it, and I certainly didn't brag about it. What if somebody asked for details? What could I say? "Yeah, an exciting high-rise fire. Of course, I never even went inside the building . . ."

Like all the uniformed services, EMS has its share of the award game. They look good on a résumé but don't really mean anything. There are Pre-Hospital Save awards, Borough Command commendations, Vice- and Presidential citations, honor awards and valor awards, each with a corresponding pin. I've never understood how they award them or why.

At that time it seemed that people were being issued these things for any big media event. I know city medics who were issued them for successful standbys without seeing a patient or even getting out of the ambulance. I came, I saw, I got a commendation.

After I worked per diem for about three months, Rosy took me on full-time. I was then working five eight-hour shifts a week but I still bounced around a lot. I'd do some midnight-to-eight shifts with two fairly steady partners and some four-to-midnight shifts with various people.

Some of the initial excitement of being a medic had already begun to wear off. I know I talked less about the job when I was home than I had in the first months. Jo-Ann had her own medical problems to deal with; she didn't need to hear about other people's. I began to keep my work life and my home life separate. When I came home from work, Jo and I would go out to eat, go for long drives, just be together. It was a happy time for me.

I could almost feel my hide getting thicker as I learned to become more detached from what I was seeing and treating. The degree of detachment is necessary. You have to acquire some emotional insulation. There are all sorts of official protocols to follow, painstakingly established and evaluated by a select group of doctors, but every EMS worker knows that the most important rule is to protect number one. The first thing to do at the scene of a cardiac arrest is to take your own pulse. New medics usually think, "Oh my God, we're in a lot of trouble here. This guy's going down the crapper." More experienced medics know that *they're* not in trouble; the *patient* is in trouble. When I was just starting out and going warp speed to even minor injuries, my more experienced partners would sometimes ask, "Does your family live in this building? No? Then slow down. We'll get there." If it's not a member of your immediate family or a coworker, it's not worth killing yourself for. You do your best, but you stay as detached as you can.

The patients are anonymous. The job is oddly impersonal, considering that you're trying to help people. You may learn the patients' names and medical histories; you may see them naked; you may see their insides; but it's never what you would call intimate. A lot of the patients you never see until they are already dead; most of the others are in and out of your life in a matter of minutes. You rarely even think of them as people. You don't stop to think about their home lives or their professions; you only care about the physical condition. It's not a middle-aged, married Jewish stockbroker having a heart attack, it's "a fifty-five-year-old rule-out M.I." It's not the captain of a high-school basketball team, it's a "a seventeen-year-old male shot." You don't want to know about the arrest's wife and kids when you decide to terminate a cardiac arrest. When I talk about a call I almost always dub the patient Mr. or Mrs. Abernathy. Why not?

A "good" patient is one who doesn't interfere with what you have to do and who doesn't present any particular problems. Good patients are nondescript: when you show up, treat and transport a patient without any hassle, he doesn't stick in your mind afterward. Patients only become memorable when things get weird or they give you a hard time.

I was mostly working night shifts and I loved it. I had always been somewhat nocturnal. The city seemed kind of mystical at night and a lot less dirty. There was very little traffic past midnight. If it just rained, everything would glisten and smell relatively good. The lights were pretty, especially if there was a bit of fog. The ships on the pier would all be lit up and the hookers would stroll in their Frederick's of Hollywood best. There were high-class call girls with the business look over by the big hotels, and lower-class ones who advertised by letting it all hang out. When I worked with a male partner, we would go around the block a few times to get a better look at the union meetings on the corners. We would wave and wish the ladies a pleasant evening. They would give us their sales pitch and point out that we did have a bed in the back.

The calls were usually more exciting at night, too, although I wasn't always prepared for them. Thank God I was working with people who knew what they were doing.

The first time I saw a serious shooting was one evening when I was working with a female medic named Kim Fallon. Mike Gebhardt was picking up some overtime by working on the basic life support ambulance with Lewis Moore, an EMT. Both of our units responded to the call. A drug deal had gone sour and there was some shooting. One of the bad guys was shot three times in the abdomen and chest and was lying in a pool of blood. My adrenaline was really flowing; I was scared. The police were running around with their guns drawn, looking for the other bad guys. I became totally incompetent. I was supposed to be making the decisions, but after a few seconds it became obvious that I was working on autopilot and not locking into the call. I knew there were a lot of things I should be doing, but I couldn't seem to remember what they were. Luckily, Mike was there to take over. He did the patient assessment while Lewis and I put the antishock pants on the patient. Kim set up most of the equipment and Mike ran the call. On route to the hospital Mike attempted the intravenous and I tried to get another set of vitals. I felt bad about blowing it, about not being able to take charge, about letting someone else run *my* call, but Mike didn't rub it in. I'd get used to it soon enough, he said.

I heard the TV click on. The volume was very low and I could barely hear it. I had worked all night and would have preferred to sleep a little longer, but I knew it was impossible. It was *Family Feud* time.

"How can you watch this show?" I mumbled, less than half awake.

"Shut up," Jo-Ann replied lovingly. "Go back to sleep."

"I can't sleep knowing that there are still people out there in the world that Richard Dawson hasn't kissed."

"Shhh. The show's on." I pulled myself up and propped my head against the wall. The top six answers to something incredibly moronic were on the board, and two idiots from two equally stupid families were trying to guess what it was. How could someone as intelligent and witty as Jo actually like watching this show? She watched both the daytime and the evening episodes religiously.

"I can't believe we're watching this," I groaned as a commercial interrupted the fierce competition.

"You don't have to. Go to sleep."

"I'm sorry. This show is just so stupid."

"Shh . . . Like the nonsense you watch is so realistic!" I rolled over and stuck a pillow over my head. She did have a point. And though I would never have admitted it, maybe I needed an occasional half hour of mindless game shows. After a night of blood, dirt, and fear in New York City, I could stand a half hour of Middle America smiling too widely, everybody a winner.

I was working a midnight shift on the West Side when a call came in for a double shooting across town on the upper East Side, just bordering on Spanish Harlem. We must have set a new land speed record getting there because we arrived about the same time the East Side unit did. It was mayhem.

There must have been a hundred people lining the streets watching the events unfold. Apparently a Hispanic guy had found out that his girlfriend had been turning a few tricks on the side for extra money. He went berserk and tracked her down to where she was working. He blasted her twice with a shotgun before shooting himself in the chest at point-blank range. He was dead, dead, dead.

The girl was lying in a large pool of blood, but the locations of the gunshots—in the shoulder and hip— weren't critical; the major organs appeared to have been spared. With a lot of blood and surgery to stop the bleeding, she might be salvageable. I had no trouble taking charge this time. I knew just what to do. We started CPR and put the medical antishock trousers (MAST pants) on her. We called EMS to have them notify Metropolitan Hospital that we were coming in with a trauma case.

We wheeled the stretcher over to the patient's side, and on the count of three we all lifted her as gently as we could. *Sploosh,* plop, plop, plop. All her internal organs fell out onto the street. This poor girl had been shot *three* times, not twice. Once in the back, right between the shoulder blades point-blank. When we found her on the ground with obvious injuries, we started CPR right away. Nobody had thought to roll her over to look at her back. A rookie mistake and a bad one.

Oh God, we fucked this up bad, I thought. What would we tell Metropolitan? With a simple medical cardiac arrest, not trauma related, after you try everything you can simply cancel the code, stop CPR, and pronounce. But with a traumatic arrest, once you elect to run the arrest you are committed to transporting the patient. There was a whole team of surgeons and emergency personnel waiting at the hospital for a girl whose lungs and heart were rolling down East Ninety-eighth Street.

I had heard a story about a coworker who responded to a call for a Man Down. It was winter and the patient was all bundled up. He appeared to have had a heart attack, so they started CPR and called for a backup. They intubated him, started IVs, put him on the EKG monitor. Everything to no avail. When they got him to Roosevelt, they discovered that the patient had in fact been stabbed with an ice pick in the back, right into the heart. He had needed fluids and surgery, but he had gotten drugs and shocks. It was an honest mistake, but the guys responsible got an enormous amount of abuse about it. I was sure we'd be in for similar misery over this one.

Happily, I was wrong. We got off surprisingly easy, partly because the patient had been very dead to begin with. All we really did by working her up unnecessarily was to dirty our equipment, waste a lot of energy, and piss off another hospital's emergency room. If the incident had occurred in our catchment area and we had taken her to St. Luke's or Roosevelt, we might never have heard the end of it. Since Metropolitan was an upper East Side hospital, one we didn't deal with very often, the staff there could only be angry with some nameless West Side medics.

My worst screw-up in my early days, perhaps in my whole career, occurred that year on New Year's Eve. For the "big three"—Thanksgiving Day, Christmas Day, and New Year's Day—the hospital puts up a request list for full-timers who want the day off, and they choose by seniority, so the newer guys usually get stuck working along with per diems. As you might imagine, New Year's is the worst, a medic's nightmare. Medics have to run their asses off all night long. Hundreds of thousands of people wander down to Times Square, drink heavily and make asses of themselves. The heaviest shift is from midnight to eight in the morning on New Year's Day as the parties break up. It's not my idea of a good time. I'd rather lock myself in my apartment, pull the covers over my head and forget the whole thing.

That night I was working with Sean on Fourteen Young. We were assigned to a report of a bad auto accident on the West Side Highway. Fourteen Adam, a BLS unit, also responded. One of the EMTs on Fourteen Adam was also a registered nurse with considerable medical knowledge. Even so, on the streets he was under the medical authority of the paramedics, and wasn't very happy about it. He was a ball buster; he would find a sore point and continually pick away at it. From a union perspective this wasn't necessarily a bad thing: the bosses could never put anything over on him. But personally, it could be hell. Everyone in the department knew that the important thing was to not piss off this guy. Luckily, he's no longer with the department.

This car accident was a bad one. An old-style Dodge had driven off the road at high speed, flipped over and struck a tree. There were two kids inside the car, one in cardiac arrest and the other with a broken leg. The fire department and police were on the scene, trying to get the kids out. We could hear one of the kids screaming, and the other only had a few minutes left before we would be unable to resuscitate him. We requested another backup.

We managed to get the arrest victim out of the car and started CPR. We immobilized his neck and back, placed a breathing tube down his throat, and put the antishock pants on him. As we moved him to the ambulance, one of the firemen told us that the requested backup ambulance had arrived.

We needed three of us to transport the arrest: one to do chest compressions, one to ventilate, and the third to drive. We took one of the EMTs with us and left the other, the ball-breaking R.N., to work on the broken leg with the backup ambulance.

This is how I learned the hard way that you must never, under any circumstances, believe anything that you don't see for yourself. The other "ambulance" that had arrived on the scene was in fact just a police emergency vehicle. The R.N./EMT had been left stranded on the highway without a partner, with a patient trapped in a car. The police and firemen finally extricated the patient, but the R.N./EMT had to work alone until the backup arrived about five minutes later. Luckily the patient only had a broken leg. If he had died, Sean and I would have been in deep shit. We were the highest medical authorities on the scene and were responsible. Leaving the EMT alone was committing abandonment of the other patient.

There were no legal or professional repercussions from that foul-up, but the ball-breaker made our lives hell for a long time. More than six months went by when all he would say to me was, "Out of my way, rookie." All he would say to Sean was, "You should

have known better." For about a year he told everyone he spoke to how we had abandoned him. He'd see
us going out to work and he'd remind us, "Be sure you
guys don't leave anyone on the highway tonight."
Over and over again. He finally got off our backs when
someone else did something equally stupid and he
decided to harp on him instead of us for a year or two.

Whatever he thought, Sean and I felt we re-
deemed ourselves soon after when we responded to a
Man Under. You see a lot of confrontational situations
in EMS: Person A fighting Person B. Car 1 versus Car
2. Truck versus Car. But there is nothing like Subway
Train versus Person. I have yet to see a person come
halfway close to winning that one. The human body is
tough and resilient, but not compared to a subway
train. The limbs come right off; the body is opened
with no resistance. People can die, and no one on the
subway would even be aware of it.

Occasionally someone falls accidentally in front of
an oncoming train. Some people are pushed. Some
use the subway as a means of suicide by diving in front
of it as it rumbles into the station. I find this extremely
offensive. Not only do I have to go down there and
pronounce and thousands of commuters are delayed,
but someone has to pick up all the parts and clean the
train.

What I find incredible is the number of people
who like to play chicken with the trains. This has to be
the stupidest game I've ever heard of. They balance
themselves on the chains that separate the cars and let
go, standing on the chains as the train races through
the tunnels and trying to last longer than their friends
do. Eventually the loser either falls forward and loses
or he falls backward and really loses.

Our Man Under was a loser at chicken who had fallen backward over the chains near Ninety-sixth Street on the Broadway line. The subway wheels ran over his legs twice, once just above the knees and once just below.

When we got there the power had been shut off and we went onto the tracks. We had to use our flashlights to see anything. Our victim was a twenty-year-old white male, or maybe Hispanic—it was hard to tell in the dark and I was looking more at his legs than his face. He had lost a huge amount of blood and had totally destroyed his legs. They were just gooey clumps. It was hard to even decide which piece belonged where. It was slow moving down there and it was so dark that if you put something down you might never find it again.

We put multitrauma bandages and dressings on his stumps and placed what was left of his torso, abdomen, and pelvis into the antishock garments. We put his "lower legs" into the MAST suit with the rest of him because, as mutilated as they were, they were still sort of attached to his body by little strands of flesh. We administered oxygen and IV lines and started to carry him upstairs.

The cops had decided that he would be going to Bellevue, which is the leading reimplant center in the city and is one of the best trauma centers around. We didn't think he'd make it that far. We also didn't think there was anything the Bellevue microsurgeons could do for our patient. With a nice, clean amputation, those guys are great, but this was a tearing/pulling/twisting/crushing injury. The cops disagreed with us, but it was a medical decision so we outranked them. It would be our tails in the sling if the patient died going to a far hospital when there was a perfectly good trauma center—but not a reattachment hospital—just fifteen blocks away. We transported to St. Luke's, calling a full trauma standby. The surgeons, anesthesiologist, radiologist, and orthopedist were all waiting and did an excellent job.

That can be one of the toughest decisions medics have to make. We saved his life by taking him to Luke's, but we threw away any chance at saving his legs. In this case, we did the right thing. The Luke's guys said the legs couldn't have been saved. Sometimes you just don't know which way to go. You can't flip a coin. The patient's life and future are on the line. Your ass is on the line. You just have to go with your gut instinct. I hadn't been on the job long enough to have much confidence in my instincts, but I had worked with Sean enough to trust his.

I was on edge a lot. Even though most of my days were filled with minor, boring, routine work, there was always the anticipation. Even when things were perfectly calm, I was excited because a good call could come in any second. And I was still new enough that the call might be something totally unexpected, something I hadn't seen before.

When I got my first drowning call—a report of a woman drowned in her bathtub—I was pretty excited. We arrived on the scene in seconds and were greeted at the door by a distraught man, about fifty years old. He led us to the bathroom where his wife was lying, splayed halfway out of the tub. She was about forty-five, naked, wet, and cold. But she hadn't drowned; she had taken an overdose of pills. As we pulled her onto dry ground and started working her up, we asked the husband if he knew what she had taken.

"Yes. Exactly," he said. "She took fifty milligrams of Valium, twenty-five Seconals, fifty milligrams of this and thirty-five tablets of that." A strange response. Usually people say things like, "A bottle of sleeping pills," or "I know there used to be a bottle of something but now it's missing," but they are never so precise. I asked him how he knew.

"We had suicide packages," he explained. "When the time came, we were going to take them together. But we got in a fight and she took hers. . . . She must have been really mad, because she took hers and flushed mine down the toilet!"

We saved the woman's life. She eventually walked out of the hospital. I never figured out if the husband was upset because his wife tried to kill herself, or because she did it without him, or because she flushed his pills.

While I saw many cases where prescription medications were abused, I quickly became all too familiar with illegal drugs, one of EMS's major plagues. Working midnights, I used to pick up heroin overdoses all the time. Addicts would shoot up a little too much, or get the dosages wrong, or have too much heroin in their system already. A slight overdose isn't too much trouble. Usually with some painful stimuli the user can be brought back to earth. Now, I do not approve of torturing patients or beating up on unconscious people. I don't know a single person out there who does this. What we do is called "using painful stimuli to elicit the appropriate neurological response." For example, sternal rubs—pushing and grinding your knuckles into the patient's sternum—or pinching his nipple, or placing a pen between his index and middle fingers and grinding his knuckles over it, will frequently bring him out of his funklike state enough for you to talk to him; at which point you either help him into the ambulance or send him on his way.

If the user has taken more than a slight overdose, the pain won't work. The effects of the narcotics will have taken over too much of his brain functions for him to distinguish pain. Heroin overdoses also frequently stop breathing, obviously a bad thing. This is where Narcan comes in.

Naloxone hydrochloride is God's gift to paramedics. It's a narcotic antagonist, which means that it reverses the effects of narcotics. It's very simple: if a person takes too much of a narcotic, Narcan will reverse it. One of the most beautiful things about this medication—"drugs" are for addicts and abuse; medics administer "medications"—is that it will not affect anything other than the narcotics in the system. No adverse reactions. It's one of the safest meds, unless you're a drug addict. Administering Narcan intravenously or occasionally intramuscularly will within a moment or two reverse the narcotics and the patient will start to breathe.

How much Narcan to administer can be a guessing game. The more of a narcotic in a patient's system, the more "Vitamin N" is needed. But if you give an addict too much, it will reverse the "normal" amount of heroin he has floating around in his body, sending him into instant withdrawal. He'll go into convulsions, have hallucinations, feel his body exploding from the inside out. I'm told it's the most horrible of hells possible. Having seen it, I believe it. He'll also probably become violent, and nobody wants to get into the back of an ambulance with a wide-awake addict in withdrawal. You try to give just enough to get the patient breathing with minimal mental status.

I've heard stories about paramedics who, for whatever reason, have a beef with a particular emergency department. When they find a narcotics overdose, they start IVs to give a little Narcan, just enough to keep the patient alive. When they reach the hospital in question, they give the patient a huge amount of Narcan. As they wheel him into the E.R., he goes into withdrawal, becomes violent, seizes, urinates on himself. The ambulance crew strolls out; Mr. Wonderful is now the E.R.'s responsibility.

Too many times you come across a patient who's unconscious, barely breathing, with pinpoint pupils—a sign of narcotic overdose—not responsive to pain. You start an intravenous line and, while mechanically breathing for him so he doesn't die, administer some Narcan. The patient starts to breathe and two minutes later he wakes up. Then he swears up and down that he didn't take any drugs. Narcan doesn't work on anything else. If after Narcan he wakes up, it was narcotics. No ifs or buts.

Parents are especially ignorant in these situations. They scream, *"My child does not do drugs!"* You can explain all day long, they'll still be saying, "It must have been a seizure," or "I think he has low blood sugar." I actually had one parent take me aside and say, "Don't worry. This is a childhood thing. He used to black out as a baby when he had high fevers. This still happens occasionally."

People try to tell you that the needle marks on their arms are from giving blood or medical tests or vaccinations. They're not fooling me; I guess they just want to go on fooling themselves. I almost have more respect for the old-time addicts I run into once in a while. There was one old black guy in a low-income housing project way uptown who shot up all the time, rarely overdosing, though I occasionally found him nodding out in a hallway, unable to get up. With a little pain I could talk to him. He always said he was allergic to Narcan. "No, man, no needles," he'd say, "I worked too hard to get this high."

My favorite Narcan story happened during a midnight shift I was working uptown. We were assigned to a report of two males unconscious on the second floor of a Harlem tenement. As we pulled up we noticed a relatively new car parked in front with New Jersey license plates. It belonged to the two white kids upstairs, both about twenty years old, both completely unconscious and impervious to pain. One was barely breathing and the other wasn't at all. Normally with one patient, one medic would provide artificial respiration and the other would establish an IV, then administer the Narcan. But tonight we didn't have time. We also only had one AMBU bag for the artificial respiration, and neither one of us was going to do mouth-to-mouth on some guy who had obviously overdosed on heroin in a Harlem building at three in the morning. So while I provided ventilation for the nonbreathing victim, my partner drew up Narcan in a couple of syringes. Instead of establishing IV lines, we just hotshot the Narcan directly into their veins. The police arrived just as we were waking these kids up.

We had to decide what to do with them. There isn't really a law against shooting drugs. Possession and selling, yes, but using . . . not really. We could take them to the hospital, but they no longer had anything wrong with them, at least not physically. I don't consider driving into Harlem to score heroin a sign of intelligence or mental equilibrium. We discussed our options with the cops. We had better things to do than drag them off to a hospital, and the kids were adamantly opposed to the idea of going to one. The cops had much better things to do than drag them off to a precinct house. We decided to send them on their way, but before we did, my partner and I gave them Narcan booster shots in the shoulder. Intravenously, Narcan works fast, but it can wear off in twenty or thirty minutes. It works more slowly intramuscularly, sort of time-released.

The guys were about to leave when one of them looked around and said, "Hey! Where's my leather jacket?" We had never seen one.

"It's gone, guy," I said. He didn't seem to understand. I simplified it for him: "While you were overdosing and not breathing, someone came and stole your jacket."

"Well, aren't you going to help me get it back?" he asked the cops. I thought they would burst something internally, they started laughing so hard.

"That was a $250 jacket. My mother just bought that for my birthday. What am I going to tell her?" he persisted.

"Why don't you tell your mommy that you got arrested in Harlem for shooting up drugs?" one cop asked him. Mr. Wizard then politely withdrew his request for additional police assistance.

I never saw them again, but I'm sure they went back to New Jersey and told their parents that they were mugged by some black guys while going to a movie in a much nicer part of town. Maybe we should have taken them to the hospital or at least notified their parents, but these idiots were technically supposed to be adults. I hope they learned something, but I doubt it.

My first yuppie-on-coke was more typical. I soon learned the routine; it's always the same. Occasional users get very paranoid. A user will hyperventilate, become very short of breath and become convinced that he's going to die. The cocaine in his system makes his heart race. He feels the pounding in his chest, feels his lungs constrict and thinks that he can't breathe. It's called a panic attack, and lots of yuppies have them.

He decides he's dying and calls 911 at two in the morning, complaining of shortness of breath (SOB). You arrive at the address given and are usually met by someone a few doors down—no self-respecting yuppie wants the neighbors to see an ambulance in front of his place. You ask what's wrong, and the patient looks around to see if anyone he knows is watching.

You walk him over to the back of the ambulance and let him in. You tell him to calm down and you ask what's wrong. It's invariably the same story, or damn close:

"I was having a little party and I took some cocaine and I'm having a little trouble breathing now . . . I'm very nervous. I have to be okay. I can't stay in the hospital. I have a presentation to give at Shearson/Lehmann tomorrow and I have to be there."

You check him out. Blood pressure, pulse, respiration, lung sounds, EKG. Everything is usually okay, if a little elevated. Most of these cokeheads just want some medical person to tell them they're going to be all right. Legally, I can't do that. I'm not a doctor. I don't have the authority to tell someone that he doesn't need to go to the hospital. I always advise them to come with us. Usually they just need to be calmed down and watched for a while. Most don't need to stay in the E.R. for more than a few hours. If someone asks my personal opinion, I might give it, off the record, but I still make him sign a release stating that he's refusing to come with us against my strong medical advice.

Working midnights, I saw the change in trends as heroin overdoses became rarer and cocaine became more popular. Maybe it does all the things they say it does for you, gives you energy, makes you feel great, does wonders for you sexually, but it's also addictive, dangerous, and kills a lot of people.

You can't always tell what drug someone is on just by looking at him. You know it's some sort of upper when his pupils are completely dilated, not very reactive to light; his blood pressure, respiratory rate, and pulse are up; the pulse is slightly erratic, and he's anxious. Nine out of ten times they'll say what they're on.

Aside from heroin and nose cocaine, you see a little LSD once in a blue moon, or occasionally some angel dust, which is a bitch because it completely separates the mind from the body. Angel dust users will put their hand through a windshield and not even know it. They climb up to roofs and think they can fly. It takes five cops to hold down a fifteen-year-old kid on angel dust, and the cops are still scared because the kid will be totally out of his mind. It's incredibly powerful. Mostly, though, you see crack. Cheap and plentiful, crack is running amok in the city.

• • •

Every night, I saw something a little different, learned something new—often something I would rather not have seen or learned. I alternated between feeling awkward—wondering if I had done everything right, if I had done everything I could—and feeling great and full of power, a life saver. And then I'd come home to Jo and it wouldn't matter what had happened on the job.

CHAPTER 4

Sean was working a double shift one day on the same ambulance, the second half with me. When I showed up at the hospital, he was methodically filling out an ambulance checkout sheet. You're supposed to complete one every day, checking about seventy-five items, but Sean was the only medic I know who actually did. Every now and then you pull it out and do a complete check, but a quick visual check is usually good enough. You need to make sure that there are enough bandaging supplies, but you don't need to actually count the triangle bandages.

"Didn't you check everything a few hours ago?" I asked.

"Well, maybe I missed something the first time," he said. He proceeded to check every single item, even the things you hardly ever use, like the twelve large safety pins which we must have under state law.

I think the rationale behind them is that they can be used to pin down the end of a sling made with triangle bandages to keep the arm from sliding out. But no one uses them; you just tie a knot in the end of the bandage instead.

I almost had to admire his compulsiveness, although I never tried to live up to it. I did get to know the ambulance very well very quickly, every corner of the bus, every item we carry. There's a whole dispensary back there, and you have to be able to find exactly what you need at the very moment you need it. I don't want to reach for bandages and find the roll of aluminum foil instead.

"What's the aluminum foil for?" an observer asked me once. "You use it to wrap your pizza in when you get a call in the middle of dinner?"

I explained seriously that it can be very useful.

"In a childbirth, you can wrap newborns in a blanket or towel and then wrap the tin foil around all of it to maintain the heat. Or if someone has a belly wound and his guts are spilling out we can cover the whole wound in aluminum foil." The observer looked at the roll of foil with newfound respect. I decided not to add the fact that I'd never actually used it on the job.

Sean was hungry, and I can always eat, so after he finished his extremely thorough inventory, we went and grabbed a slice of pizza. I gobbled down my slice in less than a minute although I wasn't that hungry. I had already learned the importance of speed eating. Medics have to eat like pigs. EMS allows its field personnel one ten-minute break per shift, but you have to be available and listening to the radio, ready to respond if a call comes in. What kind of a break is that? Since you're always supposed to be ready for calls, I usually don't even ask for the break—a "10-100". Calling in to request it only seems to remind the dispatcher that you're out there and available, and he immediately assigns you to a call.

Even if the dispatcher okays the 10-100, it's only ten minutes. By the time you get out of the ambulance, enter the fast food joint, order, wait for the food, and go back to the bus, the ten minutes is gone. If you even make it that far. I usually get called while I'm waiting for the food, and I have to say, "Oops, sorry, never mind, I'll be back later."

At least once a day I'll hear a unit being assigned to a call and the medic will cry into the radio, "How did you know I just bought lunch?" I imagine the dispatcher watching on a hidden camera and deciding the exact moment to hit me with a call. "Now? No, not yet. Wait, wait, he's got it open, he's reaching for a fork . . . the fork is in the sweet and sour pork. *Now!*" So I inhale fast food and junk food without swallowing. It's not very satisfying, so I might have two or three of these "meals" during a shift.

Now, having successfully consumed a few thousand calories, I was in a good mood and singing along with the FM radio. A teenage boy stuck his face in my window.

"Hey, how come the 'Ambulance' is backward?" he asked, waving toward the front of the bus. It was at least the tenth time I had been asked that on the job. I always thought it was fairly obvious that drivers need to read it the right way around in their rearview mirrors.

"It's for the benefit of New York's dyslexic population," I said, deadpan. "Equal opportunity and all that." The kid looked suspiciously at me.

"Oh," he said softly, and walked away. Sean looked reproachfully at me, but couldn't keep himself from laughing. He looked tired after a full day of work.

With any other partner I would offer to listen to the radios while he climbed in back to take a nap, but Sean would never sleep on the job.

The back of the bus is well-lit, but you can turn off the lights back there if one of the medics wants to take a nap on the stretcher. Unlike the St. Vincent buses, our cabin seats don't recline, so all quality napping must be done in the back, and the stretcher is more comfortable than the cushioned bench. If it weren't for the stretcher and the row of cervical collars hanging from the ceiling in all different sizes, the ambulance would make a pretty good camper. The interior, with about five feet, two inches of standing room, is beige and white with imitation-wood paneling.

We sat up front in the cockpit, the part of the bus the patients never see. It's pretty cramped. A claustrophobic medic is as hard to imagine as one who gets carsick. I had spent so many hours there already, in both the driver and passenger seats, that I had everything memorized. I could operate the radios, lights, and sirens without looking, which isn't as easy as it sounds.

The sirens have several different options. You can change back and forth from the air horn (*Ahnk, ahnk,* as opposed to a fire-truck air horn *Gronk, gronk*), to the wail (*Whoo, whoo*) and the yelp (*Yipyipyip*). St. Clare's buses have the phaser (*Drrrrrr,* like an obnoxiously loud alarm clock), but Roosevelt favors the high and low popular with European ambulances (*EEE-aaa-EEE-aaa*). There's also a public-announcement system to broadcast to surrounding traffic. You're supposed to say things like "Please clear the central lane," or "Please move to the right," but it usually comes out more like "Hey, moron, get out of the way!"

The KDT, the police radio, and the controls for our lights and sirens are contained in a panel that takes up the space between the driver and passenger seats. The KDT used to be called a VDT, which stood for "video display terminal." They changed it to "KDT," but no one's figured out what the K stands for yet. It's a computer hookup, complete with small keyboard and screen. The screen shows information about our call, such as the call numbers, the type of call, the address. We can find out where other units are, or pull up information about our previous call to complete the paperwork, to see that the call was assigned at exactly 21:01:34, that we were on route at 21:01:40, and arrived on the scene at 21:04:05.

To the untrained eye, those of us who ride around in the ambulances all day seem to be sitting around doing nothing most of the time. That is, of course, completely untrue. You drive around, go shopping, run errands, read newspapers, or write letters. You spend a lot of time filling the tanks. (Poor gas mileage, city driving, and big gas tanks add up to astronomical fuel bills. Roosevelt spends a fortune with at least three buses running twenty-four hours a day.) Going to the bank is popular, as well as buying a lot of Lotto tickets. But you keep the engine running and you're ready to roll at a second's notice, because that's what you get paid for.

While we drove aimlessly around our catchment area, we passed Fourteen Adam double-parked. The two EMTs were just coming back to their bus after a call. Sean and I waved.

It's a very sociable job, oddly enough. You would think it would be lonely, just two people riding around in an ambulance, isolated from everyone but the patients they treat, impersonally, for only a few minutes at a time. But it's not like that at all. I'm in and out of a half-dozen hospitals every day, so I get to know the E.R. staff in each hospital and all the ambulance crews. The same faces appear at the calls, the same EMTs, medics, and cops. A breakfast date on a slow night is not at all unusual. There are a few all-night places that do a good business off us.

I know where my friends like to hang out, where they like to park between calls. If I get bored and know that a friend is working on a different bus, I can go find him, hang out and talk awhile.

Years ago, crews working the midnight shift would meet at the band shell in Central Park. Upper East Side, upper West Side, Midtown, and Harlem units would come to hang out together. There were always at least three units there at any time. That doesn't happen anymore, since two Roosevelt medics got in trouble and the Rosy units were told to stay out of the park unless expressly assigned to a call there.

The two idiots in question decided to take their bus freewheeling in the Great Lawn and got stuck. They were unable to get the bus out, even with the help of the ESU officers they called. They had to wait for Department of Sanitation trucks to pull them out the following morning. Rosy got a bill from the Parks Department for the resodding of the area. The medics weren't even smart enough to lie about what had happened—they could have claimed to have been responding to a bystander report of someone injured. Old-timers at Rosy never let them forget this incident and still refer to them as "the mud medics."

"Fourteen Young for the Man Down, Fifty-seven and Eight," the radio called.

"Skell," I groaned. At Fifty-seventh and Eighth Avenue it was almost guaranteed to be a skell.

A large part of EMS's clientele is composed of what we call skells, a term which comes from the Latin word "skellum," meaning a person deserving death. Nobody ever believes me when I tell them the etymology of the word, but it's true. I don't use it literally, but it's a good word. It's not synonymous with "street person." Not every street person is a skell—some are reasonably clean, cooperative, and polite. Being a skell is mostly a state of mind, I guess, or the lack thereof. Skells are the sleazoids, the subhumanoids that wander around smelly and oogy. They're the kind of people who like to urinate on themselves, who would throw up on a sweater and then put it back on. You know one when you see one, and you see them a lot in New York, dumpster-diving to find useful garbage, lying on the street, maybe drunk or stoned, maybe just living there. The yuppies don't like it, so they call 911 and report an unconscious person. Most of the time you just send them on their way. They're not sick and they don't want to go to the hospital. They may be a big problem for society, but they're not *my* problem.

I wasn't surprised to recognize this skell. It was Donald, an undomiciled black man, about thirty-two, who drank a lot. I used to get calls almost every week for him. He usually passed out in front of the subway steps at Columbus Circle or Fifty-seventh Street and Eighth Avenue. The cops all knew him. The transit cops would force him out of the subway so he'd be a city cop problem. The city cops would sometimes push him back down the steps to make him a transit cop problem again. When he was too polluted to stumble to another, less inconvenient location, they would call 911.

"Donald! Time to wake up!" I gave him "love taps" on the bottoms of his feet with my flashlight. A crowd of interested bystanders gathered, but for once they didn't try to interfere. Usually they like to criticize my handling of this unfortunate. It's astonishing how many concerned citizens are out there, and they all seem to be lawyers or ACLU representatives. Among the comments I'd heard in the past were: "You're violating his rights," "That man has rights," "You should treat him with more respect," "He obviously needs medical help. Why don't you take him to the hospital?" Or my personal favorite: "What's your name, your shield number? I want to report you."

"What he really needs a good bath, a hot meal, and a place to stay. Is it all right if we take him to *your* apartment?" On the few occasions that I'd gotten pissed off enough to respond this way, the critic always walked away indignantly. Bloody hypocrites.

"Donald! Wake up!"

"I'm sorry, man," he mumbled. "I'm sorry."

"Hey, Donald, you okay? You wanna go to the hospital?" He mumbled something else, but I couldn't understand it. I looked at Sean. He shrugged.

"Hey, Donald," I repeated. "You wanna go to the hospital?"

"Yeah. I'm sorry," he repeated. I made a disgusted face at Sean. Normally, when we think about transporting a skell, I ask, "Honest question, honest answer: Do you have bugs?" I try to be nice about it—even people with lice deserve medical care—but I want to know about it first. Nine out of ten skells will tell me the truth, either way. If a skell tells me he doesn't have bugs, I never believe him a hundred percent because he might not know, but in general those who do will simply say, "Yeah, man, I got bugs." As long as you know about it in advance it's no big deal.

I didn't need to ask Donald. I already knew. We wrapped him up in sheets so the bugs wouldn't get out into the bus.

"You need me to go lights and siren?" Sean asked before getting up front to drive to the hospital.

"Nah, that's okay," I said bravely. I could handle the stench. Sean drove slowly and carefully, without hitting too many bumps, to minimize the risk of the bugs getting loose in the bus. If that happened we'd have to knock it out of service for an hour while we disinfected it with special delousing chemicals whose aroma would linger for days afterward. I didn't even touch Donald again or even get near him, but by the time we got to the hospital I started feeling sympathetic itching.

I dread the thought of cutting open the shirt of an unconscious patient and seeing bugs pop out. It hasn't happened to me yet, but I dread the thought of doing CPR, looking up and seeing these things going up my arm. Delousing oneself could be very unpleasant. The delouser is very abrasive stuff. Plus, you'd have to find new clothes and bag the contaminated ones for special "nuking" from the laundry.

Medics tend to assume that skells are not really sick, not in life-and-death situations. When you go to a nice apartment where someone clean and obviously well-to-do says he is in pain and having difficulty breathing, you are more likely to take him seriously and treat him with kindness, consideration, and compassion than if you get the same story expressed less eloquently from a skell in the subbasement of the Long Island Railroad who smells bad, has urinated on himself, and has bugs. But even paranoiacs may have enemies, and even skells may have heart attacks.

Ninety-nine percent of the skells in the subbasement of the LIRR do have some chest pain because of pneumonia, endocarditis, or any one of a number of infections. You automatically tune out their complaints, saying, "Oh, this person's a skell. He may be sick, but it's not a real heart attack." That's a mistake because it might be. These people are sleazy—you would cross the street to get away from them—but they may have a real heart attack or a stroke or other life-threatening illnesses.

As Jo got sicker, it became increasingly important for me to spend time alone with her. I would go to work, do my job, and rush home. Luckily, I was working with a good group of people, whom I could talk with and who understood. I really wanted to get married, but it would have meant instant financial ruin and Jo wouldn't hear of it. The hospital bills she had already accumulated were astronomical, and we both knew that there were more to come. As long as

Jo didn't have any means of support, at least on paper, most of these bills were picked up by the state.

It's a good thing Jo was sensible about it, because I couldn't think straight. I loved her more than anything in the world, and I knew I was going to lose her. Every minute counted. We didn't want to see other people. She wasn't in real pain, just some discomfort, so we could go anywhere, do anything. She took Tylenol 3 with codeine, sometimes Valium. That was enough.

When Jo-Ann starting losing all feeling in her legs, we admitted her to St. Vincent's. They asked her if she had a religious preference. She told them she was a somewhat religious Catholic; I think they were pleased. The St. Vincent's Hospital Hospice team arranged for me to have twenty-four-hour-a-day visitation rights. I turned my schedule upside down to work day shifts when possible. I would come over after work, sleep there, get a wake-up call from the staff, and head back to work. I was afforded great privileges, for which I shall always be grateful. The oncology team and the hospice group deserve more praise than I could possibly give.

On one of Jo's first nights there the head of the hospice program, Sister Patrice (a wonderful lady) stopped by her room to talk and to get to know us. As she was getting up to leave, she asked if she could give us a blessing. I didn't even know what she meant, but Jo did.

Jo looked at me, amused, as Sister Patrice blessed us. Jo knew that I didn't have anything against her faith; I just wasn't religious. Technically I was Jewish, but I never got bar mitzvahed. My favorite sandwich is grilled ham and cheese. I have no idea when the holidays are. Displays of religion tend to make me feel uncomfortable.

People who are religious probably get more so in an ambulance. Catholics clutch their beads. It can be hard to open and close their fists to start IVs because they've got their rosaries working. Some people thank God, and I want to say, "Hey, how about thanking *me*? I'm the one who gave you the IV!" But the way they see it, God sent me, I guess. I prefer to think that my orders come from the EMS dispatcher, with no help from any higher, cosmic force. Otherwise, I might have to start to wonder why God sends me on such lousy calls sometimes.

"Take it over to 330 West Ninety-fifth for adult male, Cardiac."

"Shit," I said. "Sid." This was not a good way to start the day. The address was one of the worst single-room-occupancy-transient hotels in town, and the home of a chronic caller known to every hospital in upper Manhattan. He claimed to be diabetic, to have heart problems, to be allergic to his medication. He called 911 at least every other week to have his blood pressure checked and an EKG taken.

People like this really screw up the system. We would be tied up with this clown for at least fifteen minutes if he didn't want to go to the hospital and another fifteen if he did. Poor people in the single-room-occupancy hotels tend to be chronic ambulance callers. They don't belong to outpatient clinics, Health Maintenance Organizations or other medical plans, and they certainly don't have private doctors. Medics make housecalls—no one else does these days. Frequently the chronic patients are not themselves the callers. They drink too much or do not take care of themselves and the neighbors or the social services people call 911.

When I first came rolling into an emergency room with one of our chronic patients, the staff asked, "What's wrong with Mrs. Smith today?" There's no excuse for us to know patients' names and addresses. It's criminal—or at least it should be.

Many times these people were perfectly healthy, but if they wanted to go to the hospital, they had the right to be taken there. If I were ever to refuse to take a patient to the E.R., he would certainly die. Murphy's Law. And, equally certain, he would have a sister/lover/neighbor who knows/is a lawyer and would successfully sue.

I already knew some people in my area by heart. Not just their names, but their complete medical histories. Even what positions they played in Little League twenty-five years ago. You might expect this kind of behavior from sick, old, lonely people. Sid was only twenty-eight.

My partner didn't bother with the siren or the flashing lights, just switched on the "we care" lights—completely useless box lights you can put on for garbage calls just so you can say that you cared enough about the call to put on some lights. We moved slowly uptown.

Sid was waiting for us, as healthy as ever. We treated him with a minimum of courtesy because we were, after all, professionals, but we hated every minute of it. He decided not to go to the hospital, so after he signed the release form my partner and I headed back to the ambulance, still bitching about him under our breath.

"Garbage," I muttered. "What's the difference between EMS and the Department of Sanitation? *Their* garbage doesn't talk back." New York City's Emergency Medical Service receives between two and three thousand calls a day. Some are unfounded, some are duplicates, but a huge number are just bullshit. There are calls for broken fingers, small cuts, twisted ankles, headaches, fevers, cold and flus, anxiety attacks, the most incredible assortment of minor ailments. These do not require ambulances. When I was a kid, I fell down and broke my arm. I was taken to the hospital by taxi. When I broke a finger, I walked to the hospital.

These calls are the greatest abuses of the system. Hundreds of such calls are handled each day by qualified EMTs and medics. It wastes my time, and it wastes the time of those who are really sick or injured. They have to wait longer because the ambulances are tied up. Sometimes days went by with nothing but garbage calls, and I'd wonder why I became a medic to begin with.

One repeater, John the Seizure King, came into Rosy so often he became almost legendary. He had a gimmick. He wasn't an epileptic, but he was a fine actor. He would have his "seizures" in front of Lincoln Center or Carnegie Hall just as the shows finished and the crowds emerged. He didn't look like a street person, so after he "came around," people were very nice to him and usually lent him the taxi fare to go home. Other crews warned me about him. All you had to do, they said, was to say, "Okay, John. Come on, get on the stretcher. We'll take you to the hospital." If a crew didn't know about him and rolled into the hospital with John on oxygen and IVs started, the whole staff would start laughing. John, of course, would play his part to the fullest, figuring that he could get a wash, a free meal, and maybe a new shirt. Ironically, not long after I was warned about him, John had an actual heart attack during one of his performances and died. Poetic justice, perhaps, but everyone felt rather bad about it. He was a pain in the the ass who made our department waste time and effort and do a lot of useless paperwork, but at least he was a character. Sid was just a pain in the ass.

"Fourteen Young, take it over to Fifty-sixth and Tenth for an Uncon in the street."

I kept eating as I pulled the ambulance out into traffic, wedging my soda tightly between my legs so it wouldn't spill. I had gotten very good at eating while driving. I wasn't going to throw out a perfectly good slice of pizza just because we got a call thirty blocks away. I've seen a medic finish two cheeseburgers, an order of fries, a bag of Cheez Doodles, and a soda within a sixty-block, eight-minute run. All right, I confess: it was me.

When I drive and eat as a civilian, my passenger always wants to help me hold something. If he only knew what a breeze it is to drive and eat on the Southern State Parkway. At least I don't have to answer the radio, adjust the siren every five or ten seconds, jot down additional information and worry about the call.

There was no patient at Fifty-sixth and Tenth. No one had seen anything. False alarm. It was mildly annoying, but no more than that. My partner wrote a large 10-90—no patient found—on the ACR, and I informed the dispatcher that we were available for another call. Only a few minutes had been wasted. No big deal. I'd infinitely rather have a false alarm than a garbage call.

Only a minute or two after I told the dispatcher we were available, he was calling us again. "Fourteen Young, take it over to Sixty-six and Broadway for an unconscious male lying on the street."

The patient was exactly where the dispatcher said he was, but he wasn't unconscious, just homeless, cold, and had had a lot to drink. This was before the days when police used to forceably take people to shelters. This gentleman said he wanted to go to the hospital, so we were going to take him. It was too cold to leave him on the street. He walked to the back of the ambulance and sat on the bench. He didn't need the stretcher.

I was about to drive to Rosy when the EMS dispatcher called for any available paramedic unit for confirmed CPR in progress less than four blocks away. The only unit that answered was coming out of Harlem Hospital, at least ten minutes away. We could be there in less than one. It was frustrating to hear an important call assigned to a unit farther away because we were stuck on a garbage call. Minutes can mean lives. We were much closer, but we couldn't respond.

I hated being put in this situation. It had already happened to me several times, and I couldn't get used to it. Imagine having a patient who cut his hand and needs a few stitches and you hear a confirmed call for a child hit by a car. The cops are screaming for a bus, you're just a few blocks away, and it would take at least eight or nine minutes for another unit to get there. What would be the harm if you swung over and picked up that call too? The first patient isn't going to die with a cut hand and you're not abandoning him. He's slightly inconvenienced, but so what? He shouldn't have called for an ambulance in the first place. But, of course, it is against the rules. Unprofessional.

Fuck the rules. We decided to go for it this time. We drove over. There was an ambulance on the scene from the Jewish volunteer group Hatzoloh—known in medical circles as "the Matzoh Box ambulance"; we imitate their sirens: "Oy, vey, get out of the way." They do mostly basic life support. In serious cases like this one, they call EMS for paramedics.

We were about to call the dispatcher to say that we were on the scene and were going to take our Intox upstairs with us when another Hatzoloh volunteer came running down the street carrying an EMT bag. He asked if we were going upstairs to the arrest.

"Yes," I said. "Are you an EMT?"

He nodded, trying to catch his breath.

"Great! You have to stay with our patient while we go upstairs to the cardiac arrest." He was very upset. He was a brand new EMT, this was probably his first cardiac arrest, but instead of doing CPR and helping upstairs, he had to babysit a homeless drunk. He tried to argue for a moment but I cut him off.

"You guys called for medics. We're medics. But we can't go up unless someone is taking care of our patient, and that's you." We pulled our equipment out of the bus, introduced our homeless person to the Hatzoloh EMT, and advised EMS we were on the scene and that our Intox was being taken care of by a state-certified EMT.

We went upstairs and ran the code, but the patient was too far dead. We pronounced and returned to the ambulance, but our Intox was gone. EMS had sent a basic ambulance to transport him to Rosy for us.

Other times I wouldn't be so lucky. Encouraged by getting away with it this time, I started cheating by taking garbage calls with me to real calls whenever it seemed important enough. I took minor injury patients to cardiac arrests and got the first patient to help do CPR. I took drunks to calls, and after picking up the serious patient, put them together in the back of the ambulance. The drunk got the bench, the serious patient got the stretcher. The drunks didn't mind; they seemed to enjoy the excitement. Legitimate patients were put off and confused to share the ride with an Intox, but I would explain that we didn't need to come help them, that another ambulance would have come eventually, but I thought it would be better for them to get help fast. Most appreciated it, even with a drunk making siren noises all the way to the hospital.

Another new doctor joined the team treating Jo-Ann. He introduced himself to Jo and then turned to me.

"Oh, and you must be Mr. Shapiro," he said.

I had quickly become very well known on the Spellman wing. Jo had a huge chart, and I'm sure it mentioned me frequently. Every time I met another doctor or nurse, they'd say something like, "Oh, yes, I've read about you," or "Oh . . . of course!"

I didn't mind. It would have been almost irresponsible of the nurses and doctors not to mention me to each other. I was there every day, coming and going at the most unlikely visiting hours. Half the time I slept over. And, to say the least, I was a tad overprotective.

Everyone says you need to be healthy to survive a hospital stay. But on the oncology floor no one's healthy, so what you truly need is a guardian angel. That was me. I felt sorry for the other people on Jo-Ann's floor because they didn't have me. Their friends and family, if any, were embarrassed, shy, grateful for any attention. I knew exactly what was due Jo and made sure she got it all.

Don't get me wrong. In general, the care rendered was excellent. But occasionally, just occasionally, something would go wrong. It didn't have to be much to seem like a major crisis. At this point the cancer had gotten into Jo-Ann's spine. She was unable to move or even feel her legs. She was terminal, and accepted that fact, but was incredibly frustrated about having to rely on other people for every little thing. Just needing help adjusting her position in the bed or wanting something to drink and having to wait became a terrible hardship.

Pain medication was always the highest priority. I could tolerate almost any kind of malfunction as long as Jo wasn't in pain. With her bizarre type of cancer the pain would come and go in an almost rhythmic pattern. As long as she had the proper therapeutic levels of medications, she was okay. But if for some reason the pills were late and she developed pain, it was very difficult for her to get comfortable again, even with extra meds. The Dilaudid, which had helped for a couple of months, no longer blotted out the pain. When the cancer got into her spine and paralyzed her, Jo was started on methadone. The drug addicts I saw on the streets would have been envious.

I watched Jo wince with pain, her hands clench, and I wanted to do anything I could to relieve it. It was almost two years since I had so glibly answered Dr. Sixsmith's question about looking the other way while my partner was stealing narcotics to help his grandmother, and already my opinion on the subject was changing. Would it be so terrible if a little morphine went missing? I knew I wouldn't ever have to do anything like that—the doctors were more than willing to give Jo whatever she needed—but I could understand now why someone might.

The staff at Vinny's was very understanding. They made every effort to be available for her, but there were a lot of people with similar conditions who needed extra care; not too many other young people, but everyone needed and deserved the care. There were simply too many patients and not enough nurses. When I was there, I took care of everything Jo-Ann needed, except the medications.

Watching over Jo-Ann at St. Vincent's was a very serious business for me. It almost seemed more like work than work did. When I came up to Rosy, it was an emotional vacation. I wanted lots of good calls to do, to take my mind off Jo, calls that would not be personal in any way.

My more experienced partners, seeing how enthusiastic I was, showed me ways to jump good calls. You'd hear the dispatcher assign an interesting call to another unit, and immediately radio in that you were "just around the corner" and would respond, even if you were quite a bit farther away. Of course, then you'd have to drive like crazy to get there.

A slightly more subtle way of buffing the good calls was to listen to the police radio. When you call 911, you talk to a police operator first. You tell him what the emergency is and where. He asks for a name and a call-back number before transferring you to an EMS call-receiving operator (CRO) if you need an ambulance. Since the police operator gets the call first, it is often broadcast on the police radio a minute or two before the EMS dispatcher has assigned it. The medics listening to the P.D. radio can get a jump on the call and be halfway there before it comes up on the dispatcher's screen.

You call EMS on the radio and say, "Fourteen Young, P.D. is reporting a pedestrian struck on West End Avenue and Seventy-fifth Street. We are responding." EMS will usually say okay. Then when the job comes up on their screen, they automatically assign you and call you back with the relevant information. You get there faster and the patient gets better care. The extra minute or two can make a hell of a difference. Everyone is happy.

Naturally, if the police have two calls for your area at the same time, you immediately jump the good call. Then when the call for the wino lying in the street comes through, the dispatcher has to assign it to someone else.

I enjoyed listening to the P.D. radio, hearing what was happening in the area, anticipating the good calls. My favorite P.D. entertainment was the pursuits. It was just like in the movies, except that they usually didn't end with the arrest of the suspect. My favorite type of chase was the rolling pursuit, when cops in cars chased bad guys in cars. Frequently they had to let them get away because the chase became too dangerous to the general population. It wasn't worth killing or injuring pedestrians to catch a guy who ran a red light. You could figure out how fast they were going by how long it took the cops to call in their location. If they reported the streets by threes and fours every twenty seconds or so, they weren't going too fast. But when they were at "Thirty-fourth Street . . . Forty-second Street . . . Fifty-seventh Street" in the span of one minute, they were really flying.

This may not sound like such great fun, but when you spend all your free time in a cancer ward, a little amusement goes a long way.

Jo and I had a visit from "the Jolly Priest." I think because neither of us had objected to the blessing the first night, we were put on some sort of "blessing list." Almost every night one of the priests or Sister Patrice would stop by and came into our room and bless us. At first I wasn't too thrilled about it, but I had to smile at the "the Jolly Priest." He sort of reminded me of a religious Santa Claus: plump, round face, always smiling.

The next night Jo and I were watching television. Suddenly we heard a faint, whispery sound. If Jo hadn't looked at me with a puzzled look, I would have assumed that I had imagined it. I got up and checked outside. A man in a priest outfit stood there, tall, thin, pale and calm—exactly what I always thought a priest would be like.

"Excuse me for interrupting," he said softly. He seemed almost afraid to come into the room.

"No problem," I said. "Please. Come in." I hate to admit that I had actually started to like the blessings. They were simple, peaceful. "May God look after

Jo-Ann and Paul. Keep them safe. Protect them." Not so terrible. If there is a God, it couldn't hurt.

The priest touched Jo's head, then mine, said a few quiet words and split. Jo and I dubbed him the "Priestly Priest," and he became one of our favorites. We always knew when he was at our door, but he never really knocked, just sort of rubbed his knuckles up against the door. We'd be watching TV or talking and something would make both of us stop and look at each other and say, "Priestly Priest." I'd get up or call out for him to enter . . . and there he'd be, without fail. It was uncanny.

Between calls on an extra day shift I was working, I pulled out one of the emergency magazines I had subscribed to. There on the cover was one of the action shots they liked to show to keep people interested—gory pictures of life-saving in progress. The patient in the picture was in traumatic cardiac arrest. What he needed immediately was airway control, immobilization if necessary, MAST pants, and transport. You would almost never start IVs on the scene in this case. But in this picture there were EKG electrodes on the patient's chest, which was absurd. It wouldn't matter what the EKG rhythm was: he was in arrest because of lack of fluid and the shock from the trauma.

The more I learned on the job, the more I saw the dumb mistakes in these publications. I started paying closer attention simply because I couldn't believe it. In so many of the pictures you could see some questionable medical practice taking place. It's bad enough when TV and movies show these kinds of mistakes, but these publications are supposedly run by experts in emergency medicine for experts in emergency medicine! *The Journal of Emergency Medical Services (JEMS)* and one called *Emergency* aren't bad. Every month I would skim through them and read the articles that interested me.

The dispatcher interrupted my reading with a call for a Jumper Down. A teenager had dived out a window. When we got there, he was in respiratory distress, barely breathing, and had neck fractures which ultimately paralyzed him. There was also a pillow under his head. He obviously did not jump out the window holding a pillow. Someone had wanted to make him feel more comfortable, not that he could feel anything at that point, and slipped it under his head. Not a good idea. I can't say that it caused the paralysis—most of the damage was done when he landed on his head—but it didn't help the neck injury and it closed the airway a little bit, not good for someone having trouble breathing. People breathe better when they're lying flat.

It was the wrong thing to do medically, but I had to appreciate the intention. I think people are often scared to help, scared of getting sued. There are Good Samaritan laws in most states to cover people who give voluntary assistance, but the average guy in the street isn't usually familiar with these. In New York State—according to Article 30 of the New York State Public Health Law—"any person who voluntarily and without expectation of monetary compensation renders first aid or emergency treatment at the scene of an accident or other emergency outside a hospital, doctor's office or any other place having proper and necessary medical equipment, to a person who is unconscious, ill or injured, *shall not be liable* for damages for injuries alleged to have been sustained by such person or for damages for the death of such person alleged to have occurred by reason of an act or omission in the rendering of such emergency treatment *unless it is established that such injuries were or such death was caused by gross negligence on the part of such person.*"

Don't be scared to help. If you see someone in cardiac arrest and you decide to stop and do CPR, you will not be sued if you do it wrong and he dies. Actually, you might be sued—anybody can sue anybody, and these days often will—but you won't lose. After all, he's dead anyway. If his heart isn't beating and he's not breathing, he's legally a corpse. You can't do too much damage to a dead person. You're acting in good faith, up to your level of training, doing what you think is best, even if it turns out to be the wrong thing to have done.

A true save, someone in cardiac arrest who is brought back and walks out of the hospital, only occurs if CPR is being conducted by someone before the paramedics get there. I can't stress that enough. If the heart stops, the patient only has about four minutes before brain damage starts. After six minutes or so the survival rate is almost nil. Bystander CPR is the key to saving lives. A successful resuscitation requires the ALS skills medics are trained for, but without CPR all the advanced life support in the world is a waste of time.

When it came time to do the paperwork on this case, I looked at the kid's name and felt a shock of recognition. It was somebody I knew just slightly. I hadn't recognized him at all. He looked a lot worse than I remembered. What on earth would make him dive out a window? It turned out that he had had a fight with his mother when she caught him smoking dope. I felt strangely indifferent, and that surprised me. Someone I knew was very fucked up and was likely to die. It should have bothered me, but it didn't. It was just one of the things that happened on the job, and the job was becoming more separate from my private life and my feelings.

A new intern, his first day on the job, came to start an IV to administer antibiotics to Jo-Ann. I watched him stick two catheters into Jo's right arm and miss both times. He then moved over to the left arm and missed again. I was starting to feel weak, dizzy, and furious. I couldn't watch this much longer. Finally the intern thought he was in the vein and he removed the sharp part of the angiocath. No blood flowed from the catheter. He started to put the sharp back into the plastic catheter still in her arm. You *never* do this—it's one of the first things they teach you about starting an IV. It could cause catheter shear, which means that the sharp point could tear through the tiny plastic tubing, ripping it off and leaving it lodged in the body to do all sorts of damage. I stepped forward, took his hand and said, "No more."

I think he was as upset as I was. He tried to explain that they needed a line and that someone was going to have to do it. I tried to be nice as well as firm. I wasn't going to let him do it.

"Do you think you can?" he asked in a huff.

"Yes."

He got up, walked out of the room and returned with more alcohol preps and some new IV catheters.

"I don't want to see this," he said. "I'll be back in a few minutes."

When he returned with the antibiotics, the IV was running. It was the first time I'd stuck Jo, but I wasn't a bit nervous. I couldn't do any worse than he had.

This guy, despite his problem with needles, became our favorite intern. It became routine for me to do the sticking. He'd walk in, toss a few blood tubes and needles on her bed and say, "Two red tops and a blue-top tube please. Back in a few minutes."

He was a good guy and would occasionally come hide in our room. He'd plop down in a chair and watch TV or just chat. It was really the most anyone could do for her; she wasn't going to get better.

Most of the new interns were good, but a few were horrible. Our favorite didn't have a clue about a lot of stuff, but he admitted it. I'd ask him something and he'd give us a dumb look and sheepishly admit, "I don't know . . . But I'll come back later with the answer." And he did! Some docs would try to bullshit us with medical gobbledy gook. Unfortunately for them, Jo-Ann's cancer was so rare that I had read *all* of the medical literature on it. Sometimes I'd lend my articles to them. I might not have a clue about the proper treatment of lung cancer or leukemia, but I knew my paragangliomas.

The docs tended to have attitude problems. I understood where they were coming from: they suffer through college, bust their tails to get top grades, get into med school, study more, and finally get to be doctors. Now they're supposed to be in charge. They don't need or want some wise-guy medic getting in their way and questioning them. Too fucking bad.

They seem to develop the attitude before they

even finish med school. One woman in a white lab coat with a stethoscope and a covered-up ID badge came over to me and introduced herself as the new "subintern."

"Isn't that the same thing as medical student?" I asked her. She got pissed.

"No, I'm a subintern," she insisted. "I'm in charge of Jo-Ann's case." Now I got pissed.

"Yes, or no," I demanded. "Did you graduate medical school yet?" She had to reluctantly admit that she had not.

"So why don't you just admit that?" It wasn't unusual or inappropriate for fourth-year med students to be put in charge of patients, always answering to the residents or Attendings, of course. A lot of the students probably use the subintern scam to make the patients feel more confidence in them. It backfired with us. We didn't need people playing games with us.

Paradoxically, doctors often make the worst bystanders at accidents or medical emergencies. They have a lot of medical knowledge and training that paramedics don't, but most of it won't help them out on the street. Don't ask for my advice if you have a kidney infection, but if you're hit by a car or stop breathing, you're better off with a medic who knows the latest emergency techniques than with a specialist who hasn't had experience with any emergencies in the last twenty years. I wouldn't want a sixty-two-year-old dermatologist to treat me if I were to stop breathing. He had an emergency room rotation in medical school thirty-five years ago, but times have changed. Even an E.R. doctor doesn't have the training or experience to climb under a subway train to start IV lines. Medical school doesn't teach the best way to remove someone from an overturned car when he's got spinal cord injuries and internal bleeding. If you take too long, he'll die of blood loss; if you hurry, he may be paralyzed for life.

Most of the E.R. M.D.s know the full-time medics by name and have a good working relationship with them. It's relatively recent that doctors started specializing in emergency medicine, so these M.D.s tend to be younger. Other, older doctors haven't worked directly with paramedics and don't trust their medical opinions.

I was working a midnight shift with Sal Gonzalez, a supervisor who was working a street shift for a change. We got a call for a Cardiac in the lobby of a fancy hotel on Seventh Avenue. The patient had chest pain, was pale, cool and moist, and was having trouble breathing. I opened his shirt and applied the EKG leads as Sal took the vital signs. They weren't good: the pulse rate was about forty beats a minute, the EKG showed a second-degree heart block, and he had almost no blood pressure. The police were keeping the bystanders back as I started the IV and got the patient on oxygen. Suddenly, one man pressed forward.

"I'm a doctor . . . let me through." The cop looked at me, and I gave him a nod. I quickly explained what was going on while I finished taping down the IV line. As Sal got the atropine out of the drug box, the M.D. went nuts.

"No, no! What do you people think you're doing? You can't be doing this here! Take him to the emergency room!"

I tried to explain that New York City paramedics

have a protocol for bradydisrhythmia that includes atropine and Isuprel.

"Listen to me," he said. "I'm the chief of Endocrinology of a hospital in Massachusetts. I don't think it's a good idea for you to be doing that. It's too dangerous. You're wasting time. You should be letting the doctors in the hospital do that."

He was wrong. The only time I was wasting was the time I spent talking to him. It's true that the cardiac meds are dangerous, but the risk to the patient is smaller than driving at the speed of light to get to the hospital when he's got no blood pressure. You've got to stabilize where you are first, then transport safely. I explained what we were doing but he continued to object.

The police officer in charge stepped forward and nearly pushed the M.D. across the room. With a snide Boston accent, the cop said, "Hey! What does this look like? Massachusetts?" He then came back over to us and whispered, "If this guy dies, I'm going to have your asses." The patient did fine.

I was a young and relatively inexperienced paramedic, it's true, but that only showed in the fact that I took the time to argue and explain with this doctor and that I accepted him as a doctor without proof. Now I'd be more careful. As the law states, they must be properly identified. Too many people call themselves doctors: professors, Ph.D.s, psychologists, dentists, and lots of wackos.

Father Daniel Berrigan came by Jo's room, but she was feeling very tired that night. Usually she enjoyed his company. I had heard of him, but I didn't know much about him until he first came by the room to talk. Jo was interested in his life, and he seemed very interested in ours. The first night he came by, he blessed us, made himself comfortable and sat and talked for ages. The next time, he brought us an autographed copy of his book, *Prison Poems*, which he had written while in jail for his activism against the Vietnam War. He stayed even longer that time. I got the idea that he really didn't like having to do hospital time. He didn't say so, but he didn't seem to want to leave our room to see other people.

"I'm sorry, Father," I told him this night. "Jo-Ann's really too tired tonight." He nodded his head.

"Well, let's you and I talk, then," he said, taking me by the arm.

I looked up at the schedule posted in the crew room. "Damn." A few of the other medics glanced over at me.

"Fuck! Shit! Damn!" I sputtered.

"Something wrong?" one of them asked.

"When did Bob call in sick?"

"A couple of hours ago," said another.

Damn. I was scheduled to work the four-to-midnight shift with Bob. Now, because he had banged in sick, I was forced to work with Ted. I had been looking forward to working tonight, but now I just wanted to run away. After a long, difficult day dealing with M.D.s with attitude problems, the last thing I wanted to do was spend eight hours stuck in an ambulance with the worst attitude problem of all.

I glanced at my watch. Was it too close to four to say I felt ill and had to go home? I'd rather go hungry than work with Ted again. I would never have signed up for the shift if I knew I'd be working with him. But shit happens. People get sick or hurt; they're late or stuck on mandatory overtimes. I was trapped.

Ted pulled the ambulance over to the side of the street and parked.

"Wait here," he ordered. "I'll be back in a few minutes."

"Where are you going?"

"Out. I'll be back in a few minutes."

"How do I get ahold of you in case we get a call?"

"Don't worry. If we get a job, hit the siren and I'll be out in a few minutes."

He climbed out of the bus and slammed the door. He started to step away, then suddenly turned around and stuck his head back into the cab.

"And don't volunteer for any jobs! Only touch the radio if they call us."

And he was gone, God knows where, visiting someone, or shopping, maybe. I sat there like an idiot, worrying. What if he didn't return? What if we got a job and he didn't hear the siren? I started thinking again, as I always did around Ted, about burnout.

Most of the horror stories you hear involving EMS are due to burnout. The newspaper story about the EMTs in Brooklyn who told a lady with abdominal pain that there was nothing wrong with her and refused to take her to the hospital without even doing a physical exam or getting a complete history—she later died of massive internal bleeding—is an obvious example. My guess is they were just lazy; they didn't want to carry her. I doubt they work anymore, and EMS may still be involved in the lawsuit.

In another reported case a man in the Bronx supposedly died of an asthmatic attack immediately after the ambulance crew told him he would have to walk out to the ambulance. He was in acute respiratory distress. He collapsed, stopped breathing, and died. Critically ill people cannot walk to the ambulance. We have stretchers, stair chairs, and other carrying devices for that. I certainly don't carry everyone I treat, but if someone needs to be carried, he gets carried.

The line between a veteran medic and one who is burned out is as blurry as the one between a rookie and a veteran. It's an easy job to burn out in. Most medics try not to bring the job home with them, psychologically speaking. (Practically speaking, they bring home bandages, aspirin, and other supplies—none of the really expensive items, of course.) If there is an exciting or weird call, you might want to tell people about it—I've been known to go on at great lengths—but you can't let the work get to you. You can't go to bed thinking, "Oh God, that kid died in my arms. I feel like shit." You'd go crazy.

Actually, it's the volunteer medics in the boonies who probably suffer the most psychologically from the job. They only handle a serious call once in a blue moon, so if it's a bad one, it sticks with them. The medics on the streets every day see too much of it. When you have something really nasty, like a little kid run over by a truck, it's horrible; but ten minutes later, after you've done the paperwork and cleaned up the ambulance, you've got another call to do.

Every once in a while the collective horror wells up and you go out and get smashed or kick your dog or something. But in general you just don't let it bother you. Most medics blow off steam by griping about the job, by making all sorts of sick jokes, constantly laughing at death, gore, and themselves. EMS came up with a bumper sticker that showed an EKG line progressing from a flat line to a normal pattern and ending up as the New York City skyline. The medics at Rosy turned this around to show how New York had a normal EKG until we arrived, at which point it died.

But in a job where a bad attitude is the norm, where bitching and moaning are par for the course, you can't always tell when someone crosses the line and is too burned out for the job. In Ted's case, there was no question.

I was getting nervous about how long Ted had been gone. How long should I wait before I called EMS and reported my partner AWOL? Then he came back, and after a few minutes of stony silence, I began to wish he'd go away again.

"Fourteen Young, you've got an Uncon at Fifty-seventh and Broadway." Ted didn't move.

"Uh . . . Ted?" I said quietly. "Aren't we going to respond to this call?" I knew better, but I couldn't help myself.

He didn't even look up, but his long mustache twitched. "I'm not done with this page yet."

How foolish of me. And how inconsiderate of the person on Fifty-seventh Street to be unconscious.

"I'll be done in a few minutes," he said. "We have ten minutes to get there before they start to ask for updates. We'll be there before then."

It was true. Even with the three- or four-minute delay, we'd get there within the time allotted. But somehow it seemed like a good idea to get there faster, like in five minutes instead of nine. The time discrepancy probably wouldn't make too much difference. The odds were that the case wouldn't be life-threatening or even an emergency; probably just a homeless or skell. But you never know, and sitting in the front of the ambulance, looking out the window, waiting for Ted to finish his page, was incredibly frustrating.

God, I thought, I hope I never get to this point in my career. If I find that I no longer want to treat patients the way they should be treated, I hope I'll be able to walk away from it. Most do—there are very few fifty-year-old medics. Mike Roth was the only one I knew, and he was a different story altogether.

"I don't see anything," Ted said quickly as we came screeching to a stop at Fifty-seventh and Broadway. He was all ready to fill out a 10-90.

"Oh shit," I mumbled.

"What?"

"There," I said, pointing through the windshield to the opposite corner. "Right under the Duane Reade drugstore sign."

"Fuckin' Donald," Ted said. "I'm not getting out for this."

Donald was crumpled up on the street, passed out, facedown. Dirty, but somewhat less disgusting then usual. A pretty businesswoman was standing over him, waving at us. I shook my head and climbed out of the bus. It was the third time I'd been called for Donald that week.

"I'm not sure if he's breathing," the young woman said. She was carrying a leather briefcase that probably cost more than I made in a week.

"Oh, sure, he is," I said calmly. "Donald's indestructible."

"You know him?" She seemed surprised.

"Of course." I reached out with my foot and gave him a slight nudge. "Donald! Time to wake up!"

"*Uummm*ppphhhh," Sleeping Beauty groaned. "I'm okay."

"I know, Donald. But you have to get up. *Now*."

He rolled slowly over and looked up. He reeked of alcohol, but I would have been surprised if he hadn't.

"Hey, man, I know you!" he said, with something approaching animation.

"Of course you do." I pulled him into a sitting position. "You want to go to the hospital?"

"No. No, I'm okay today. I don't need no hospital." He wiped his face with his hand. Traces of snot stuck to his sleeve.

"Okay, then you know the rules. You have to get up and walk away." He stumbled to his feet. I watched him carefully in case he fell.

"Aren't you going to take him to the hospital?" the woman demanded.

"No. He doesn't want to go." I was still watching Donald for any sudden movements. He seemed pretty coordinated today.

"But doesn't he need medical care?"

"Oh, sure. But he doesn't want to go."

"He'll probably just lie back down on the street somewhere else," she protested.

"That's where he lives."

Donald started to shuffle away eastward.

"See you later, Donald," I said.

"Bye, man. See you later," he muttered back.

"And you're just going to let him wander away?" the woman asked, getting angry.

"Yup."

"And what happens when he lies down and some-one else calls 911?"

"We'll come back and see him." I was getting bored with her. "But it probably won't happen. He'll probably head over to the Park and sleep it off there. If we're lucky he'll cross Fifth Avenue."

"Why?"

"Because then he'd be in New York Hospital's catchment area and they'd get called for him."

Ted played the same waiting game on the next call, but this time it was for an asthmatic citizen who needed some real treatment and who would have appreciated a faster response. When we finally ar-rived on the scene, Ted treated the asthmatic per-fectly, which reminded me what a good medic he could be if he only wanted to. I've seen many such cases since. Some of the worst medics have the most knowledge and the best skills. They've been medics for years, have seen everything, treated everything, have more experience than anyone else, and try to avoid doing the job at all costs.

As soon as we turned the patient over the E.R. staff, Ted decided to take a mini-vacation.

"Roosevelt Young on the air for an update?" EMS called us for the third time. "Fourteen Young in the hospital for forty-five minutes . . . Yankee/Young/Roosevelt medics for an update, please."

"Shouldn't we give a signal, Ted?"

"In a few minutes," he said, leaning back on his chair in the ambulance crew room.

"I finished restocking about ten minutes ago," I prompted.

"Switch the oxygen?" he asked, uninterested.

"Yes. And restocked the drug box. And replaced

the LifePak batteries. Cleaned up the back of the bus. *And* logged the call on the envelope."

"Hmm," he mumbled through his mustache. "Okay, I'll be ready to go in a minute."

I really hated working with him. Everyone occasionally holds a signal while they grab a cup of coffee or a bite to eat. Unlike police officers, medics do not get a lunch break. After thirty minutes of CPR, I need a soda or a snack. If I don't take care of myself, I won't be able to take care of anyone else. But that's every now and then for a few minutes, not every call, every day. Ted was impossible. He held signals every call, waiting till the EMS dispatchers called us to give a signal instead of just expediting and giving them an update on our own. He was a master at manipulating the system.

"We've been in here for forty-five minutes," I reminded him.

"Don't worry about it," he said. "I'll take care of it."

"I don't like holding my signals."

"Hey! I said I'll take care of it." There wasn't any arguing with him. By the end of the shift, I was happy to return to St. Vincent's, where, in comparison, everyone was helpful and friendly. When I walked onto Jo's floor, the nurse at the desk smiled and waved. It was amazing what a difference that made.

Besides tolerating my constant presence, the nurses at Vinny's also taught me how to take care of Jo. I was a hot-shit paramedic, but I had no clue how to change the sheets on a bed with a patient still in it. Medic school never taught me how to insert a foley catheter or how to change a bedsore dressing.

I seemed to get along with almost all the nurses.

One of the midnight nurses was married to a medic, so that helped. After they got to know me and felt comfortable with me, we developed an excellent working relationship. We were all there for the same reason, except I was more like a private duty helper. And I took my duties seriously.

I was at home one night sleeping when the phone rang at some absurd hour of the morning. Jo-Ann said she was sick and the handheld buzzer to summon the nurse wasn't working. I had been deeply asleep and I wasn't dressed, but I arrived on her floor in fifteen minutes. My name was with the security people at the door and I had permission to enter after hours, but I didn't even bother with that. I just grabbed my medic jacket, EMS shield, and hit the door running. The guards assumed I worked there. I was probably out of control, because I don't remember now who I yelled at or what I shouted, but it was effective. I got things straightened out in a hurry and spent the rest of the night at the hospital.

Jo only had to call me for help a few times. The staff was relatively young and probably sympathized more with Jo than with the other, older patients. But I also think the staff made a conscious decision to avoid giving me a reason to show up. If there was just one nurse available and Jo and some other patient needed help, the nurse would have to choose which one to treat, and they knew that if Jo was slighted, I'd come storming in, no matter what the time. Was I wrong? Abusing my position? Probably. Did I care? Not really. I felt bad that other people were possibly not receiving the highest level of care because of my ability to influence things. Sometimes I felt bad that no one else had someone who could just pop in at four in the morning and bitch if something wasn't right. But I wasn't in love with any of the other people on that floor. This was family. Nothing else mattered.

Father Bill Kilody was assigned to ride an orientation shift with me. He seemed like a neat guy, a minister who had become a E.R. nurse at St. Luke's, a broad-shouldered fellow with thinning gray-blond hair and a mustache. I wanted to give him a good shift, but we were all out of luck. We got garbage call after garbage call, skells, false alarms, minor bullshit.

Finally, after almost eight hours of boredom and frustration, we got a call that sounded like it had potential, a G.I. bleed in lower Harlem. We raced up there to find a big, fat, black woman in cardiac arrest on the floor of her one-room studio apartment. Her neighbors, who had made the call to 911, stood anxiously in the hall.

The patient was covered with coffee-ground-like vomit, a textbook symptom of a G.I. bleed. We could assume that the arrest was due to hypovolemia—blood loss—not a heart attack. Instead of administering cardiac drugs, we needed to get the MAST pants on her, give her lots of fluids, and get her to the hospital as quickly as possible so they could give her blood.

I had a horrible time trying to intubate this lady; there was too much vomit, and she was so fat that it was very hard to manipulate her head and neck. Father Bill was a big help, doing CPR compressions while my partner and I attempted the advanced life support. With each compression, more vomitus shot out of the patient's mouth. Everyone got splattered, but Father Bill didn't flinch.

There was no unit available to back us up, so we had to carry this huge lady down three flights of stairs by ourselves while she vomited nonstop. We continued the resuscitation attempt until we got to the E.R. and the doctors there pronounced her dead. Welcome to the streets, Father Bill.

After work I hurried back to the hospital, always in a hurry to squeeze out the moments with Jo. I stopped off and picked up Japanese food, mostly the more exotic, spicy dishes. By this time our choice of activities was seriously curtailed, but we spent great quality time together. When it got bad, at least we were together. Mealtime became an event. Jo never lost her appetite, and I've never had that problem either. Japanese food was one of our favorites. We'd feast at St. Vincent's at weird hours.

A night nurse wandered into the room and looked around with a "what do I smell?" look on her face. I told her that Jo and I were taking the night off, we were off-limits. After the midnight rounds and pain meds, no more contact, please.

We shut the door and pretended we weren't in a hospital. The staff didn't worry, because I was there. Of course if we needed them, they would have been only too happy to help. I climbed onto her bed—by this time she didn't take up a lot of room—and we just watched TV, ate, held hands and slept.

CHAPTER 5

It was a windy fall day. A long board—four by six inches by ten feet—blew off a new skyscraper going up on Eighth Avenue and Fifty-seventh Street. A young man was passing by, in the wrong place at the wrong time. It looked like an animated cartoon, when one character hits another with a pot and you can see the indented shape of the pot in the head. Except that it wasn't funny and it wouldn't just bounce back a second later. This guy had his two ears intact, but not much in between. There was a goofy expression in the one eye that was left, as if he were wondering what happened.

Colleagues had recently told me of a DOA they had pronounced, a Columbia College student who was killed when a gargoyle fell off a building and hit her. She was just walking down the street and a moment later she was dead.

It's a cliché, but every now and then I get an extremely vivid and gruesome reminder of how true it is: you've got to live life for right now, for today. I felt it more than ever with Jo getting sicker and sicker.

It also crossed my mind, just for a second, that maybe this wasn't such a bad way to go. Maybe Jo would have preferred this kind of death to the kind that was coming. At least this guy with half his head on the sidewalk didn't have to deal with the certainty of impending death, the pain, being at the mercy of everyone around him. One quick blow, and that's all, folks.

By then, Jo had developed an obstructed kidney. She wasn't in too much pain because of all the medication she was already taking, but she was spiking very high fevers. She was depressed about it, worried that the really bad times were beginning.

Urology was called in for a consult. A young doctor, short and thin, barged into our room late one night, very businesslike, clutching her clipboard. She introduced herself as the urology resident and ordered me to leave the room. I didn't usually leave the room when the doctors were talking to Jo. I had hardly ever been asked to leave. I had certainly never been ordered to leave. I fought to remain calm and polite.

"I'm sorry," I said. "I don't usually leave. I'd prefer to stay."

"Sorry," she said. "I don't examine patients with other people present."

At this point Jo-Ann and I were very familiar with the rules and regulations. We could recite the Patient's Bill of Rights by heart.

"I'm sorry too," Jo stated. "I don't feel comfortable

having you examine me without him being present."

Now we had a standoff. The doc refused to examine Jo with me present, which was more or less her right. But Jo-Ann also had the right to refuse any examination.

The doctor started threatening us. Not physically, of course. But very clearly threatening.

"There will be serious ramifications because of this," she said. "The Attending will not accept this reasoning."

I tried to explain that we both felt it was important for us to participate in everything that happened to her medically. Jo explained that if I was in the hospital, I was present for everything, including examinations.

The doc repeated that the Attending, who would be coming over tomorrow morning, would not allow me to be present. He would not tolerate this type of behavior. She implied that Jo's care would be compromised unless we gave in to her pronto.

Finally I asked who this all-powerful Attending was.

"Dr. Robert Furey," she announced reverently. I almost fell over.

"Dr. Bob Furey?" I gasped. "About five feet, eight inches? Short-cropped hair? Receding hairline?"

"Yes, that describes him," the doc said, confused.

"Jo," I said, somewhere between a yell and a laugh, "you met him last summer. Remember? Dr. Bob. The medical director of my volunteer fire department."

It was a beautiful coincidence. I had known Dr. Bob for years in the other context and had completely forgotten that he was also an Attending in urology at St. Vincent's.

"There won't be any problem with Dr. Furey," I told the resident, who got mad and split.

The next morning I was sound asleep in my chair, head back, mouth open, feet up on Jo's bed, when the urology team wandered in. Dr. Bob tapped me on my leg.

"Dr. Bob!" I exclaimed, jumping up, shaking his hand. The line of interns and medical students following him, including the witch of the night before, were shocked by my familiarity with the boss. Bob and I talked about our rescue squad. We were interested in purchasing some additional equipment and I needed his authorization. We discussed the pros and cons of MAST pants as opposed to additional oxygen supplies. After about ten minutes of this, he said, "Okay, now let's check on Jo-Ann."

He didn't throw me out of the room, although I'd have left if he'd asked. For Dr. Bob, anything. Occasionally, I glanced over at the resident who had tried to turn a simple examination into an unnecessary power struggle. She was clearly uncomfortable. Good. I never mentioned it to Dr. Bob. I didn't have to. Our resident turned into the sweetest, most considerate doctor in the hospital. It's all about who you know.

After the kidney obstruction was surgically corrected, Jo-Ann decided to come home and forget about any more surgery or radiation. We only had so much time left together; we didn't want to spend it all at Vinny's, friendly nurses and priests or not. She had been in there more than three months and was sick of it. This was a difficult decision for Jo, not just because it meant admitting defeat and waiting for death, but because she didn't want to be a burden to me. I wasn't worried about that. I wanted her home.

I converted our bedroom into a mini intensive care unit, with large oxygen tanks, a hospital bed, IV pole, even the sliding table that fits over the bed. And medicine. Lots and lots of medicine.

The St. Vincent's team was instrumental in getting us home health aides so someone could be with Jo while I was at work. Home health aides are people hired to sit with someone who needs help doing normal day-to-day functions such as eating, cleaning, going to the bathroom. They are not medical personnel, just babysitters for adults, usually for the elderly. Sadly, ours were idiots. Some of them could barely read. I have no idea how they actually found their way to our apartment. I wouldn't let them do anything. I told them they just had to be there, to get her something to eat or drink if I wasn't home. Jo couldn't stand to have them hovering over her, and they weren't exactly stimulating company, so she usually asked them to stay in the living room unless she called them for something. One of them took to compulsively cleaning the apartment out of sheer boredom. The place was never so clean, before or since.

When I went to the pharmacy St. Vincent's deals with to pick up Jo's drugs, the pharmacist took one look at my order and went nuts. All the paperwork was properly completed, with forms in triplicate and a previous request by the hospital, but nobody ever gets that amount of drugs per month. He double- and triple-checked, made call after call. Jo was taking enough methadone to keep a few addicts happy and the doctors at Vinny's had also arranged for us to have Levo-Dromoran, an injectable synthetic narcotic which usually cannot be had outside the hospital.

I didn't mind waiting while the pharmacist triple-checked everything. I knew how unorthodox it was, and frankly, I was as scared as he was. What if I got mugged on the way home? The street value of these drugs would have been impressive. I took taxis door to door.

When it was time to go to work, I kissed Jo good-bye and loaded up a syringe with a few mg. of Levo for her. She was now taking between 80 and 100 mg. of methadone a day. If she needed an extra shot of Levo, she could give it to herself.

I had taught her how to administer the medication herself in case I wasn't there to do it for her. It wasn't pretty to watch. Since she didn't have any feeling below her belly button, she just jabbed the needle blindly into her leg, then, while holding the syringe, she pushed the plunger down with the other hand. She didn't feel a thing, but I got goose bumps just watching her.

We were called off the streets at three A.M. for an in-service training at the hospital. Legally, ethically, the department is obligated to provide us with a formal update or class on each new piece of equipment the department plans to use. Not that it requires much training to use a new brand of head immobilizer or cervical collar. Most of the time we already know how to use it or are already using it out in the field, but we have to sit through the in-service anyway. Sometimes it's as simple as viewing a fifteen-minute videotape. This time, a service rep from the company that manufactured the equipment actually came over to the hospital to give a small presentation.

Most of these sessions are greeted with less than an enthusiastic response. It's an opportunity to get off the streets for an hour or so and kick back in the E.R. conference room with a soda or cup of coffee, but most of us would prefer to skip the "lesson." At three A.M., when the streets are quiet, all you really want to do is relax, maybe take turns snoozing.

I had to feel bad for the company rep. Here he was, at an absurd hour of the morning, all excited and enthusiastic and ready to talk about his product. A handful of tired EMTs and medics staggered in, plopped themselves down with food and drink, put their feet up and faced him, bored and tired, with looks that said clearly, "Okay, we're here. Let's get this over with."

The home health aides were incredibly underpaid. I almost didn't mind them not being able to read or speak understandable English. For four dollars an hour, what do you expect?

But I did expect more from the Visiting Nurse Service of New York. I've actually heard people say nice things about them, and maybe there are some great nurses out there, but I didn't meet any of them.

To benefit from the home health aide service, we were required to submit to a weekly visit from the Visiting Nurse Service, partly to check up on the patient, but partly to make sure that everything was okay with the aides. We scheduled the weekly visit to be on Wednesdays, my usual day off.

A nurse arrived, clutching a great big file. Picture

Nurse Ratched in *One Flew Over the Cuckoo's Nest*. I assumed this file contained some information about "the Patient." I assumed the nurse could read. After all, she did pass the R.N. test. Maybe she just didn't like to read. She certainly knew nothing about Jo's medical condition. Zippo.

She entered our room, walked over to the hospital bed and barked, "Okay, let's climb out of the bed and get you moving."

Jo gave me a look that silently screamed, "Don't you dare say anything!"

"I'm sorry," she politely informed the nurse. "The cancer has gotten into my spine and collapsed it. I'm quite incapable of getting out of the bed."

That came as a shock to the nurse, who began frantically rummaging through her files to find out if we were telling the truth. I was seething. I desperately wanted to toss this person out of our apartment.

To regain control of the situation, the nurse started telling us what we were doing wrong. The physical therapy, such as it was, was "inappropriate." We tried to explain that the St. Vincent's hospice team sent a nurse over each week and we were following their routines. Quite happily, thank you very much.

She didn't understand or care. I don't know how we got through that visit without me punching her out, but we did.

Toward the end of the month, I got nervous that we'd run out of drugs for Jo. I called the hospice team and they sent Jo's nurse, a great guy named Graham Bass. Graham had been following Jo's case since her hospital stay. Far from an inconvenience, he was a welcome guest. He brought Jo's prescriptions, stayed, chatted, and checked us both out. He was ostensibly there to check on Jo-Ann, but he never left without having a little talk with me, to make sure that I was holding up under the strain.

Sean and I got a call on the upper West Side for a one-year-old child choking. We flew up there and arrived in about a minute. The time elapsed from when the call was placed was about three minutes, tops. A young girl, about fifteen years old, opened the door of a basement apartment in a lovely brownstone.

"I think everything's okay now," she said. The baby had turned blue and started to gag. The girl, a babysitter, had flipped him over and managed to dislodge a marble that was stuck in his throat. The baby still seemed to have trouble breathing, so the babysitter called 911, which was absolutely the right thing to do.

When we checked the kid out, he was fine; alert and oriented, no distress. The problem was that the parents weren't there to sign a release form. Legally, we had to take the baby to the E.R. Minors, except for legally emancipated ones, are not allowed to sign release forms. If you're called to an accident, you must transport the minors, even if they're perfectly fine, unless a parent or legal guardian is on the scene to sign for them. It is, quite literally, kidnapping. Legal kidnapping. And it's a pain in the ass for everyone involved. The kid doesn't want to go because there's nothing really wrong with him, but he has no choice. You take him to the emergency room, and his parents eventually get billed for both the ambulance and for the E.R. visit. If the kid lives nearby and someone can go get a parent or responsible guardian to the scene to sign the release form, fine. You sometimes make that effort, but you can't wait too long for his mother to show up when it would only take you a few minutes to get him to the hospital, do the paperwork, and be ready for another call.

It wasn't a bad idea for this baby to go to the E.R. anyway. There was a chance that the marble might have torn something when it was lodged in the throat. The problem was that the babysitter, who was also looking after the baby's older sister, didn't want us to take him. She was terrified of getting in trouble for all this. She insisted that she had been left in charge and should make the decision. From our standpoint she was a minor and not even legally responsible for herself, let alone for anyone else.

The cops showed up and decided to help us track down the parents. They were supposed to be at some friends' house, but when we called there, we got another babysitter who said that both couples had gone to dinner in Greenwich Village. We called the restaurant, but their phones were out of order. Meanwhile, we were spending far too long on this call.

The cops contacted their boss, who contacted an officer in the restaurant's precinct, who sent a patrol car to notify the parents. In case the parents were already on their way home, I left a message on the door which stressed that everyone was fine, and we took the whole crew to the hospital.

When we rolled into the St. Luke's pediatric emergency room, the nurse handed me the phone. It was the baby's father and he sounded pretty hysterical about hearing from the cops that his kids had gone to the E.R.

"Calm down, sir," I said. "Everyone is fine. Don't kill yourself trying to get here at breakneck speed.

Really. It's okay." He still sounded like a wounded seal. "Your babysitter did everything exactly right. You should give her a raise. You should adopt her and put her in your will."

Another Wednesday, another jousting match with another Nurse Ratched clone from the Visiting Nurse Service. This one didn't know Jo-Ann was paralyzed either. She also found fault with the program the St. Vincent's hospice people had established. In her opinion, we weren't treating the bedsores properly.

I tried, unsuccessfully, to eliminate the duplication of nursing visits. Graham, Jo's hospice nurse, also tried, but without success. He was really all we needed. Besides having control over the magic prescription pad, he supplied us with most of the other hardware we required. Perhaps equally vital, he had a somewhat calming influence over me when I wanted to explode.

"Ignore them," Graham said, meaning the visiting nurses. "They're necessary to keep the aides. Don't let them upset you."

"I know," I grumbled. "But I'm sick of having all these people traipsing through my house."

Another visiting nurse came. This one did know Jo-Ann was paralyzed. Surprise. She thought we should change the pain medication schedule, though.

The line between a rookie and a veteran medic can be thin, but knew I hadn't crossed it yet. Sometimes it felt as if I'd been doing the job forever, for too long, but I still had a lot to figure out. It wasn't the medical emergencies that confused me so much as red tape and paperwork. And the wackos.

You deal with a lot of crazies. Especially at the full moon. I'm not superstitious, but full moons really do bring out weirdness. I'm not saying it's due to the moon and the tides. Maybe people just think, "Hey, it's a full moon. Let's go out and do something and do something stupid. It's expected of us."

It's bad enough when the patient is obviously wacked, but sometimes you can't even tell at first if a patient is crazy. I had a call for a Cardiac at Forty-second Street and Eighth Avenue, across the street from the Port Authority. The cops said, "He's a citizen," meaning that he was a "real person," not a skell—which is always a surprise at that address.

"He was chased by some guys and now he's complaining of chest pain and difficulty breathing," the cops said. It sounded legitimate. The patient was in a suit, overcoat, hat and tie; he was clean and polite. We got him in the back of the ambulance, put him on the EKG monitor, started to get a history, prepared to run an IV. He was very agitated, which is a common symptom for people having heart attacks or angina.

"Can we start to go? Can we start to move?" he asked. That's common too. People don't realize that medics can do almost everything the E.R. can do. They just want to get to the hospital.

"Just relax, we have some things to take care of first."

"No, they may still be after me! They could still get me!" he gasped.

"Don't worry about it. We're here. The police are here. No one's going to get you. You're okay with us."

"No, no, you don't understand! They have access

to me in the subway!" His eyes started to bug out. "They almost got me with the guns."

"Shooting?"

"No, no." His voice got hushed. "It's real CIA-type stuff. It's a ray gun. If they could get me down in the subway, we're sitting ducks here in the ambulance!"

We called the sergeant over.

"We have to get to the hospital right away!" the patient insisted. "They'll get us with the ray gun. We're sitting ducks here. We're not even a moving target."

He hopped out of the ambulance and bolted down the block. I was left standing there with a needle in one hand and an IV line in the other—I had been about to start the IV and administer cardiac meds.

He might just have been a loony-tune psychiatric case, in which case he should have gone to the hospital anyway. Or he might have been stark-staring mad, but still having a real heart attack, in which case he definitely should have gone to the hospital. Or, worst of all, he might not have been crazy. If they could get at him in the subway with a ray gun, we really were sitting ducks in the ambulance on Forty-second Street . . . so we got the hell out of there.

At the time, I was probably out of my mind myself. I would go to work, deal with life and death in a high-pressure environment, then I'd head home to spend every free minute with my private patient. Between the job and my volunteer fire department, I had always been busy, but now I was literally a twenty-four-hour-a-day medic. Instead of household chores like doing the dishes, which I let the home health aides take care of, I would do physical therapy, change the foley catheter, empty the urine bag.

The weird part of all this is that I loved it. My time with Jo-Ann was the best thing that ever happened to me. I still wanted to get married, but if it had been impractical before, it would have been impossible now. The home health aides, as stupid and underpaid as they were, were a fortune. The medicines, oxygen, and hospital bed alone could have bankrupted me.

I felt important, as I never had before. I was needed. For the first time, I was afraid for my health and safety: What would happen to Jo if I got hit by a car?

Being a medic is certainly safer than being with the police or the fire department. You don't see headlines about medics killed in shootouts, or four medics killed when roof collapses, or the like. But depending on the shift and the area, it can get hairy. Would you feel safe riding around Harlem all night with thousands of dollars worth of equipment and drugs? You don't have enough narcotics for anyone to make a lot of money selling them, but there is enough morphine and Valium for a fix, and that might be tempting to some people. Naturally, medics are very careful with the narcotics. We wear them in a small pouch strapped to our belts. You have to sign them in and out, and there's almost a ceremonial handing-over of the narcotics between shifts.

I wear a bulletproof vest every day that I work 911 on the streets. EMS is field-testing some vests that they're thinking of issuing to everybody, but it's not standard procedure yet. I bought mine when crack became epidemic. I felt self-conscious about it at first, but now I like it. It's not too bulky or heavy, just a snug security blanket wrapped around my chest. It hasn't saved my life so far, but I like knowing it's there.

On Wednesday, I was psychologically prepared for another moronic nurse to invade our privacy. And she didn't come. Reprieve! The week went by without incident. Wednesday rolled around again, but the nurse didn't. When they missed the third week in a row, I was pretty ecstatic. I should have called or something, but I was too happy.

I was snoozing the next Tuesday, off that day for a change, when they called.

"Mr. Shapiro, this is Nurse Whatever, and I need to come over right now for an on-site visit." I knew it had been too good to last.

"Okay, how about tomorrow?" I offered. "That was our usual day."

"No," she insisted. "You have not had an on-site checkup in four weeks and I have to come over *now*."

"I'm sorry about that," I said, trying not to sound aggravated. "But this isn't a good day. I'm not feeling well. Jo-Ann's not feeling well. Tomorrow is the normal day we have these visits. Couldn't you please come over then?"

"Mr. Shapiro. There are rules and regulations. If I don't come over today, I will have no choice but to remove the home health aides." There it was, the ultimate threat. As worthless as the aides were, they were indispensable. Someone had to be there with Jo when I was at work.

Jo-Ann jumped in. "Fine," she said through clenched teeth, "tell her to come over."

"Fine. Come over, then," I told the nurse, and

slammed down the receiver. I knew what Jo was going to say before she said it.

"Don't say anything to her," she ordered.

"I don't care what—"

"Listen to me," she repeated. "Don't say anything to her. *Nothing*. Is that clear?"

I nodded weakly and tried to not think about killing the nurse when she arrived. I was not going to lose those aides. I was not going to make Jo go back to the hospital, which was what she would have to do if we lost the aides. But I hate being powerless in my own house, and I was not going to take shit from some stupid visiting nurse. I was very hot, almost out of control. Not a loud, screaming, out of control; more like the calm, deadly quiet of "a nice guy" who one day axe-murders his whole family.

I got myself and the apartment cleaned up before the nurse from hell arrived.

The conversation was polite and guarded. As upset as Jo-Ann was, her control was far superior to mine. She wasn't going to say or do anything that would threaten the continued presence of the illiterate aides. I could tell she was much more worried about what I might say or do, so I tried to stay calm. After the cursory exam, the nurse left us to go talk to the aide for a minute.

"She'll be out of here in a minute," Jo said to me.

"I know," I said calmly.

"Don't say anything to her," she ordered.

"I won't. I'll just go see her out."

"Please," Jo begged. "Don't say anything to her."

"I won't. I promise."

I caught the nurse just as she was leaving, still clutching Jo's thick file. I stood in the doorway.

"You know I don't make the rules," she said. "But we all have to follow them."

"I understand that," I said. "But it was your fault the VNS didn't send anyone for three weeks, not ours. So I don't think it's right to punish us for your company's oversight." I was calm, but this was probably using up my few remaining shreds of self-control.

"Now listen to me," she interjected sharply. "We have the right to show up any time we deem necessary. Just because you belong to a hospice program doesn't give you or them the right to interfere with our services."

I kept silent, trying hard not to kick the living shit out of her. She mistook my silence for compliance.

"Fine. As long as we understand each other," she added snidely.

As she turned to walk away, I cleared my throat and, as calmly and seriously as I could, told her, "If you ever threaten to remove the home health aides again, I swear to God I will go to your office and burn the place down, killing everyone there." I watched her face for a moment as I slowly closed the door. I didn't know if she thought I was serious or crazy or both, but I expected trouble either way.

Jo was waiting for me in the bedroom (of course).

"What did you say to her?" she demanded.

"Nothing," I said halfheartedly.

"*What* did you *say* to her?"

I couldn't lie to her.

"I threatened to burn down their office and kill everyone there."

"Oh . . ." She shook her head. "Well, I'm glad you didn't say anything to her."

• • •

I waited. I expected a call from the agency telling the aides to get the hell out of there. Or maybe a call from the police. Or the fire marshals. What I got was a call from Graham.

"Did you really threaten to kill everyone in that office?" he asked, sounding half impressed.

"Burn the place down, too," I added.

"They're pretty upset," he said, somewhat unnecessarily. "You know, you really can't say stuff like that."

I tried to explain what had led up to my going overboard, but he already knew, and it wasn't really important anyway.

"Will you at least apologize?"

"I'm sorry," I said sincerely.

"Not to me, you idiot! To the Visiting Nurse Service."

That I would not do.

I was somewhat nervous when Wednesday rolled around the following week. When the phone rang, I was actually prepared to apologize. Amazingly, so were they.

"Hello, Mr. Shapiro? . . . Hello, sir, this is Nurse Whatever, from last week. If it isn't too much of an inconvenience, could I possibly come by today? I could make it another time if that would be better."

"Now will be fine," I told her. She came and was as sweet as could be, an absolute angel. The next week, the Visiting Nurse Service made a deal with Graham and the hospice program. VNS would no longer need to send anyone over to check up on us. Son of a gun. Threats really do work.

• • •

Jo-Ann was an incredible patient, independent and uncomplaining, and she always kept her sense of humor. I don't think this made me less patient with the people I dealt with on the streets, but the contrast was evident.

A medic named Luis Negron and I were called to an office for a woman who was having trouble breathing because of a bad asthma attack. She wasn't on death's doorstep but she needed some aggressive therapy. Unfortunately, her seven coworkers wouldn't leave the lounge where she was waiting for us. A seizure in an office building often turns into a spectator event. The patient all of a sudden has a hundred "best friends" who refuse to go back to work.

In order to get a patient's medical history, medics have to ask a lot of personal questions. You might not want your coworkers to know the date of your last menstrual period, the type of birth control you use, your history of drug use, etc. I try to ask people politely to please back up, to please give us some room, some privacy. But I can only ask so many times. If the patient requires quick medication or IV lines, I don't always have the time to be polite. In this case, we needed to listen to all the patient's lung fields and apply the EKG monitor, which involved opening her shirt. Undressing a person in front of her whole office is not going to make her breathe more easily. I finally had to physically push the coworkers out of the room and shut the door.

Of course, when we arrived with the patient at Rosy, our supervisor was waiting for us.

"I was just on the phone with the president of

Company X and he accused you guys of being incredibly nasty, rude, and of physically assaulting him."

"He's full of shit," I said. Luis nodded along. "The guy wouldn't give us any room. We needed some privacy, and the coworkers just wouldn't help us out. . . . Go ask your patient if she thought we were out of line."

"Actually," he chuckled, "they're really only complaining about one of you. They're really pissed off at the tall medic with glasses, dark hair, and the mustache." Luis and I looked at each other. At five-eleven, he was barely an inch taller than I was; we both had dark hair, glasses, and a mustache. Our patient backed us up, of course, even going so far as to say that we were great and that she would have thrown out "those idiots I work with" herself.

Sean and I were working a four-to-midnight shift with a paramedic student. A lot of observers come ride on the ambulance. Most of them are students, bright-eyed and eager to do their ambulance rotations: medic students, EMT students, first-year medical students, fourth-year medical students, and first-year interns doing their E.R. rotations. Normally, I don't mind observers. But medic students are a real hassle. Medical students, interns, doctors, and nurses don't actually do anything, they just observe what you do, so all you have to worry about is them getting lost or hurt. Observers are easy to misplace. Normally, when you lose one, he finds his way back to the hospital, usually pretty pissed off or at least confused.

I've also had trouble with observers falling out of the ambulance. They get very excited when you're going to a good call. The siren is blaring, the bus is hurtling through the streets, the radios are squawking. If you stop for any reason, the observer thinks you've arrived and starts to get out. When you accelerate again, he goes flying down the street.

But paramedic students pose the most problems because they're not there to observe, but to practice the skills under a controlled environment. Two veteran medics are there to make sure they don't kill anyone or, if worst comes to worst, to throw them out of the way and take over. Most of the time they're pretty good. The ambulance rotation is one of the last steps in the training, so if they get that far, they're usually okay. Their downfall is that their eagerness to practice the advanced skills makes them overlook the basics they learned as EMTs. All the advanced life support in the world won't do a damn thing if you don't take care of the basics first.

When it's time to start an IV or intubate, I let the student have the first shot at it. If he misses the vein on the first stab or fails to pass the tube after one look down the throat, I take over. Patient care has to come first.

You get some students who will make great medics. Unfortunately, there are also the rare and dangerous cases who can't diagnose their way out of a paper bag, and there's the occasional prima donna, like the one we had this night. This guy thought he was God's gift to the medic world. He was ready for anything and wanted to deal with cardiac arrests, stabbings, and all the great medical emergencies. Luckily, it started as a very quiet night. Sean and I tried to shut him up by quizzing him on his protocols.

"Okay, you come across a patient who is in V-Tack

with a pulse. B.P. of 80/palp. What do you do under standing orders?" He was supposed to be able to spit out what the good book said, verbatim. He would start to recite protocols, and as soon as he'd get something wrong Sean would do a game show buzzer. We nitpicked for close to two hours and *aahhnnkked* him throughout the upper West Side.

We were finally assigned to a CVA (stroke) at the Plaza Hotel. The employees were half-carrying the patient out of the hotel toward the ambulance as we pulled up and it was obvious that he was having a cerebral bleed right in front of us. An artery or vein had popped in his head, spilling blood into his brain. The skull is a fixed-space cavity; any extra fluid or blood can't escape. It fills up the space and presses down on the brain, causing brain damage and then death, so we had only a few minutes to do all the things we had to do.

Sean started using the AMBU bag to hyperventilate the patient, who would soon have to be intubated. I got a quick set of vitals as I told the student to set himself up for an IV. The patient had great veins and was thus an easy IV case, but somehow our genius baby medic missed the vein by a mile. That's not such a terrible offense: it happens to every medic at one time or another, but he was very embarrassed. I got him out of the way and popped the IV in place.

Sean was in the process of placing the breathing tube as I got the medications to administer. I handed the student one of the drugs and told him to push it intravenously, calling out for Sean to hear, "Here's 0.8 mg. Narcan." I then drew up the Thiamine and handed to the student, saying "Thiamine is going in now." Sean nodded as the student administered it. I grabbed the final drug on the altered mental status protocol and said, "Here, quick, give the D-50," referring to dextrose, a sugar. The student was panicked by now. He was trying to get over the disgrace of having blown the IV by taking control of the medication administration. He grabbed the Abboject, a prefilled container, and said, "D-50 going in now." As he was about to insert the needle into the IV line, I grabbed his hand.

"What are you about to give?" I demanded.

"Twenty-five grams of a fifty percent solution of dextrose," he said confidently, quoting the protocol word for word.

"Look at it," I advised him. The words on the Abboject read "Sodium Bicarbonate." Rule number one about medication administration is to read the label. Always. No matter who hands it to you. If he had taken my word for it and stuck the medication blindly into the IV, it might have killed the patient.

Sean looked up from intubating the patient to say "*Aahhnnkk.*" The student was shaking and looked almost worse than our stroke victim. He shut up for the rest of the shift and was very subdued when he thanked us for letting him ride with us. He never showed up for another Roosevelt rotation.

I was always terrified that something would happen to Jo while I was at work and the idiot home health aide would call 911. I listened intently to the radio any time Dispatch gave out a call at an address that started off like mine. I would have hit light speed getting to my apartment if I had ever heard the call come over, whether I had a patient in the back or not.

I wasn't about to let some crazy ambulance crew work on her.

At that time, "Do Not Resuscitate" orders were not accepted outside of the hospital. They've always had DNR orders inside hospitals for terminally ill patients. The doctor decides that the patient is a "no code" or a Do Not Resuscitate, so then if he stops breathing and his heart stops, you don't do CPR, you let him die.

After much discussion between me and Jo-Ann, I wrote my own DNR order for her. It wasn't legal, but I like to think that other medics would have respected it. It identified myself and Jo-Ann, showed a copy of my EMS shield, and included a letter telling them not to do anything except to call me on the radio and I'd be there in minutes. Thank God it never came to that.

It's important to be able to separate one's personal life and beliefs from one's professional attitude. I know that. Each case is different, with different factors that we may or may not understand. But watching Jo-Ann die bit by bit changed my ideas about a lot of things and couldn't help but affect the way I do my job.

Dealing with dead people is not the most upsetting part of the business. Even watching patients die isn't as disturbing as you might think. You do, of course, attempt to resuscitate them, but it becomes easy to say, "It was their time." A defense mechanism? Probably. The truth? Possibly. An excuse? Not really.

The truly distressing calls, the ones that haunt me after the shift is over, are when I watch people become vegetables.

There isn't a medic on the streets who is pleased

when he "saves" someone who spends the rest of eternity hooked up to a machine. It hits you hard to watch patients go from active members of society—hardworking, conscious, alive people—to comatose, permanently vegetative gorks, something you turn and water once a day. Broccoli.

I don't necessarily want to resuscitate a comatose elderly person with oxygen and IV feeding tubes. When the family tells you to "Try and save them," you do what you can, but you can't help thinking that it's just their time to die. I've pulled patients like this off their beds and subjected them to the abuse of advanced life support intervention—doing CPR compressions on a bed isn't very effective because the whole body just sinks into the mattress when you push on the chest—but it was painful, probably more so for me than for the patient, who was only trying to die.

This is not only true for very elderly patients, but also for terminally ill patients with no hope of recovery, including AIDS victims. A lot of times these people want to die in peace at home, but the family can't handle watching them die. I know how painful that can be. But it becomes a real problem if the family calls us when the patient isn't quite dead yet, when he's comatose or just about to die. I'm always really sorry when that happens. I don't want to sound flip, but these people are going to die. There's nothing I can do to save them. It's not a secret; there are no surprises. But when I arrive, if the patient is still alive, I don't have the authority to withhold treatment. He probably wanted to die at home, but now I have to take him to the hospital. I also have to do a lot of work, IV lines, intubation, etc. So, please, if you don't want paramedics to take a terminally ill or very old patient to the hospital and do painful, humiliating, and completely useless things to him, DO NOT CALL 911.

Recently, New York State finally decided to let medics acknowledge Do Not Resuscitate orders outside the hospitals for patients who want to die at home. Up until 1989, if you were transporting a patient for whom a DNR order was in effect inside the hospital and he died in your ambulance, you were still required to do everything possible to resuscitate. Now, if the family presents you with the DNR order written and signed by a doctor on hospice stationery stating that the patient is terminally ill, is a member of a hospice program, and that resuscitation should not be attempted, you can respect that.

My attitude about suicide has also evolved in a parallel sense. From an EMS perspective, suicides are just like any other call. If Joe College jumps from his window because he's flunking chemistry, you treat his injuries the same as if he were a construction worker who slipped from a scaffold. In fact, you refer to the patient as a "Jumper" whether he actually jumped, fell, or was pushed. It's none of your business how he got where he is.

I've come to realize that if they're alive when you get to them, they didn't really want to die. Very often someone will take a lethal dose of prescription medication and then immediately call his best friend to tell him so. Of course the friend calls 911 and the paramedics save the patient. Someone who climbs onto a ledge and jumps without saying a word to anyone obviously wants to kill himself. Someone who waits for the police does not. Anyone threatening to jump is usually "salvageable," provided the rescuer manages the call properly.

I used to think suicide was always wrong. I still think that most of it is sheer stupidity and it angers me. But after the things I've seen, I have become a card-carrying member of the Society for the Right to Die. It's not a conflict of interest. I will do everything in my power to save someone's life, but if he's brain dead and going to spend the rest of time on a respirator in an irreversible coma, I think the family should have the right to disconnect him. Especially if it was the request of the victim.

I have a living will, which New York State does not recognize. Yet. It simply states that "when it is medically confirmed that there is no reasonable hope for recovery, I wish to die naturally, receiving only comfort care. I do not wish to have my life prolonged by artificial means."

Obviously, if I'm critically injured in a car crash, I want to be saved by whatever heroic measures possible. If, however, after the rescue, I'm a vegetable, I would want them to turn off the life support. If I were, God forbid, to come down with cancer or another horrible disease, I would do anything to fight it, chemo or radiation. After all that, if the treatments were unsuccessful, a time might come when I decided that enough was enough. I don't want to be stuck in a hospital with tubes and wires. Let me die peacefully, preferably surrounded by stewardesses from Thai Air and a couple of UCLA pompom girls.

It's possible to keep someone alive on machines with breathing tubes, feeding tubes, tubes taking urine away, bringing fluids in. Not many people would look forward to this kind of old age. Some countries have active euthanasia. I'm not supporting that. But passive euthanasia—just giving pain medication and not treating the illness or disease—is another story.

A lot of older people see it that way. Sometimes you find an elderly suicide who left a note along the lines of "I'm eighty-seven, I've had a good life. This has been my house for sixty-two years. I can no longer take care of myself and I don't want to subject myself to the care of others. I've always made my own decisions about my life, and I want to do the same about my death." So be it.

One lady I know about express mailed her keys and a copy of her note to the local police precinct. When the police and EMS arrived, the apartment was clean and organized. Copies of her will were laid out along with the names of her lawyer and doctor and a note apologizing for any inconvenience she might have caused. She had taken a couple of bottles of pills mixed in with a bottle of antinausea medicine. She had even laid out large plastic sheets so if any of her body fluids leaked out it wouldn't be a problem for the morgue people. Most of our clients are not nearly as considerate.

The day before Jo-Ann died, I was away. For the first time in I didn't know how long, I decided to get away for a weekend. I went to a fire drill for my volunteer department on Fire Island. When I left, she seemed okay and had no objection to being left with the home health aide for the night. She called after I had been on the island for about five hours. She sounded tired, distant and weak, not like she had a few hours before. She told me to come home. I figured there was a problem with the aide—maybe she had tried to broil the ravioli again or something equally stupid—but that wasn't it. Jo told me to come home because she was dying. I don't know why, but I said, "I know that, but can you wait till I get home tomorrow?"

"Please come home. I'm scared," this tiny little voice replied. Now I was scared. Throughout everything, Jo-Ann was *never* scared, or at least she never admitted it. I jumped on the next boat and got home as fast as I could.

In the few hours I was gone she had deteriorated considerably. She was nearly comatose and didn't even want her pain medicine. She was too tired to swallow the pills. She was right—she was dying.

I was with her the next morning when she died. It was quiet. And strange. I had dealt with death every day on the job, but here it was in my apartment, in my bedroom. I was freaked out. I checked for a pulse. Nothing. I checked again. Still nothing. I listened for heart sounds, breathing, anything. Nothing.

I didn't call anyone for a long time, but I did send the home aide away. I didn't want them in my house ever again. They were a necessary evil while Jo was alive; now they had to get out. I kept checking for a pulse. I knew there wouldn't be one but I had to keep checking. All I kept thinking was, Boy, is she going to be pissed if I call up people and tell them she's dead when she really isn't.

It took another hour before I was finally convinced, and then I couldn't get ahold of anyone. It was Sunday; her doctors were off. No one seemed to answer their pagers. Now I was completely crazed. The funeral home couldn't pick up the body until there was an official death certificate signed or until a physician notified the home and stated that he would sign a certificate. I certainly wasn't going to call 911. After another couple of hours I finally reached the hospice people, who were great. I think I probably babbled incoherently to them, but ten minutes later I got a call back from a doctor I had never even heard of who told me that someone from the hospice program had called him. He had met Jo-Ann once and would call the funeral home. They would then track down the real physician of record, but this way she could be picked up immediately.

Rosy gives medics three days off for a death in the family, and they're fairly good about extending it when requested. I asked for the time off, but they said that Jo-Ann wasn't family. We should've gotten married, I thought, kicking myself. I didn't have the heart to argue, but it really hit me hard. How dare anyone say Jo wasn't family? I took two personal days. The guys I had been working with didn't know a lot about my home life. They had never met Jo-Ann. I don't know if they knew about her death. They didn't mention it, and neither did I.

A week after Jo-Ann died, her brother Keith came to New York to pick up her cremated remains to take back to Hawaii for a family burial. He was a pretty good sport and agreed to take Jo out to lunch with us. We did it right: we went to her favorite deli, asked for a table for three, and plopped that hard container right on the seat between us. Mealtimes were still very important to us.

It was easy to get caught up in "I wish." I wish Jo

was still alive. I wish she wasn't sick. But then again, if she hadn't gotten sick, then she wouldn't have been in Bellevue for tests and I would never have met her. I wish Jo was never sick, but came to New York to study and got the apartment next door to me. I wish. . . .

It didn't matter what I wished. Jo-Ann was dead. I started getting rid of her stuff. I no longer needed to be living in an intensive care ward; I wanted to get my own life back, and the fewer painful reminders the better.

After about a week, the job was mostly done. The hospital bed was gone and so was the rolling table that fit under the bed. The oxygen tanks were gone. Her clothes were gone, donated to a local Catholic charity. The few personal things she had went back to Hawaii with her brother. All that was left was the wheelchair, on long-term loan to us from a surgical supply house. And I couldn't get rid of it.

I called the supply house. "Hello. My name is Paul Shapiro, I have one of your wheelchairs that I need to return."

"I'm sorry, sir, we have no record of you having one of our chairs," a woman responded.

I was sitting in it at the time, so this seemed a little absurd to me. "Look under the name Kitagawa," I suggested.

"No, I'm sorry, we have nothing listed under either name."

I climbed out of the chair and looked at the metal label that was soldered onto the back support. "Look up the chair serial number," I advised her, and recited the ID code.

"Please wait a moment." I waited. "Oh yes, here

we go. According to our records that chair was returned six months ago."

"How the hell can it have been returned six months ago?" I demanded. "I'm sitting in it right now."

"I don't know, sir. But according to our records it was. You must have someone else's chair."

Normally I have more of a sense of humor, but this was a hot summer day and I was tired, depressed, and alone. I was trying to do the right thing, although I was pretty sick of always trying to do the right thing. I was not in the mood to play games.

"Look," I said, "obviously the chair is in my possession. I couldn't have made up the serial number. I wouldn't be wasting my time and yours. Obviously your records are mixed up."

"The records are not mixed up," she insisted. "That chair was returned in February. You must be mistaken." That did it.

"I guess you're right," I snarled. "I guess I'm just having a fucking hallucination." I slammed the phone down.

I contemplated throwing the chair in my car, driving over to the supply house, and tossing it through their front window. Then I debated igniting it with lighter fluid and launching it from my eighteenth-floor terrace. But common sense won out. For the next hour I banged and pried and finally pulled the label off the chair. Now it was mine. I contacted the St. Vincent's hospice program for the last time and told them I had a chair to donate.

A week later, I got a call from the surgical supply house.

"Mr. Shapiro, we understand you have one of our chairs," a different person stated confidently.

"I don't think so," I answered honestly.

"I understand that you called us last week, informing us that you have chair number whatever-it-was and would like to return it."

"Hmmm." I paused for dramatic effect. "According to my records, that chair was returned in February." I hung up.

Jo's Medicaid card and Social Security supplemental check arrived in the mail, although both agencies had been notified about her death. They were obviously a bit behind in their filing system. I wrote them a letter reminding them that they shouldn't be sending these anymore.

I have trouble remembering what the next few months were like. I know I drank a lot. I didn't know what to do. There was nothing for me to do. I could come and go as I pleased, without worrying about getting hit by a truck or getting sick. I must have been doing all right at work, because I still had the job, but for months I came home right after work and did nothing. I just sat in the bedroom, as I had been doing for so long.

CHAPTER 6

Little by little I came back to life. After months of working on autopilot, I found myself beginning to enjoy the job again. If you call that living. A lot of people still thought of my career as something I would grow out of. They would ask, "Are you still doing that paramedic stuff?" as if it was a dance that had gone out of style. Can't you just hear them asking an attorney if he's still doing "that law stuff"? "That paramedic stuff" was all that kept me going, and the most fun I could have.

I had enjoyed working nights, but I had never had a steady shift. I had had a "Ping-Pong" schedule, bouncing back and forth from the four-to-midnight and the midnight-to-eight shifts. I could never really get a rhythm going and I was getting a little wacked. I thought a change of pace would help. A slot opened up to work steady days and I jumped on it. Having a regular schedule might help me feel more stable, and having free evenings might even allow me to have a life outside of work.

I would be working about half of my shifts with a medic named Gene Epstein. I had worked with him a few times before, enough to know that we'd have fun together, and we did, although our ongoing feud began on the first shift we worked together.

"Take me to McDonald's," I said when I got hungry.

"No," Gene said.

"No?" I repeated, stunned.

"No!"

"Please?" Maybe he just wanted to hear the magic word.

"No." He pulled away from the curb.

"Where are we going?"

"Seventy-second and Broadway."

"Why?"

"I want to go to the health food store. It's lunchtime." Gene looked the part of a vegetarian and a health food freak. He was sort of a retired hippie and still wore his hair a little too long, with a goatee and mustache. He lived in a commune for a while where they grew their own food and started their own ambulance crew.

"That's why I wanted to go to Mac's."

"How can you eat those things?" Gene wondered aloud.

"It's easy," I answered. It was a silly question to ask a devout carnivore and a junk food addict. "You unwrap them, squish the ketchup from the little packets onto them, sprinkle with the pepper packets, and stuff them into your mouth."

"Sure . . . complete with gristle, bone munchings, and God knows what else." We pulled up in front of the health food store. If I didn't like Gene, I might have killed him.

When he returned to the ambulance with his larva sandwich, and a side order of mulch, I had to ask, "How can you eat those things?"

"It's easy," he replied. "You cover with all-natural dressing, sprinkle some of the organic flavoring onto it, and stuff it into your mouth." I eventually got my burger, but by that time I had almost lost my appetite from watching him eat his fertilizer. I vowed to get revenge.

Early in my career on the day shift, we were called to a private doctor's office for a heart attack. Working evenings and nights I had been able to pretty much avoid private docs, except for an occasional doctor/bystander. I soon realized how lucky I had been.

We found the scared gray-haired lady alone in an examination room, without oxygen and without any attempts to stabilize her. She wasn't being monitored by the doctor or by a nurse, although they should have known the importance of taking the vital signs every few minutes.

I wish I could say that this was unusual, but while I was shocked at the time, I have learned since that this is the rule and not the exception. Many doctors border on negligence when a real emergency presents itself in their offices. Nine times out of ten the doctor diagnoses a heart attack and doesn't do a thing for the patient except call 911. The most crucial time is spent making arrangements for the admission to the hospital, and it's usually *his* hospital, not necessarily the nearest one.

Normally before you transport a heart attack, you put the patient on oxygen, start IVs, monitor her closely and administer cardiac medications. Gene and I would do all this while still in the doctor's office. But this doctor didn't want us to do any of these very necessary procedures.

"Just take her to the hospital. I have made all the arrangements," he told us.

Gene explained that we have protocols to follow before transporting. The doctor didn't listen. He forbade us to intervene, stating that this was *his* patient and that *he* was the highest medical authority there, so we should obey *his* orders. Gene and I looked at each other, amazed.

"Uh, if we're going to disobey our protocols, you'll have to accompany us to the hospital to explain your order." I knew he wouldn't leave a room full of paying patients to go with us.

"Just take her to the hospital," he snapped. "They'll take care of everything there."

We didn't have time to argue. Gene and I put the patient on a stretcher and rolled her out the door.

It closed behind us. Gene looked around. "I don't see a doctor," he said. "Do you see a doctor?"

"Nope."

"Well, that makes us the highest medical authorities on the scene, I guess." We followed our normal protocols.

What really makes private doctors go ape is when you decide that the patient isn't stable enough to go to the hospital with which the doctor is affiliated and instead has to go to the nearest hospital's emergency room. This means that the doctor won't be paid for the patient's hospital stay. He yells, screams, whines and/or begs. It's embarrassing, but you can't risk the patient's life just so the doctor can make money. Luckily Rosy has an excellent medical director who backs his medics up a hundred percent.

Doctors have complained about medics in my department to our medical director, to the hospital administrator, and to the NYC Medical Advisory Committee doctors, the ones who establish our protocols and standing orders. Most of the doctors complaining are just concerned about how it looks to their other patients when an ambulance crew has to be called in to treat their patients. If they cared about the patients half as much as they do about their images, they would be glad to have the medics show up.

I checked the mail when I got home. There was another Medicaid card and Social Security check for Jo. I wrote "Deceased" on them and sent them back. Were they trying to rub it in?

Gene and I were parked in the traffic circle off the West Side Highway overlooking the Seventy-ninth Street Boat Basin, my favorite place to park in the Roosevelt area. You have to be in a good position to move quickly. In this particular spot, the highway would let you get uptown or downtown fast, and since Seventy-ninth is a major street, you could also get across town. I'd park up against the wall and overlook all the wonderful houseboats. It was nice and quiet.

"Take me to the health food store," Gene said. "I'm hungry."

"No," I said calmly, as I started up the ambulance and pulled into traffic.

"No?!"

"No," I said definitely. Paybacks are a bitch.

"Then where are we going?" he demanded.

"Kentucky Fried Chicken."

"Oh God, how can you eat those things?"

"Easy. Very easy."

"Could we at least stop on the way? I'm starving."

"No."

"Why not?"

"Because I'm driving."

Logically, the two of us shouldn't have gotten along. It wasn't just the difference in eating styles; we disagreed on everything except medical decisions. I liked the Mets; he was a Yankee fan. I liked the Rangers; he liked the Islanders. We both seemed to enjoy arguing about all these things, though.

In the hospital between calls, we ran into one of the newer medics.

"Hey, are you working tonight?" I asked.

"Uh, I was," he said, looking embarrassed. "I, uh, got a really bad headache. Just registered in the E.R. They told me to go home." I checked my watch. We were two hours and twenty minutes into the shift. If you work two hours, you get paid for the entire shift.

"You working with Dunn tonight?" I asked.

He nodded miserably. You must work with the partner assigned to you, unless you document the reasons why you refuse. This usually involves ratting on someone for violating a policy or a code of conduct. No one wants to actually write up a coworker, so medics "get sick." If a medic says he has a headache and doesn't feel up to giving a hundred percent out there, no doctor will send him back to work, even if there's nothing really wrong with him. If he were to screw up and mistreat a patient, the doctor's license could be called into question.

"Feel better," Gene said. We understood perfectly.

No one wanted to work with Ted. Being stuck in a small ambulance for eight hours with someone you didn't like is horrible. It's a Catch-22 situation: If the supervisors assign a good worker to ride with someone who's burned out, the good one often gets corrupted. Burnout is very contagious. It's like a cancer. Either the good worker burns out himself or he will start calling in sick all the time to avoid working with the bad one. If the shift assignment isn't changed, the good worker may eventually quit. The department loses a good employee and is left with the bad one. But if the supervisor pairs up two people who don't care anymore, you might as well not have the ambulance out there. Maybe they'll answer a call. Maybe they'll get there eventually. Maybe they'll treat the patient appropriately. Maybe they'll notify the dispatcher afterward that they're ready for another call, but certainly not right away.

I walked into the crew room and noticed a new memo posted on the wall. It said that Roosevelt ambulances should no longer park in the traffic circle overlooking the Seventy-ninth Street Boat Basin. The people in the boat basin had complained that they didn't like always seeing an ambulance when they looked up. Damn. Some folks have no civic spirit.

I tried parking at a bus stop on Seventy-second Street. It seemed like a good spot, convenient trafficwise, and with good access to bathrooms. That's another important consideration. I take most of my pit stops in the hospitals, but it's never a good idea to put it off until you're in the hospital next. With my luck, I'd probably get stuck on a job for two hours.

A middle-aged lady with a hatchet face came up to the window.

"You shouldn't be parked here," she said. "We have to walk out into the street to catch the bus. It isn't safe." Where did she expect us to go? Did she want us to drive around without stopping for eight hours in Manhattan traffic? I was annoyed, but I left the spot.

I was parked outside a Korean deli where I had stopped for some soda, when a St. Clare's bus pulled up. A medic I knew by sight hopped out and came over to the window.

"Hey, guys, how's it goin'?" he asked.

"Pretty quiet," I said.

"Yeah . . . listen, uh, we're having kind of a slowdown over at Clare's. . . . Try not to bring any patients there, okay?"

"Sure." I shrugged. It was all the same to us. "What's the story?"

"Problem with the administration. They didn't want to listen to our complaints, you know, we tried writing letters as a department and all. . . . We're going to send them a little message this way."

"No problem," I said. I didn't even ask what the complaints were about. Solidarity is solidarity. The Clare's medics were very effective in spreading the word. For a couple of days all the ambulances in the area—not just the Clare's buses, but the Rosy buses, the EMS units, everybody—avoided the Clare's E.R. when possible. Of course, no one would drag a life-and-death patient farther than necessary, but most cases aren't that critical.

The strategy was sound. Most hospitals get twenty to twenty-five percent of their admissions through the E.R. At Clare's, the percentage was much higher. Many private docs brought their patients to "nicer" hospitals like Roosevelt, Lenox Hill, or St. Vincent's for elective surgery. With the ambulances bringing the emergency cases to other hospitals, admissions at Clare's would drop through the floor.

At the start of my next tour a couple of days later, I asked my partner if we were still supposed to avoid Clare's.

"Nah," he said. "Word's out, they're cool again. Their administrators must've gone nuts with the E.R. empty. All of a sudden they're dying to meet with the ambulance department and hear their complaints."

After a lot of riding around and experimenting with different corners, Gene and I finally found a good parking place: in front of Ray's Pizza at Seventy-second and Columbus. Aside from the fact that Ray's made great pizza, this was a prime girl-watching spot. Ray's didn't seem to mind, although you might think having an ambulance planted by their door all the time would be adverse publicity.

We had just finished our slices when we got a call for a "skell on a stick." It was a cold winter, full of "skellcicles," skells who freeze to death. A "skell on a stick" is a skellcicle stuck to a bench.

"Can you get a pulse on him?" I asked.

"No," he said. "Let's give him to the E.R." It can be very difficult to tell if a skellcicle has a pulse. The heart might be beating just a little bit, but because his veins and arteries are so constricted from the cold you can't feel it. Which gives rise to the medical expression, "He ain't dead until he's warm and dead." The E.R. sometimes has to perform CPR for hours before the person is warmed up enough to allow a safe pronouncement of death, even though everyone there knows he's dead. It's a drag because unless you have a "thumper," a machine that performs CPR automatically, it has to be done manually, wasting a lot of time and energy. St. Luke's and Roosevelt shared a thumper which hadn't worked in years. Every once in a while they would borrow one from New York Hospital or Jacobi, but it could take up to thirty minutes to show up.

You can't do a lot for the skells that aren't dead yet. If you find someone lying in bed in a hotel room or an apartment barely breathing, his heart beating very slowly or erratically, you can start IVs, give cardiac meds, intubate, whatever. But if a skellcicle suffering from severe hypothermia has the same symptoms, you have to be extremely careful. If you warm him up too quickly or do anything invasive, his body will go completely haywire. If someone is freezing cold, his absorption rates get screwed up, so it's harder to judge how much medication to give him. If organs are shut down from the cold, what you give might not work at all, or might work too fast. So you have to just control the airway and transport quickly to the hospital, where they can raise the body temperature gradually without causing a massive shock. When it's 20 degrees Fahrenheit outside, you can't really warm someone up on the street.

Our next patient, a lady in a mink coat, had probably never before lain in the street until she dropped dead in front of the Hilton Hotel. On TV and in the movies, women never have really bad asthma attacks or go into cardiac arrest. We couldn't have medics ripping open their blouses on screen, could we? Well, in real life these things do happen, and on the street in the wintertime, when you have to take layers and layers of clothes off them.

Bystanders were doing CPR on this rich lady when we arrived. I tried to pull her arm out of her mink coat so I could start an IV. I really did try. It's always hard to undress an unconscious person, but getting the arm out of a sleeve while people are pounding on the person's chest is just about impossible. I didn't have the time to play games. So, after a brief attempt, out came the shears. Snip, Snip, snip.

I try not to trash people's clothes, but I do sometimes have to cut them off. The shears medics carry can cut pennies; they do the job quickly. As a simple courtesy you try to cut along the seams so the clothes can be resewn later. I hate cutting off down coats because the feathers fly everywhere and make it difficult to work. I've got to admit that I did get a kick out of cutting this mink coat, though. I don't like them, and I couldn't afford them even if I did. I also had to cut through a silk blouse and a bracelet she had around her arm. In case you were wondering, the coat didn't make it. But that's okay. Neither did the lady.

On the subject of clothes, I'd like to add that, contrary to popular opinion, ambulance crews do not check to see whether a patient's underwear is dirty or not. They don't even see it usually. I don't know whose mother started the myth. Besides, if you've just gotten hit by a car or shot in the belly, your underwear isn't going to be clean anyway.

I went home that night and turned the ringer off the telephone and turned down the volume on my answering machine. No point in screening my calls; I didn't want to talk to *any*body. It had taken me a long time to be able to do this. The ringer on my old phone couldn't be turned off, and I had never been able to let it keep ringing. I had had an answering machine for years, but I could never bring myself to screen the calls. If I was home, I picked it up. Now, after a long day, I just wanted a little peace and quiet. It was beautiful.

I thought about what I would have for dinner. I liked to cook, but I hated doing dishes and I wouldn't bother for just me. Why spend an hour preparing a gourmet meal, trash the entire kitchen, only to then toss it onto a TV tray, jump into bed, and eat it in front of the tube in ten minutes? My diet was consistent if not balanced: junk food on the job, junk food off the job. Frozen ravioli, frozen pizza, noodles and cream cheese, hamburgers. . . .

I began to worry that I was spending too much time sitting alone in my apartment. But I enjoy it, I argued with myself. Or do I? Maybe I've just convinced myself that I enjoy the solitude when I really don't. But isn't thinking that I enjoy it the same thing as enjoying it? I decided not to worry about it.

Going through my mail, I found another Social Security check and a Medicaid card for Jo. They continued to arrive every month like clockwork. I understand why the system is so fouled up: they're just incompetent. Of course people abuse the system. They make it hard for you not to. I didn't have any use for the magic green Medicaid card, and the thirty-some dollars a month the Social Security people sent wasn't enough to tempt me to cheat and risk getting caught. But after ten months of watching them issue checks to a dead girl, I started thinking about a quick trip to Aruba or someplace. The package deals were only four hundred bucks or so, and the government was throwing this money away.

It had gotten to be a game. I sent back one check ripped, folded, spindled, and mutilated. I sent back another taped to a copy of Jo's death certificate. I even taped one to a postcard from some exotic place where I claimed to be spending their money. No response.

I was sitting in the bus, humming along to the radio, when a city EMS ambulance pulled up. A young guy hopped out and came straight toward me. I didn't recognize him, but he remembered me.

"I rode with you last year," he said. "You and Sean. You guys busted my chops for the whole damn shift. You handed me the wrong medication syringe, remember?"

"Sure," I said, looking more closely at him. He had gotten scruffier since he became a pro. "Did you ever learn the protocols?" I asked.

"Sure did. And I always look at the syringes before I push them." He grinned, so I guess he appreciated the lesson. After a potentially lethal experience like that, you never forget. I know I didn't, and I can thank Jim O'Kelly for that.

It was a slow day, plenty of time to talk, until Gene and I got a call for a forty-one-year-old black man with AIDS. Lay people assume that medics must hate and fear working with AIDS patients. Not really. All medics treat AIDS patients all the time, I don't think too many are scared of contracting the disease from a patient. You wear gloves. You watch what you do with the needles. And, most important, you don't have sex with the patients. I'm just as concerned when I have a patient with TB or hepatitis. The real problem is that AIDS patients stay in the hospital longer, require more attention and time, and often need private rooms. The system is overrun.

This guy had pneumonia and was unable to keep food down. He was wasting away. He had also been throwing up blood. Gene and I were careful, as always, wearing gloves and not getting his body fluids on us. But the guy was a pleasure to treat. No arguments, no complaints. All he wanted was for us to check him out, give him the reassurance he needed and take him to the hospital.

After we got him there, we responded to a call for an old bedridden black guy who had been peeing in empty beer cans and stacking them up by the bed. It was a small room, his garbage was piled up everywhere and the stench was overwhelming. I was never a smoker and Gene quit a few years ago, so we had to bum cigarettes off a cop. Keeping the smoke in our mouths to deaden the smell was the only way we could get close enough to treat the patient.

This was the sort of patient I'd love to hate: fat, sick, idle, reeking . . . but he was actually a very pleasant, apologetic, personable guy. I can't really dislike a patient who is friendly and cooperative, no matter how dirty or smelly he is. We didn't even mind carrying him down three flights of stairs.

Cases like this gave me a whole different perspective on society: if you never deal with skells, street people, the poor, the smelly, you're bound to have prejudices, to hate and fear them. But any medic in this city will tell you that these people can be more personable and cooperative than upper class upper West or East Siders.

I walked into the crew room and scanned the walls for new memos. Rosy was a paper factory; there were always new memos for every occasion, no matter how insignificant. Meetings, warnings, in-services, new pieces of equipment, new rules. . . . This time it was a bit different. There were several small, framed calligraphic certificates, departmental awards "honoring" some outstanding Rosy medics.

The first time the bosses had the bright idea of giving departmental awards, they made a big deal out of it. They sent all the department members letters requesting our presence at an award ceremony, refreshments to be served, etc. Nobody took it seriously, so this time they didn't bother. They just slapped the things up on the wall of the crew room.

Each award was worded slightly differently for a personalized touch. It was a nice thought, but it probably resulted in more hurt feelings than pride. Two medics were given awards that cited their "intelligent contributions and outstanding integrity," but Sean received official recognition for his "outstanding integrity and loyalty to his duties," with no mention of intelligence. When I saw him the next day and congratulated him offhandedly about the award, he sounded even more sarcastic than I did.

"Yeah," he said. "I'm loyal, I'm like a puppy dog, but I guess I'm not too bright. . . ."

For days afterward, when asked anything, Sean merely replied, "Duh? . . . I don't know. . . . I may not be intelligent enough to answer that."

Even the people giving these things out at Rosy didn't take them seriously. Not too long after awarding Medals of Excellence to two medics who talked a Jumper down off a ledge, citing their "professional application of crisis intervention techniques with unusual faithfulness and perseverance to the spirit of the service," they canned one of these "faithful and persevering" medics for less than professional behavior.

In the mail, yes, again, Jo-Ann's Medicaid card and Social Security checks.

"I'm sorry, Mr. Shapiro," the Social Security clerk said, "I don't know why you are still receiving checks. Our records indicate Ms. Kitagawa died almost a year ago."

"Well, could you get them to stop?" I asked.

"Please hold. I'll transfer you to another department."

"Billing, please hold."

I held.

"Billing adjustment, please hold."

I held.

"Investigation department, please hold."

The hell with it. I hung up.

The checks eventually stopped coming. Every once in a while something still gets delivered for Jo from some government agency that obviously hasn't gotten the word yet.

A medical student was riding with me and Gene one fall day, a clean-cut, baby-faced kid. He and I might have been the same age, but it was clear to me that he had been safe in a well-lit classroom while I was working midnights on the city streets. I felt ten years older than him. As we were checking the bus, I read him the riot act.

"You're not supposed to get involved with the medical decisions," I said, "just to watch. We might ask you to take a blood pressure or hold an IV bag, but that's it." He nodded earnestly.

"Take a good look at the bus," I continued. "If there's a really big call, several units might show up. They all look alike, so remember our number. If anything really crazy happens and Gene and I split up, choose one of us and stick with him." The kid kept nodding.

"Also, make sure you exit the bus from the back *only*. You can't see the traffic when you open a side door, and a truck might come by and remove it." You have to do a ton of paperwork if the bus gets damaged. That's how I judge the relative seriousness of offenses. When I think about doing something stupid or wrong, I figure out how much paperwork I'd have to do. It isn't always worth it.

This student was a good guy, cooperative, helpful without getting in the way. He was just dying for some real action, but the tour started out as a complete bust.

Then we heard some interesting radio activity. We hadn't heard the original call assignment so we didn't know what the problem was, but two basic life support units were on the scene. They were calling for the Emergency Service police to respond and asking the EMS dispatcher to call the fire department for a ladder truck. Something big was going on.

"You want to go?" I asked Gene.

I knew he would. The medical student in the back of the ambulance was starting to get excited.

"Fourteen Young," Gene said into the radio as he started to pull out into traffic. "You need medics on that job?"

The EMS dispatcher thought for a moment. "Fourteen Young, I think that call is a little south for you."

"Central," Gene said. "We're already halfway there."

"Ten-Four, Young, if you're already on the way. You need the info?"

"Just the ID number," I said to Gene as I began writing the call info down on the ACR pad.

"ID number only," Gene advised the dispatcher. "Three minutes out."

The EMS radio was squawking. The P.D. radio was blaring updates. I cranked up the volume on the FM stereo as K-Rock began its psychedelic six-pack, six songs from the sixties. I'm pretty good at listening to everything at once.

According to the updates, a construction worker, suspended up on a scaffolding, was struck in the head with something heavy. He was knocked off the scaffolding, but landed on another platform. Gene and I exchanged happy "this is going to be good" glances as he weaved in and out of traffic. I think the medical student was starting to hyperventilate.

We found more than just a crazed scene. We found a media circus complete with police cars, three fire trucks, two BLS ambulances, EMS supervisors, and mobile mini cams from all the networks.

There was just one patient, though, and he was very fucked up. He was on a wide ledge about ten feet above us. One of the BLS crews was already up there while the other stood on the roof of a truck handing the immobilization equipment up to them.

Since the BLS crew seemed to have the C spine and oxygen supplies well in hand, we grabbed our airway equipment and trauma bag and headed over to the base of the building.

"Don't get lost," I reminded our medical student. He was really getting into this. "Stick with us or stay with the vehicle."

The EMS supervisor was running around trying to give orders, but with only one patient, the ALS unit on the scene was supposed to be in charge. That was us. Gene and I climbed up onto the roof of the truck and finally got a look at our patient. He was a white male, about forty, very unconscious. He had an obvious depressed skull fracture. There were other fractures, but none of them was as serious as the head injury.

It seemed foolish if not downright dangerous to stay up on that ledge for too long. The patient needed a trauma center right away, and it wouldn't help matters if one of the rescuers took a fall.

Before we could move him we had to immobilize his neck and back. Once the longboard, C Collars, oral airway, and oxygen were in place, we started to lower him to the street.

By this time hundreds of people were watching. Everyone wanted to give a hand—police, firefighters, the victims' coworkers, even bystanders. Most of the police were busy just keeping people back.

As we rolled the patient to one of the waiting BLS ambulances he started to gag and vomit, a common symptom of severe head injuries. His pulse was becoming erratic and I thought I detected some slight seizure activity. This guy was crapping out right in front of us.

As important as getting him to the hospital was, we had to get control of his airway *now*. We also needed to get a few lines in place, but that could wait a minute. We lifted him into the back of the BLS bus and Gene and I both hopped in.

First we suctioned the victim's airway. Aspiration of vomitus into the lungs was not going to help him. We had to clear a passage for air to get into his lungs before we could think about other treatments.

Sometimes discretion is the better part of valor. Sometimes it's best to take all the advanced life support stuff you can do and say the hell with it, let's get to the hospital. You can try to do some of it on route.

Considering how unstable this guy was, Gene and I decided both of us would ride in the back with him instead of splitting up. We would both work on him.

"Here!" I said, tossing my keys to one of the EMTs. "You drive ours to the hospital."

"St. Vincent's?" he asked. It was that or Bellevue.

"Yeah, Vinny's," I said, pulling the back of the ambulance door shut.

"I'll lead the way," he yelled as he ran over to our bus.

Our ambulance ran interference as the other EMT pulled this one into traffic. The siren was wailing as Gene attempted to intubate the patient and I started an IV.

Suddenly it dawned on me.

"Hey, Gene!"

"What?" He was trying to stick the E.T. tube in place.

"Where's our med student?"

"I think the tube's in," he said, as if he hadn't heard me.

"I don't know," he added a moment later. "I thought he was following you."

"Not me," I said, sticking the IV catheter into the man's arm. "I don't know where the hell he is."

"Oh well."

"Shit happens."

We had more important things to worry about just then, but still, when students ride with you, they're your responsibility. It's embarrassing to go back to the hospital at the end of the shift and tell the supervisor that you've lost another one.

On the bright side, losing med students doesn't require you to fill out too much paperwork. Med students are a dime a dozen—everybody wants to be a doctor—so losing one only calls for one page, maximum.

The trauma team was waiting for us as we pulled into the ambulance slot. This guy had neurosurgery written all over him. After a quick stop in the E.R. for C Spine and skull X rays, a few more IVs and a foley catheter, he was on his way up to the O.R.

As I was finishing up the paperwork and Gene was retrieving some of our equipment, I looked up and saw our medical student walking toward us. I was all ready to apologize, but he beat me to it,

"I'm so sorry," he blurted out. "I was trying so hard not to get in the way. I didn't realize you weren't going to go back to our ambulance."

"How did you get here?" I asked him.

"Took a cab. It was great!" he announced to the E.R. "I was watching you guys in the back of the other ambulance. Then I figured one of you would go back to ours. Then I saw our bus pull out, and the back door of the ambulance you were in slammed shut and you pulled out. I asked a cop which hospital you went to." I had to hand it to him. He was a good sport. And I didn't have to apologize or do any additional paperwork.

Gebhardt came up to me afterward and said, "You know, Young Skywalker, you're good . . . but you're not a Jedi yet." I appreciated the compliment, backhanded or not. He was right. I was getting good—good enough to impress a student—but I still had things to learn.

I got stuck working Thanksgiving Day. It's worse than Christmas but not as bad as New Year's Eve. It can be a headache, though, because of the Macy's Thanksgiving Day Parade. Just my luck, we got a call for an "other" right smack in the middle of it. No one was sure what the call was about; maybe a Jumper, maybe a Man Down. We tried to charge to the scene, but the parade was going down Central Park West and there were a million people there. Traffic was blocked off and we couldn't get through the band and the floats. We parked about halfway down the block from the call, grabbed our equipment and did the rest on foot.

It turned out that some poor guy had been standing in the street with his kid on his shoulders. A lady watching the parade from her second-story window had leaned out too far to see an interesting float and fell right out, crash landing on the guy and his son. Suprisingly, the kid was perfectly fine. The lady only had minor bumps and bruises. The father had a dislocated shoulder and a couple of other non-life-threatening injuries.

You always check out a patient's mental status as an important indicator of what's going on. If the person has good vital signs but is confused, you know something else is wrong. If his vitals are lousy but he's still mentating, oriented and alert, it's not as bad as it could be. On the call report, you write "A&O×3" (alert and oriented times three), which means the patient is aware of person, place, and time. You ask: Do you know who you are? where you are? what time it is? I also used to ask peole a fourth question: Do you know the first name of [then] Vice-President Bush's wife? I figured if they knew Barbara, it didn't really matter if they got one of the other questions wrong. Well, this guy was completely confused, but he had every right to be. All he knew was that he had just seen the turkey float go by when something went *whump*, his kid started screaming, and he felt his shoulder dislocate. The guy had to go to the hospital, which really upset his kid. He wanted to watch the rest of the parade.

Gene and I were having one of our endless good-natured arguments when we were interrupted by the radio.

"Fourteen Young, take it over to the Fifty-ninth Street station of the IRT Lexington line for an arrest."

"I hate subways," I said disgustedly as Gene started to drive over. My announcement didn't surprise him. I made it every time we got a call in a subway, and he always agreed. I'll admit that as a mode of transportation subways are excellent—fast, cheap, and contrary to popular belief, safe. But they're underground. There are tons of walk-ups in New York, and it's not fun to carry a patient down five flights of stairs along with an oxygen tank, IV lines, an an EKG machine. But it's much worse to carry them up from inside the subway. It's usually hot down there and much too crowded. When the train comes in, you can't hear anything.

Most of the calls in the subway are bullshit. There are a lot of homeless people down there, keeping warm and dry. The transit police try to keep them moving along, but when they find one who's too unconscious, they call EMS to take him to the hospital. The drunk, homeless guy isn't happy about it. The cop isn't happy about it. I'm definitely not, and neither is the hospital, but that's the system. You have to watch out for these patients: they often have fleas, lice, or whatever other oogy things might be spawning down there.

Then there are the dreaded Subway Sicks. An awful lot of people get sick riding the subway to work. It's partly psychological, I'm sure. It's technically called a vaso-vagal response. Something stimulates the vagal nerve, causing the heart to slow a little. A drop in blood pressure results, the patient feels weak, dizzy, sick to his stomach, and passes out. Five minutes later he's fine. The heat and lack of fresh air contribute to this. Men whose collars are too tight may rub their necks at the arteries, contributing to this response. I usually recommend that these people go to the hospital to be checked out, especially if they're over fifty. At least they can usually walk to the ambulance themselves.

When the call is "legitimate," you have the problem of finding the patient. You can get to the station within five minutes, but finding someone in a madhouse like the Columbus Circle station or Forty-second Street is not so easy, particularly if the caller can't specify if the patient is on the uptown or downtown platform, the express or the local side.

We knew that this case was not bullshit and we knew exactly where it was because the transit police were on the scene. They confirmed that CPR was being done. We arrived a moment after a BLS unit did and followed a cop down four flights of steps to the deepest part of the station. We found the patient on the floor of the Number 6 train. Two people were doing CPR and mouth-to-mouth. It amazed me that good samaritans would do that for a total stranger on the subway. It's conceivable in a small town in Maine, but you don't expect it on the NYC subway. One of the CPR givers was a doctor from Columbia Presbyterian.

The BLS crew continued CPR, but hooked the AMBU bag up to oxygen. EMTs and medics don't do mouth-to-mouth. I cut off the guy's shirt and Gene put on the EKG. Nobody knew the patient or his medical history, so we were working blind. There was a scar across his chest that looked like an open-heart-surgery scar. That was it. The EKG showed a rhythm of Ventricular Fibrillation (V-FIB), meaning that he had chaotic electrical activity in his heart instead of an organized rhythm. Gene charged up the defibrillator paddles and we shocked the patient, trying to override the heart's inactivity and send it back into a normal rhythm. We must have shocked him eight or ten times and administered every antidisrhythmic drug we carry, to no avail. As we were about to give up, a pulse registered. He just came back to life, even starting to bite down on the tube.

We were drenched in sweat, exhausted from the strain of getting to him and saving him, and now we had to carry him up four flights of stairs. We put him on the scoop stretcher, which is designed to carry people who must be lying flat. With four people carrying the stretcher, one at each corner, one carrying the IV lines, and one carrying the oxygen and the EKG monitor, we started up the stairs. The other policemen who had arrived were busy keeping people out of our way. Halfway up all those stairs, we seemed to be in worse shape than the patient. All I kept thinking was, Why couldn't he wait until he was out of the subway before he did this?

The patient eventually made a complete recovery. We went to see him in the hospital. The first thing he asked for when they took the breathing tube out of his lungs was a drink of whiskey. He was a confessed alcoholic who later admitted to living in the subway. I wonder if the good samaritans would have stopped to help if they had known he was a street person. He looked okay when he collapsed, wearing nice, clean clothes.

When I saw the BLS crew again, they seemed pretty excited about the save.

"Hey, we nominated all of us for a save award," they told me.

"Oh. Okay," I said indifferently. I didn't want to bring them down, but I couldn't take it too seriously. Everyone likes recognition for a job well-done, but I'd received awards for really stupid things and never got any credit for the times I did something truly outstanding.

As far as I was concerned, EMS had gone overboard on the award concept. At one point they were issuing commendations to the EMS communications department for conduct above and beyond every time they stayed at their posts during bomb threats. Considering how many crews were phoning in bomb threats against the communication center, it's amazing that the call-receiving officers and dispatchers could sit up straight with all those medals pinned on their chests.

The "Pre-Hospital Save" award was the worst of all. It drove me absolutely batty. This "honor" was given to EMTs and medics for saving someone's life. Wasn't that what they're paid for? For a while everyone was getting put in for this award. EMS doesn't even differentiate between patients who are really saved and those who become vegetables. As long as he wasn't breathing and had no pulse when you got to him, but he had a pulse when you got him to the E.R. you qualified. He could die the next day without regaining consciousness and it still counted as a save. In my book that's only a resuscitation. A save walks out of the hospital.

In this case the EMTs had done good CPR, Gene and I had run a textbook ALS code, and the patient did come back from the dead to eventually walk out of the hospital. I guess if anyone ever deserved a save award, we did. It didn't mean much to me, but if the EMTs wanted it, fine.

Of course, I wasn't always up to award-winning standards. I was thankful that there weren't any witnesses on some of the calls I went on, like the day when Gene and I had a patient with a fractured femur. I went back to the ambulance to get the Hare traction splint, the brand I had always used, and was shocked to find only a Sager splint, a different brand. Damn, I thought, I should have paid more attention at that in-service. I'd have to let Gene handle this one.

Suddenly I heard Gene's voice, anguished, yelling at me from the fifth floor window: "Not that one! Get the Hare!"

I could only hold up my arms in desperation and yell back, "It's the only one there."

It took a few minutes of debate and a little trial and error, but we did manage to apply the splint appropriately. I only hope the patient had no idea how uncomfortable we both felt doing it.

I paid extremely close attention to the next inservices.

Radio City Music Hall, the home of the Rockettes, has a corporate contract with FastCare, Roosevelt's private ambulance service. Also, for insurance reasons, their basement medical office is manned by EMTs for every show. Somehow, they hired Mike Roth to run the medical department. He tried to recruit me for shifts every time I ran into him at Rosy. In addition to his other dubious qualities, Mike was a suprisingly successful wheedler.

"Come on, Paul, don't you want to do a shift at Radio City? It's a piece-of-cake job."

"Hey, Mike," I said, "if I want to work an extra shift, I could do it at the hospital and get paid time and a half. Doing a shift at Radio City would be the equivalent of throwing seventy bucks down the drain."

"No," he argued. "You're looking at it all wrong. You get to watch a great show and you get paid to do it!"

What the hell, I thought. I might as well check it out. I worked at a Bill Cosby show and a Pretenders concert, both of which I really enjoyed, but I would have enjoyed them more in a good seat, with a date, knowing I was off duty and wouldn't be interrupted. The only calls I had were minor things. If anything major had come up, I was only expected to stabilize the patient until the FastCare ambulance arrived. One teeny-bop rock act I didn't even bother to watch I went in, snoozed in the medical office, answered a false alarm or two and went home.

I was in a particularly good mood the morning after the teeny-bop show, making fun of Gene's taste in food, his whole lifestyle, when we got a call for a Cardiac at a fairly conservative hotel off of Central Park. A beautiful blond babe was waiting for us in front of the hotel, wearing a black outfit that looked like a combination leotard/nightie and flowed in the wind as she waved to us. Yes, I thought, it's going to be a good day.

"CPR's in progress upstairs," one of the cops on the scene told us, so I didn't have time to give the blond the attention she deserved. When we reached the patient's floor, a short, thin man greeted us and said calmly that they'd "really like to keep the whole thing quiet." Gene and I looked at each other, surprised and confused. What "whole thing" did we have here? Gene assured the man in a very serious voice that our work is always confidential.

We entered the tastefully decorated suite where a large burly man with a long ponytail was doing mouth-to-mouth resuscitation on the patient lying on the floor. We pulled out our equipment and Gene did a double-take.

"Oh, wow," he said. "Is that—"

"Yeah," the small man said, sounding almost bored. I got the impression that they'd been through this "whole thing" before.

"Wow, cool, he's one of my favorites!"

The rock star, who had come into the city to do a commercial against drugs, had obviously overdosed on narcotics.

"What's he on?" I asked.

"Uh, he took some painkillers," the small man, the star's agent, told us.

We brought the star right back with Narcan. He was very obnoxious when we woke him. He didn't want to go to the hospital, but we told him he had no choice. Before we left, I told the burly guy who had been doing mouth-to-mouth how lucky the star was that he was there and knew what to do.

"Oh, yeah," the big guy said. "We're all trained in CPR." It seemed to be a job requirement for the members of the star's entourage.

The agent took our names and addresses and told us we'd get wonderful gifts and letters of commendation, etc. The star signed himself out of the E. R. a few hours later against medical advice, and I think he even performed that night. The newspapers reported the next day that an ambulance had been called to his suite for "cardiac problems," which was almost true since that was what the dispatcher had mistakenly told us to expect.

A few weeks later I got a package at the hospital. Surprise! It was one of the overdosed rock star's albums and a key chain with his picture on it, which I will never in my life use. Unlike Gene, I was never crazy about this guy, and I liked him even less after he was so rude to us for saving his life.

"Hey," Mike told one of the other medics at Rosy, "did you hear Paul got fired from Radio City for dancing with a concertgoer?" I didn't bother to explain.

"Hey," Mike told another, "did you hear Paul got fired for making out with a concertgoer in the mezzanine?" I laughed.

"Hey," he continued to someone else, "you know Paul got fired from Radio City? Yeah, he got caught having sex in the aisles with a concertgoer. Really. Wild sex. Out of control."

Maybe I should have set the record straight. The truth is that I was standing in the back of the Radio City mezzanine watching Crosby, Stills and Nash give a great concert. I was minding my own business, wearing my stupid white lab coat, holding my radio next to my ear in case someone actually needed help—there were, in fact, no calls that night. A very attractive, scantily clad and obviously spaced-out blond beauty came bopping over, dancing her little heart out. She tried to dance with a few of the ushers, without success. She tried to dance with one of the security people, also without success. I was next in the dance parade, and I thought what the hell.

Just as she and I were starting to dance, some

Radio City executives happened to walk by. They were not pleased, but they didn't fire me. Instead, I was fired for a different reason, by a computer operator who couldn't get off her tail to look in the files.

Radio City had written to me saying that I had to provide proof that I was a U.S. citizen. I wrote back reminding them that they had photocopies of my passport on file. The same paper pusher wrote back saying that if I did not provide proof of my citizenship, I would no longer be allowed to work there.

It would have been simple enough to produce my passport for another inspection, but incompetence and pointless bureaucracy get on my nerves. I might have to put up with some degree of it from my "real" employers, but in a job I don't need, for very little pay, forget it. I wrote another letter, very formally worded, saying that if they just checked the stupid file, they would find the proof, which I had provided when hired only a couple of months before. I wondered if this clerk had ever worked for Social Security or Medicaid.

A few days after the CSN concert, I got yet another letter saying that until I showed them proper proof that I was a United States citizen, they would no longer let me work at Radio City. I had had enough of the job anyway, so I let it slide.

One of the EMTs who worked at Radio City before me, one of their star employees, conscientious, eager, competent, had to stop working there when he was arrested and convicted of blowing up abortion clinics around the country. He had proved his citizenship, though, using a fake name and identity. I'll bet the clerks never gave him a hard time.

• • •

Pete Robinson came on the regular day shift with me and Gene. He had been hired about a year before to do vacation relief and had then done steady nights, but I had never worked with him. I had seen him around the hospital and I definitely liked him, though I couldn't pinpoint why.

"Of course you like him," Sal Gonzalez said. "He's just like you."

"Oh, come on," I exclaimed. "There's no one just like me."

"Oh yeah? You're both buffs. You're both volunteer fire fighters out on the island. You both have the same warped sense of humor. You even look alike."

It was true that Pete and I were roughly the same height and size. We had the same length of dark hair, mustache, glasses. He was a captain in the Seaford Fire Department, and I had made captain in my volunteer department in Saltaire (I'm an assistant chief now).

On the other hand, maybe Sal was just making excuses for his inability to tell anybody apart. He always got both me and Pete mixed up with another medic named Gary Pollino who didn't look anything like either of us, apparently because "Pete, Paul, and Pollino" all sounded alike to him. It wasn't very flattering, considering that I had worked a few shifts with him when the administrators had decided that supervisors should work occasional street shifts.

Pete and I were riding around, trading fire stories and looking for good fire calls to jump on, when we got a call for an unconscious man in the lobby of a building on Amsterdam. When we arrived, he was sitting in the lobby, looking like shit. That's not a

·precise medical term, but it was true. He had passed out, tried to stand up and passed out again. But he didn't want anything to do with us.

"I'm fine. I have to get back upstairs." He seemed alert and oriented, but we asked him to just let us check him out, and then if he didn't want to come with us, no problem. He was a little pale and cool, his belly was tender and his blood pressure very low in the sitting position. His pulse was fast and he seemed shocky. He had a drinking history and an ulcer history, so we figured he had an internal bleed in his belly. But he still refused treatment.

Now if someone doesn't want to go to the hospital, even if he's really sick, that's his business. He just has to sign the forms releasing the medics from any responsibility. You can't knock him down and take him against his will. That's called kidnapping and there are laws against it, unless the person is clearly a threat to himself or others, in which case a police officer can place him under protective custody while you take him to the hospital.

We were putting our stuff away when this guy, still waiting for the elevator, started to sway. We barely caught him before he hit the floor. He had practically no blood pressure and his pulse was racing. He clearly had an active gastro-intestinal bleed and needed to go to the hospital. When lying flat, there was enough blood to feed his brain; he was lucid and continued to refuse treatment. But as soon as he stood up the blood would pool in his feet and he would pass out.

He stood up and went back to the elevator, but it had already gone upstairs. He passed out again. We caught him, put him down . . . and once down he became lucid again. He not only refused treatment, but now he started getting irate at our insisting he come with us. He stood up and started to throw a punch. It was the easiest fight I ever fought: I just had to duck the punch and wait for him to fall down all by himself. Pete called for the cops, but when they showed, the patient seemed perfectly rational since he was on the ground again.

"If he doesn't want to go, don't take him," the cops said. I told the patient to go ring for the elevator. He did and collapsed before it came. The cop told him he'd have to go with us, but he continued to refuse. Finally a police sergeant had to show up and we had to go through the same demonstration before they agreed to handcuff the patient to the stretcher and make sure he got to the hospital.

A slot opened up at the hospital for a paramedic supervisor and Sean got the job. No surprise there. With his exaggerated organizational skills he seemed born to be management. It did surprise me, though, that once he got the job he never worked another shift out on the streets. Not one. It's too bad for the new people coming up at Rosy that they'll never get to work with him. I can understand that someone might get tired of being on the streets full-time, but I can't understand how you can give it up cold turkey once you get used to the excitement.

Both Gene and Pete were off on the day when I got into the one fender-bender that I'm almost proud of.

With the traffic in this city, it's surprising that I haven't gotten in more accidents. I've been in a few fender-benders, but luckily no one has ever been hurt. Usually the ambulance isn't going fast enough to cause significant damage. People think that ambulance drivers are speed demons who enjoy tearing around recklessly. It *is* a thrill at first, but that wears off pretty quickly. You see too many tragic car accidents not to be very careful yourself. I used to think I'd want a small sports car, but not anymore. Small cars tend to be death machines. In a mid-size car, you at least have a chance of surviving an accident. Legally, drivers of emergency vehicles are not required to wear seat belts, though the patient must be strapped in. I always wear mine. I wear it when I'm driving, when I'm a passenger, often even when we're parked and not going anywhere.

Most of the accidents with ambulances involve being rear-ended. There are laws about following emergency vehicles too closely but they are rarely enforced. I've been hit twice, once by a car, once by a truck. I don't particularly mind if people jump behind the bus and try to drive with us, but they shouldn't forget that they don't have the right to run lights. The idiot truck driver in question actually had the nerve to tell me: "I didn't think you were going to stop at that intersection." A ridiculous excuse—even if I hadn't stopped, *he* had a red light.

This time I was working with a medic who tended to get on my nerves. When circumstances required us to work together, we would pretty much ignore each other for the whole shift. This guy was just sitting in the passenger seat, reading the paper and paying no attention to what I was doing. Until the crash, of course.

As I was driving across town to respond to a call on the East Side for an unconscious woman, a red

Plymouth mini van kept getting in my way by creeping up into my blind spot. The lights were on, the red flashers were flashing, the siren was doing all it could. I was signaling like crazy and this idiot still would not get out of the way. I couldn't believe that he didn't notice me.

I was blasting the air horn (*ahnk, ahnk*), and switching back and between the yelp (*YipYipYip*) and the high-low (*EEE-aaa-EEE-aaa*). You'd have to be playing the radio awfully loud with the windows rolled up and the air-conditioning on not to hear. But even if you managed not to hear all the noise, you had to see the ambulance. It's big. It's got AMBULANCE written in large letters on the front. I think it's safe to say that this guy knew the ambulance was trying to get by him. He just didn't want to move. Another medic might have handled the situation differently, but I remembered back when I was a brand new per diem and the veteran medic I was riding with rammed the cab. I remembered both how satisfying that was and how we never got in trouble for it.

As we approached the scene, I figured the jerk might get out of the way if I pulled over to the left. He didn't. I hooked my left rear fender with the front right part of his mini van. There was a wonderful crunching crash sound and a quick stop. That got my partner's attention all right. He looked at me as if I had lost my mind. The asshole driver, who was almost too white and preppy to be true, was raving mad. He demanded my license and registration and kept babbling about how it was a brand new car. I thought it was mildly amusing. I told him that the police would arrive presently.

Since we were sitting in front of the patient's

office, I went to check on her. She was fine and didn't want to go to the hospital. When I got downstairs, my adversary was calmer and I completed the necessary paperwork with him.

As per department policy, my partner and I had to remain on the scene until the police arrived. Our tour was over, but we couldn't leave. My partner was furious; I thought he was going to pop an aneurism. Because he and I never spoke more than necessary, he hadn't told me that he had important plans for that evening. How was I to know? Just his luck, the cops took about forty minutes to show up.

After we drove back to the hospital, I had to write out an incident report. Roosevelt loves incident reports. I've written hundreds of them. This one read: "While responding to a report of an unconscious female, a red Plymouth wouldn't get out of my way. So I hit him." Signed Paul Shapiro. After the supervisor on duty had his fit, I handed in the real report. It was a page and a half longer, detailed, explaining about blind spots and a lot of other nonsense, but it basically said the same thing.

Accidents medics sustain while driving the ambulance don't affect their personal car insurance policies, so don't get in the way. We've got little to lose and we're bigger than you are.

Gene and I were sitting in the bus in front of a store on Amsterdam Avenue, minding our own business. It was an unusually warm day for March. People were walking around, shopping, enjoying the city. Everything was as it should be except for the old lady being dragged down the street.

It was incredible. An old lady, maybe seventy-five

or eighty, was being literally dragged down the street by a somewhat younger woman. The old lady was lying on the sidewalk, conscious and obviously resisting the efforts of the younger woman to drag her away.

I think Gene and I thought the same thing as they came closer and closer: Why us? We didn't want to get involved. We're not police officers. But this wasn't the sort of thing we could just ignore.

We got out of the ambulance and stepped over to the two women.

"What's going on here?" we asked the younger woman, who looked about fifty.

"Nothing," she said. "I'm just taking her home."

It didn't look that way to me. The old woman was gripping a fire hydrant for dear life. I tried to talk with her, but the younger one wouldn't let me.

"I'm her nurse and I'm responsible for her," she said. "She's only giving me a hard time. She could walk if she wanted to."

I'm not Sherlock Holmes, but I looked over at the lady refusing to let go of the hydrant and I was sure something was not right. I tried again to talk to the dragee, but as luck had it, she didn't speak English. Her face had a waxy, pained expression.

Gene and I decided that we couldn't let this old lady be dragged down the street. We would take her to the hospital. When we told the nurse so, she became irate.

"I'm in charge here!" She stomped her foot. "The family has hired *me* to take care of her."

A small crowd had gathered and seemed to have mixed opinions. Some agreed with us, but a few thought that the nurse ought to be allowed to do as she thought best. The bystanders were somewhat vocal, but far from dangerous or hostile.

We informed the EMS dispatcher that we had been flagged down for a street job and requested that the Twentieth Precinct send a patrol car to give us some assistance. It wasn't an emergency situation, so we didn't call directly on the P.D. radio and we did not put in the request as a priority.

Unknown to us, however, a store owner on the block had called 911 and told the operator that there was a crowd of people who appeared to be fighting with an ambulance crew. This elevated our call to a 10-85—officer in need of emergency assistance *now*.

Other EMS units listening to the P.D. radio heard the report. They called the EMS dispatcher and advised him that we must have called a 85-forthwith over the P.D. radio and they started to respond.

The traffic on the radios was flying. EMS was trying to call us for an update, but with all the radio traffic and the noise on the street, I didn't hear. Some other bystanders called 911 to report some sort of situation. When EMS still couldn't get hold of us, they put in a second request for the police to respond forthwith. This upgraded the call to a 10-13, an officer's life being immediately threatened. The reaction was impressive.

There is a lot of family feeling on the streets. You have to save number one before you can save anyone else. Whenever a medic hears a cop call in a 10-13 on the P.D. radio, he starts to respond without waiting to be assigned to the call. After hearing every available police car report that they're responding, you get on the P.D. radio and say quickly, "Paramedics also responding." It's a simple line, but it means a lot to them. The street cops know that if any of their guys are hurt, the medics will be there immediately. The police dispatcher knows that with all the craziness, he doesn't have to worry about calling for an ambulance.

A 10-13 scene is wild and dangerous. Cops run around with guns drawn; hundreds of them seem to come out of the woodwork. Streets are closed off, Emergency Services cops take over the scene, and if an officer is hurt, you get escorts to the hospital. There's no question who's treated first if a cop and a suspect are both injured in a shootout: you care for the injured officer. Another ambulance will have to be called for the suspect.

This situation, although a false alarm, proved that the courtesy extends both ways. The cops thought Gene and I were under attack, and the army came riding in to the rescue. We heard sirens everywhere, loud, coming from all directions, and we wondered what all the commotion was about. When the first patrol car arrived, an officer bounded out with gun in hand.

"Where's the Thirteen?" he demanded.

Gene and I had no idea. We looked around, confused, at our two little old ladies, the older one still clutching the fire hydrant, and the small, certainly not violent, crowd. Then we realized what was going on and felt like idiots.

It all got sorted out. The first P.D. car told the other cars not to bother, except for the sergeant. They thought he should witness us prying the old lady from the fire plug and taking her to the hospital. Which was all we wanted in the first place. I apologized for all the confusion, though it wasn't really our fault. In some ways I felt good about it. I've never felt that my life was in jeopardy on the job, but I know now that if I did, there would be a lot of help. Fast.

Pete and I were working on St. Patrick's Day and hating it. The unofficial holidays are worse than the real ones: St. Pat's Day Parade because of the drunks; Puerto Rican Day Parade because of the drunks; New York City Marathon Day because of the runners. I now avoid working these days at all costs.

Are people required to drink to excess during certain parades? What the Puerto Rican Day Parade lacks in sheer numbers, it definitely makes up in decibel level. I don't understand how speeding wildly through the city in cars with flags taped to the antennae, blaring music at top volume and honking their horns, adds to the feeling of self-pride. I don't want to sound like a bigot or deny the right of anyone to celebrate his heritage or homeland, but where does it say you have to be bombed out of your mind to do it?

The St. Patrick's parade is at least as bad. Don't Irish people find the stereotype of the drunken Irishman offensive? I wouldn't mind if they all blasted themselves quietly into La-La-Land in the privacy of their own homes, but way too many end up falling down and needing my help. The emergency rooms get stuffed with intoxes who fall and then need stitches or X rays. Most drunks are obnoxious. They're loud, belligerent, occasionally violent, and they seem to enjoy throwing up.

Plus, the parade makes traffic impossible, which keeps medics from getting to any serious calls. That St. Pat's Day, Pete and I got a priority call for a cardiac arrest on the East Side. The parade goes up Fifth

Avenue, so most of the park is closed off, and Fifth is closed off. So how could we get across town? We thought we were going to have to go up to 125th street to do it. We tried one of the Central Park transverses but it was completely closed, emergency vehicle or no. We were pissed off about being delayed on such an important call, but we had received an update saying that the arrest was in a doctor's office with CPR in progress. There was still hope for the victim, despite the parade.

We finally found a transverse open at Eighty-sixth Street. The parade had already started but was only up to about Fifty-seventh Street, so we zipped up Fifth Avenue in front of it. All the traffic was stopped, millions of people were lining the street waiting, and we flew by with lights and sirens like we were part of the parade. We even waved to people as we went.

"They're in Examination Room One," the receptionist told us when we arrived at the doctor's office. "Just down this hall and to the left."

"Thanks," I said as I trudged through the office, lugging the drug box and oxygen. Pete had the EKG monitor and the paperwork.

I pushed open the exam door and saw our patient lying flat on his back. He looked pretty dead, and the doctor was looking a little flushed himself. Sweat poured down his face as he stood over the patient, doing CPR compressions.

"I'm glad you guys are here," he said, completely out of breath.

"What happened?" I asked as Pete and I started pulling our equipment out.

"I was giving him a stress test and he just collapsed." The doctor looked annoyed that we didn't spring to relieve him on the compressions.

"How long has he been in arrest?" Pete asked, quickly hooking up the EKG monitor.

"About twelve minutes." The doc glanced at his watch. "It was a witnessed arrest. I've been doing compressions since he coded."

"Who was doing ventilations?" Pete asked. I had a bad feeling about that. There wasn't anyone at the head of the stretcher when we walked in.

"Uh, there haven't been any ventilations," the doc admitted reluctantly. The EMTs backing us arrived, took over the compressions and started to bag the patient.

"Hey, Doc, if you weren't breathing for this guy, we don't have much of a chance of bringing him back." I wasn't overstating the case. Doing compressions without any ventilation does no good at all. There's absolutely no chance of resuscitating that way.

"Do you want us to try and resuscitate or would you prefer to pronounce before we get started?" It was a rude thing to say and my tone was even ruder, but I couldn't help myself.

"Uh, no . . ." The doc seemed at a loss. "I'd like you to try to resuscitate."

"Okay, we'll try." I said.

As the doc started to leave the room, Pete asked, almost accusingly, "How come no one was ventilating?"

The M.D. stopped short. "We don't have an AMBU bag," he said, seeming not at all apologetic that he had just let this patient die right in front of him.

One of the EMTs said, "What? A big-shot doctor never heard of mouth-to-mouth?"

The doctor had really pissed me off with his incompetence, so right before we decided to terminate I told the EMTs to take off and get themselves put on another call. BLS crews sometimes get stuck taking bodies away if they're in public view or if there are extenuating circumstances. Paramedics never have such duties; an advanced crew can't be tied up like that. Pete and I finished the paperwork and were halfway out the door when the M.D. asked, "What about the body?"

"He's in the examining room," I said.

"But I need that room!" he protested.

Too bad. We left.

The guy might not be a bad doctor in his field, but he had forgotten the basics. We always record problems like this in our reports, but nothing comes of it. If we have trouble with a doc associated with St. Luke's/Roosevelt we can take it to our medical director or associate director, who will intercede for us, but outside our small universe we can't do diddly about negligent doctors.

I saw that again the following week when I was working with a female per diem. We got a call for a female Uncon, possible reaction to medication.

"Nice building," my partner remarked as we walked in. She ran her hand along the wood paneling. The apartment door flew open as soon as I rang the bell. Two women in their early twenties, dressed in blue jeans and sweatshirts, practically pulled us inside.

"Hurry, hurry," they pleaded, as they led us into

the bedroom. Their mother was lying on the bed in a nightgown, very unconscious.

"What happened?" I asked the shorter girl. She seemed marginally calmer than her sister, who was pacing rapidly.

"I don't know," the girl wailed. "She wasn't feeling very well. She called her doctor and he sent a prescription to the drugstore." She was starting to shake.

"Okay, calm down," I said. "She's going to be okay. Go on. Slowly."

"I picked up the prescription for her a few hours ago. She took the pills and went to lie down. I tried to wake her up a few minutes ago and she wouldn't wake up."

"Where is the medication now?" my partner asked.

"Here," the other sister said, thrusting the bottle into my hands as if it was poison.

"This is pretty strong stuff." I passed it to my partner for inspection. The patient, a fiftyish woman, was really out, responsive to deep painful stimuli only. When I held her hand over her face and let it drop, it came crashing down right onto her nose. Usually people with a shred of consciousness can somewhat deflect the self-punch.

"There's no blood pressure," my partner announced. She tried to get vital signs. "Pulse is very weak. Irregular too. Resps are shallow."

"But there is a gag reflex," she added a moment later as she tried to insert an oral airway. I pulled the oxygen out and slapped a high-concentration mask on the unconscious woman. The EKG monitor was beeping. We both started looking at her arms for IV sites.

"When was the last time your mom went to her doctor?" my partner asked. Both girls shook their heads.

"Today? Yesterday? Last week?"

"No. Not for a long time," the younger girl finally answered.

"So how does he know what he's prescribing for?" my partner whispered under her breath.

"It's called Russian Roulette with a prescription pad," I said. The patient had described her symptoms over the phone, and her doctor prescribed some medication. Stupid. Many patients will overemphasize some medical conditions; others will underestimate their symptoms. It's impossible to prescribe accurately without actually examining the patient. I wasn't sure if our patient's present medical condition was worsened by the medication or whether she was truly ill and the prescription was too little, way too late. Either way, she could have died.

"We're going to take her to Roosevelt Hospital," I said. "Put on some shoes if you're coming with us." The girls sprang into action, grabbed their purses and put on their shoes. By the time we reached Rosy, the patient's vital signs had improved somewhat. She had even regained consciousness enough to answer some basic questions. She was admitted to one of the ICUs for the night for observation, to make sure there wouldn't be any relapses, but she would eventually be okay. If her daughters hadn't been with her to call 911 she might have died.

It's very frustrating to come across cases where a doctor has clearly been negligent, even to the point of killing a patient. You document it thoroughly, but there are never any repercussions. Doctors don't want to act against other doctors.

Gene and I were parked in front of Ray's watching the world go by when a city EMS ambulance pulled up. It was the BLS crew we had worked with on the cardiac arrest in the subway months before.

"Have you guys gotten your awards yet?" they asked.

"What?" I asked. "No. What are you talking about?"

"You remember, the save in the subway. We each got a save award, a borough command commendation and a transit police citation for that call." Gene and I had gotten nothing.

"What?" I said, ticked off. "How can they do that? We were the unit in charge, the medical authority at the scene, the advanced life support. . . . How can they give you guys all these awards and give us shit?" It's true that I never took the awards seriously, but this was a matter of principle. I don't like being screwed over.

"EMS," Gene said, shaking his head. That said it all. In the several months that I had worked with them, Gene, Pete, and I had been nominated for a whole bunch of awards, and I actually got one pin months after the save in question. As far as I know, Gene and Pete never got theirs. I received letters from the EMS awards review committee informing me that I had won two more such awards, but I never got the pins. The mail isn't that slow between Maspeth, Queens, and Manhattan; EMS just hates giving awards to the voluntary hospital medics.

"You know," I said, "I may drive out to Maspeth

with my letters and demand the other pins they owe me just to give them a hard time."

The call info just said a male stabbed, P.D. requesting a rush. So much for the quiet morning Gene and I had been enjoying. Our backup BLS ambulance was also assigned once the police on the scene called for a rush, confirming the severity of the injuries. We shot up West End Avenue and converged upon the scene with Fourteen Adam right on our tail. Two police cars were parked in front of the building, one facing uptown, the other downtown.

As Gene pulled over and stopped, we hopped out and began pulling equipment off the bus; stretcher, oxygen, trauma bag, MAST pants.

The victim was slumped over and bleeding on a bench in the lobby. He had been stabbed in the elevator, and made it to the lobby before collapsing. We had to push by some interested bystanders. The Twenty-fourth Precinct police were trying to get information from the victim, but if the patient told them who stabbed him or why, I didn't hear it. I wasn't really listening. The injuries were potentially critical. We had to get him to a trauma center forthwith. We moved him over to our stretcher and slapped some multitrauma dressings over the stab wound, administered high-concentration oxygen, and began rolling him to the ambulance.

"Can you describe the assailant?" the police were asking. "What was he wearing?"

I could sympathize with them; they weren't finished getting the necessary information. With the proper facts they would have a much better chance of catching the guy who did this. But from a medical perspective, if we delayed too long this would go from an assault and attempted murder case to a confirmed homicide. There was internal bleeding and I was pretty sure the knife had hit something important, maybe a lung. I pushed the cops aside so I could work.

Gene started to drive to St. Luke's and called for a trauma team standby. I started a large IV line and began running Lactated Ringers into the patient's veins, trying to supplement his blood supply. The officer who rode with us to the hospital wanted to continue questioning the victim, but my questions had to take precedence, even if they were just basic medical history stuff: Do you take medication? Allergic to medication? Any medical problems in the past? Basic, but essential.

We arrived at Luke's within minutes, and the trauma team was waiting for us. They started working on the patient immediately as Gene and I gave the report.

"His spleen's lacerated!" one of the doctors shouted. The chief surgical resident grabbed the phone and slated the patient for immediate surgery. An intern started another IV.

"Order blood," another doc called. "Have it meet us in the O.R." They did some quick X rays and raced the stretcher upstairs. As the E.R. fell relatively quiet, I finished my paperwork while Gene restocked and cleaned up the ambulance. It took him a while to wash all the blood out.

Medics have to have very strong stomachs, obviously. I've never tossed my cookies over something I've seen on the job. All the stories I tell sound horrific, but quite frankly, they're not much worse than assisting a childbirth, which is a very oogy process. Babies are bloody and mushy. Nobody's happy: the mother's screaming, the baby's screaming, the father looks like he's going to keel over and seize. It's a mess, but medically it's not a big deal. Women have been doing it alone for centuries.

Gene and I were called for a woman giving birth in the projects at around 101st and Columbus. A birth is a basic life support call—EMS tries to send EMTs—so I hadn't responded to many.

We got there just as the baby was coming out. I don't even remember if it was a boy or a girl. We caught it, cleaned it, made sure it was breathing, suctioned its nose and mouth, made sure the mom was okay. We clamped the umbilical cord, but left it for the doctors to cut. We waited about ten minutes until the placenta came out—it looks like someone vomited up their liver—bagged it, and transported to the hospital. Very disgusting.

Just two days after the stabbing, a fine spring day, Gene and I were sitting in the ambulance reading the papers when we got a report of an Uncon in a car on West End Avenue. This sort of call is usually legitimate, but sometimes it's just someone taking a nap.

We found a man, about fifty-five, lying in the street, with a lady doing perfect CPR on him. She looked up at the St. Luke's/Roosevelt ambulance.

"I'm an O.R. nurse at Luke's," she said, continuing the compressions. "I was just walking down the street and I found him slumped over the wheel in cardiac arrest."

"How long have you been working on him?"

"About three minutes." We went to work. A

Luke's/Rosy BLS unit showed up moments later and pitched in.

I looked up a minute later and saw Dr. Andy Leiffer, a St. Luke's/Roosevelt Emergency physician, walking by, pushing his baby in a stroller. When he saw us he came to lend a hand. We then had two Luke's medics, two Luke's EMTs, a Luke's doctor, and a Luke's nurse all working the arrest. This patient seemed to be a magnet for Luke's personnel. As luck or skill would have it, we were able to start his heart. We put him on the stretcher.

"We'll take him to Luke's, I guess," Gene said. It seemed only logical since we had an entire crew from there. Gene called ahead so the E.R. would be ready for us.

When we arrived, I started to give the report to the staff. "Fifty-year-old male, postcardiac arrest. Patient found in arrest, unknown down time, CPR started, in progress three minutes prior to our arrival. Initially asystolic, we tubed him, dropped a line, gave two mg. epinephrine, one mg. atropine, one amp D-50, got a pulse. . . ."

When it came time to mention the patient's history—previous medical problems, current medication, allergies to medication, etc.—I could only say that I had no idea.

"It's okay. I know all about his history," one of the E.R. nurses said. I looked at her, amazed, and asked how.

"He's my husband," she said.

Everything seemed to come to a stop. Even the machines sounded quieter. Some coincidences are just too big to swallow. You would think that with all this, some divine power was looking after this guy, but his luck ran out. A few weeks later the patient died in the cardiac care unit.

Summer arrived with a bang that year. A few bangs, really. The first came one July day when Gene and I were hanging out at Roosevelt between calls, talking to Mike Gebhardt and Mike Roth, who were working on another unit. We were walking down the hall from the ambulance crew room toward the main E.R. when there was a huge crash. The place erupted, everyone shouting, and a young man came flying through the E.R., jumping over people, making for the door. A cop, blood pouring out of his head, was giving chase, gun drawn.

People under arrest are frequently brought into the hospital, either for a quick psychiatric evaluation or for medical reasons. If a "perp" (perpetrator) is cut or hurt during the arrest, the cops have to treat him with compassion and appropriate medical care, no matter how heinous the crime. A policeman brings the perp in, handcuffs him to a chair or bed, and stays to watch over him. It looked like this time one had gotten away.

Some EMS people are police wanna-be's. Most of us don't have a secret desire to be cops, but, as I said, there's a lot of family feeling on the street. Cops, fire fighters, EMTs and medics are "us," everyone else is "them." So although it's not technically our business, we do occasionally get caught up in the excitement of a good chase or the glory of a collar. Without hesitating, certainly without thinking, the four of us took off after the bad guy who ran out of the E.R. and dived off the loading platform where the ambulances back up to unload patients.

Gebhardt reached him first and tackled him around the legs. Gene and I followed and helped hold him down. Roth arrived last and landed on us all. That hurt. Remember, he's a big guy. The cop screamed a 10-13 into his radio. The perp was struggling like crazy. The four of us had a hard time keeping him down, but we knew we'd just have to hold him for a minute until the backup cops arrived.

It turned out that a brand new intern had told the cop to uncuff the patient so they could take X rays. The cop didn't want to but the intern said it was necessary. After the X ray the cop went to handcuff the suspect again, but the suspect had other ideas. He grabbed the chair and swung it, hitting the cop full, and hard, in the face. The cop eventually needed about thirty stitches. The perp had committed armed robbery, was wanted on other charges, and had just assaulted an officer, so he knew he would go away for a long time if caught. No wonder he struggled so hard.

We got a big thanks from the police department. At first the hospital was very proud that their paramedics helped save the day, but they were a lot less thrilled when they found Gebhardt getting X-rayed for potentially busted ribs, me getting X-rayed for a twisted ankle, and Gene all banged up. Nothing was broken, but Gebhardt and I had to go on disability for a couple of days from injuries sustained while collaring this bank robber. Roth walked away without a scratch, giggling as usual. The hospital suggested that in future we stick to treating patients.

Back on the job a few days later, my ankle still hurting a little, Gene and I were reliving our big moment of glory when we heard a call for a male shot in Central Park. We raced over to the Great Lawn to find a very dead guy sitting slumped over in a motorized wheelchair. He had apparently driven his chair into a nice, shady part of the park, placed his gun in his mouth and pulled the trigger. It was extremely effective as suicides go. He might have thought it was a pleasant place to die, but it probably ruined the day for plenty of people who went to the park to relax.

The phone was ringing and I was hung over after a rare night of carousing with old friends. I had to stop and think where I was, what was happening, where was the phone?

"Hello," I croaked out.

"Hello. Is Paul Shapiro there?" I didn't recognize the voice and I was sure that no one I knew would be so cheerful in the morning.

"Yeah. I'm Paul."

"Hi. My name is Ahmadou," the stranger announced, as if that was supposed to mean something to me. I had no clue. "Your sister Mary and I work together in Morocco," he explained. "She told me that I had to call you when I got to New York and that you would take us out and show us the town."

I was way too sick for this. Us? Who was us?

"I'm sorry," I said quietly. "Who are you?"

"My name is Ahmadou, and your sister and I work together."

It was starting to come back to me. I had gotten some sort of letter from my sister telling me that someone might be showing up. Swell. Remind me to kill her. I didn't need this today. I shook my head clear.

"Okay," I groaned. "How long are you going to be in New York?"

"We are leaving tomorrow. So we have to get together tonight!"

I wanted to tell him to go to hell. If I hadn't been half asleep I would have thought of a good excuse to get out of it. But nothing sprang to mind, and before I knew it, I had accepted.

Ahmadou turned out to be a chubby and jolly mustached Moroccan, the head of my sister's university English department. He spoke good English, although it sounded like he had cotton in his mouth. His friend Mohammed was also an English teacher, but at a different university. Once I really woke up I started thinking of all the different places I could take them. As it turned out, they had their own itinerary.

"We want to go to Harlem," Ahmadou announced.

"What?" I had to double-check. "Where do you want to go?"

"Harlem. Our tour guide wouldn't take us."

"Of course not," I blurted out. "It's not exactly showing New York at its best."

"But that's where we want to go."

We piled into my car.

"Lock the doors and roll up the windows tight," I ordered as we started heading north.

"That's a crack house," I pointed out. "Do you see the hole in the wall? That's the entrance, since they boarded up the front door." My Moroccan charges aahed and oohed and jabbered Arabic and French to each other, leaving me out of the conversation until they remembered that Americans don't usually speak three languages at the same time, and decided to fill me in on whatever they were babbling about.

"Over there is a hotel where I once responded for two people shot."

"Why?" they cried avidly. They really seemed to like this stuff.

"Drug deal went bad," I said, cruising past a small crowd of people standing around the otherwise deserted streets. I was praying that the car wouldn't break down. I didn't usually worry about being in Harlem when I was driving around in my ambulance, but as a private citizen with two North African university professors, I was concerned.

"This is Harlem hospital," I pointed as we continued up Lenox Avenue. A few moments later I gestured toward a boarded-up windowfront. "I was recently here for a car that drove up onto the sidewalk and ran three people over before crashing into that store over there."

The Shapiro tour of New York City. You can't find it in *Michelin*. It isn't for everyone, but these guys loved it. During the tour, I started to wonder how much this job had warped the way I look at things, whether I was getting too morbid. Maybe I was. I have to admit that I enjoyed taking them around, seeing New York, and myself, through different and amazed eyes.

The call came in as a "pedestrian struck," someone hit by a car, but I didn't particularly hurry, because the address given was on the fourth floor. Unless the car had torn through the fourth floor, this was not a case of "pedestrian struck"; it did not require advanced life support. If the victim was able, as this one was, to walk to the elevator, go upstairs and call the ambulance, it should be categorized as a minor injury. If he were really hurt, he'd still be out on the street.

I started keeping track of the misclassified calls I got. I figured it was about fifty percent. The Call-Receiving Officers (CROs) determine whether the call requires basic or advanced life support, what type of call it is and what priority. It should only take them about thirty seconds to classify the call so the dispatcher can assign it to a crew on the streets. To do this, they're required to ask the caller certain questions, such as, "Is the patient having difficulty breathing? Is he/she having chest pain?" Many people say yes even when it's blatantly not true.

Callers inflate the importance of their call because they think that this will guarantee them a faster response. This happens a lot in the low-income housing projects because people there don't believe they'll get police help or medical care as fast as they would in upscale white neighborhoods like the upper East Side. If someone falls down and gets hurt, a caller from the projects might say, "My God, I think he was shot!" EMS calls will be generated as "possible male shot." You end up flying around trying to find a phantom patient.

The dispatcher can say if there is a call-back number. When there isn't, when the call is anonymous, it's much more likely to be bullshit. When someone is willing to give his name and phone number and to take responsibility for the call, it's probably legitimate.

To an extent these people are right. There are more ambulances downtown. There are only four medic units north of Ninety-sixth Street. There are fourteen south of Ninety-sixth Street, where the nicer neighborhoods are and where the residents have more influence with respect to demanding services from the city. They need more ambulances and more resources uptown.

It's less understandable and a lot more annoying when a minor call is upgraded simply because a caller in a "good" neighborhood doesn't want to wait an extra minute or two. A lot of calls get unnecessarily upgraded to advanced life support calls, from "female sick" to "cardiac," for example. If someone has a drop of blood in his stools or in his vomit, the call will come in as an "internal bleeder," which it usually isn't.

"Major injury" is perhaps the most currently abused category. The CROs have obviously changed their criteria: When I first started, if I was assigned to a major injury, it meant that someone was caught under a subway train, had a limb caught in machinery, was hit by something that fell twenty flights off of a construction site, or was in comparably dire straits. Everything else came in as "injury" or "minor injury." Nowadays, if an old lady falls and cuts her chin, they call it a major injury.

Lately, EMS seems to be inexplicably upgrading "emotionally disturbed patient" calls to "altered mental status." You hear the call on the police radio as "fifty-eight-year-old lady with psych history acting weird," classified as an EDP call, which a BLS unit could handle. A minute later it comes over the EMS radio as an "altered mental status," an advanced life support call. Go figure.

The CROs need new protocols and the call categorizations should be reviewed. There has to be a way to phrase the necessary questions without positively inviting the caller to lie about the patient's condition. There has to be a way to convince people that they *will* get an ambulance promptly, even if the call isn't immediately life-threatening, and that it's in their best interests to be both honest and accurate.

I was sound asleep when I heard all hell breaking loose in my apartment. Hell, I thought foggily, the damn cats. My parents had just left for jobs in China, and stuck me with their two cats, Para and Medic—an illustration of warped parental humor. "It's only for a year or two," my mother assured me. "They'll be good company for you."

The beasts scratched and howled at my bedroom door like they'd been stabbed in the heart. They didn't stop until I got up to feed them, at which point I noticed that they had knocked over two plants, a lamp, and the garbage.

The next night I tried leaving my door open. The cats started bouncing up and down on my head as soon as it got light out. They were absolutely undaunted by threats, smacks, or even being thrown across the room. Great company.

I didn't realize just how much I wanted to get away from everything, from work and bureaucracy and the city, until the chance to get away from it all for a while was dangled in front of my eyes. Steve Moffett, one of the Jersey guys from my medic class and a pretty good friend ever since, had the annoying habit of calling me bright and early in the morning, about an hour after I got to sleep following a night shift. This time, though, he actually called me at what I would consider a decent hour in the evening.

"Hey, big guy, you want to go to Kenya on a safari?" Steve asked. He had been approached by a travel agency setting up a large incentive trip for a major Wall Street company. The firm's highest earners would be going on safari in six months, and the bosses were very concerned about the lack of medical care available. On one of their last trips, there had been some medical problems, and they didn't want them repeated so far away from any organized medical system. Was I interested in going along? Was I ever. It sounded too good to be true.

Telephone calls flew back and forth for weeks as Steve and I discussed what medications and equipment we'd need on safari. Steve had recruited another Beekman medic and Dr. Diane Sixsmith, Beekman's Emergency Department director, who had overseen our medic training. Approximately two hundred people were going, divided into four subgroups, one for each of the four of us. We would get a first-class trip plus a salary. Definitely a good deal.

I didn't tell anyone at Roosevelt about the possibility of my going on safari. I didn't want to brag about it and then have it fall through. Plus, there were a few medics at Roosevelt who were much more qualified for something like this than I was; I was just lucky that it had fallen into my lap. I didn't want to get on anyone's bad side by bragging about it, and I didn't want any competition for my slot.

I came rolling into a snooty upper East Side hospital with a patient in critical condition. A nurse looked up from whatever she was doing and whined, "We're closed."

This is a phrase I hear too often from emergency

rooms. It isn't true, of course. The only times a New York State E.R. is legally allowed to close is if it's on fire, if there's a lunatic with a gun taking hostages there, or if some other truly catastrophic event occurs.

What the nurses mean when they claim to be closed is that the hospital has requested a diversion. If the E.R. is completely full, with no more available beds, monitors, or other equipment, the E.R. can request that the ambulances on the street be notified so that they won't bring any more patients to that particular E.R.—"request" being the operative word.

Diversions are sometimes specific to one department. If the E.R. isn't full but the labor and delivery rooms are, the hospital can request an OBS diversion, asking that the ambulance crews take pregnant women elsewhere.

Of course, even if the hospital is on total diversion, that only affects the incoming from the ambulances working 911. People still walk into the E.R., private ambulances continue to arrive, cops still bring in patients.

Certain requests for diversion are not granted. Trauma centers are never allowed to close to trauma. Burn centers must always stay open. If there is a snow emergency in the city, no diversions are allowed. If the driving conditions are dangerous, EMS doesn't want its units going any farther than necessary. The most common reason for EMS to refuse a diversion is when all the hospitals in that area are trying to divert. Ambulances can't drive thirty minutes out of their way just to find a hospital that isn't crowded.

From the medic's perspective, patient condition is the bottom line. You try to honor requests for diversion because it really can get crazy in the E.R., but often you can't. If you have a critical patient around the corner from an E.R., you'll take him to that E.R. whether they're on diversion or not. If you don't think the patient can safely make it to a hospital farther away, you'd be an idiot to try, not to mention that you'd just be inviting a lawsuit.

"Yes, I know," I told this nurse, holding up the patient's two IV bags. "But he's pretty unstable."

"But we're supposed to be on diversion," she whined, still standing behind the counter.

"Yes. I know." My tone was a little sharper. I could hear the EKG machine beeping irregularly.

"We don't have any unit bed upstairs."

"Yes. I know." I was almost shouting now.

"Well, why did you bring him here?"

"Because he lives down the block and he's *barely breathing*!" I almost always had trouble with the nurses at this hospital. "You're not closed," I snapped. "You're not allowed to close. You are requesting diversion. Request, request, request. Period."

"Oh, all right," the nurse said in a huff. "Let me see if I can find a bed for him down here. But we'll just have to transfer him to another hospital later."

"I don't care about later," I told her. "I just don't want him coding on *our* stretcher *now*."

The hospitals that seem to work the hardest are the ones that bitch the least. St. Luke's, Bellevue, and Metropolitan, which are always swamped, hardly ever complain when you can't honor a diversion request. I've seen them running cardiac arrests in the hallways at Luke's because there were no available rooms. When they are supposedly on diversion and you roll in with a serious patient, they roll their heads back.

"Did you know that we're sort of on diversion?" they ask.

"I know. I'm sorry. I don't think this guy'll make it downtown."

The Lukes's nurses are usually understanding. "Just hang on a second," they say, "I'll try to find a stretcher." The St. Luke's E.R. is old, small, drab, broken-down, underequipped and understaffed. They seem to handle more patients, and sicker ones, than Roosevelt, which is a big, bright, airy, new, clean facility with better equipment and more staff. And in my personal opinion, Luke's is by far the superior emergency room. It's a question of attitude. Our department sometimes refers to the Roosevelt E.R. nursing staff as the Olympic Whining Team. Most of them are good nurses who do their job well. They just like to complain about it.

I got home from work, exhausted from doing battle, to find that the cats had vomited in three different places and had pulled down two bath towels to use instead of their litter box.

I screamed death threats at them, meaning every syllable, but they just looked up at me adoringly, asking, "Aren't we going to get something to eat?" If they weren't so cute they'd have been lunch meat. As it was, I spared their lives, but I had to find something a little less cute to call them. I tried "Beast," which fit most of the time, or the generic "Cat," but finally settled on "Muttley" for both.

CHAPTER 7

My thoughts were increasingly turned away from the streets and toward the Kenya trip. Having the trip to look forward to should have made everything on the streets easier to deal with, except that I still couldn't believe it would really come about. One problem was how to get the time off from Rosy. I had lots of vacation time coming to me, but in a job like this, you can't just take off whenever you want to. You have to have staggered vacations to ensure coverage. Someone has to mind the store. Vacations are scheduled by seniority, and I was still pretty low on the totem pole.

All I knew was that I was going to go on this trip, no matter what. A chance like this wouldn't come often; I wasn't going to blow this one. I didn't want to have to quit over this, but I was prepared to if need be.

Every December thirty-first the vacation list comes

off the wall. Up to that point the medics with most seniority could choose their vacation time with no competition. As of 12:01 A.M. January first, it's open season. By luck, or perhaps divine intervention, the Kenya trip was scheduled for March, a month nobody else wanted. I snatched it up and committed all my accrued vacation time toward it.

Medics in New York City are highly trained for medical emergencies, but you don't learn many relatively simple medical procedures because they are not emergency techniques. When someone cuts his hand and needs stitches, you cover the injury with sterile dressings and take him to the hospital where a doctor in the E.R. will do the suturing. It's not that suturing is too hard—it's just not a question of life and death, and it takes too damn long. You can't stay on the scene for an hour setting up sterile fields, administering anesthetics, and stitching people up. You take them to the E.R. and you're back in service in a few minutes.

In NYC, if you can't establish an IV for some reason, you get the patient to a hospital ASAP. If they can't get a line there, they do a cut-down: a surgical procedure in which a doctor cuts through the skin, down to where he sees the vein and can stick the needle into it.

In Kenya there wouldn't be a local hospital to take the people to. If someone cut himself, I'd have to do the sewing myself. If I couldn't start an IV when it was needed, I'd have to do the cut-down. On the other hand, to look at the bright side of the situation, there wouldn't be any snooty nurses to say "we're closed."

Dr. Sixsmith arranged to send me and Steve to

Brookdale Hospital for a quickie class in advanced trauma life support. Moffett and I drove out there that morning, pretty excited about learning real trauma surgery stuff. Two interns and a medical student were also taking this class. We practiced the procedures under the watchful direction of the Brookdale Emergency Department director.

The lab looked like a standard operating theater, with surgical tables, medical equipment, respirators, IV lines. We were scrubbed, gloved, and gowned. The only thing wrong with this picture was the patients: on each table lay a large, unconscious dog.

Obviously you can't practice complicated surgical techniques on living human beings. It's possible, but not as effective, to do it on corpses. You want to see how much the patient bleeds, to know if you're doing it properly. After performing a cut-down, you want to see if the IV runs properly. So you work on large dogs, the closest thing anatomywise. They have more fur than most people, bigger noses than some, but the insides are much the same. The one I worked on was an attack dog, a doberman or rottweiler. If it hadn't been in a coma, I'd have never gone near it, let alone with a needle and a scalpel.

The dogs were knocked out, placed into deep comas and put on respirators. At first I felt somewhat uncomfortable. I like dogs. I understand people's objections to these types of labs, but there is no way to get this level of training without animal practice. I'm against tossing acid in bunny rabbits' eyes to test perfumes and other nonessential experiments, but with this training I might be able to save human lives, and that has to take priority. And these guys really couldn't feel a thing. When we finished, they'd be given a lethal injection.

I must have done two dozen cut-downs on my dog, slowly marching up the inside of its leg. Every once in a while the doctor would wander over and give some helpful piece of advice. Mainly he just said, "Good. Now do it again." It wasn't a high-pressure environment like much of my medic training had been. No one would be flunked out; there would be no grades, no certification, not even any record to show that I had received this training.

We placed chest tubes between each rib of the animal. Then we started on surgical cricothyrotomies. A cricothyrotomy, like a tracheotomy, is a hastily made surgical incision in the neck allowing us to breathe for a patient in cases where we were unable to intubate him.

The dog bled less than I thought it would, which meant that I was doing pretty well, although it was my first stab at anything like this. We spent the entire day practicing, and I started feeling more confident. Part of me was terrified that I might have to actually do some of these things out in the jungle, but another part of me had its belief confirmed that the skills involved in being a doc aren't that tough. The huge amount of schooling, learning about what to do, is the hard part. Once you get to the actual doing, the skills involved aren't all that difficult.

It was about this time that I looked around and realized that I wasn't a rookie anymore. Maybe getting the extra surgical training showed me how comfortable I was with the skills I already knew. There was a lot I could take for granted. I felt prepared for anything that could come my way. That didn't mean that I wouldn't have any surprises—as long as I work 911 in New York City, there will always be surprises—but I would be able to handle them.

Gene and I were assigned to treat an elderly male who had fallen, fracturing a hip and an arm. When we tried to question him, his daughter kept answering for him and then yelling at us for delaying. Sometimes it's almost impossible to treat a patient because of his family. Even if the family members are sane, they're usually frantic with worry, and they have no idea what you have to do.

Medics ask their questions for a reason; it's not just small talk. It's important to know if he simply tripped or if he fell because he was dizzy. Maybe he had had a heart attack that would kill him while we treated the fracture. It doesn't take long to check, but his daughter, who was obviously not the brightest bulb in the chandelier, made it very difficult.

When Gene and I splinted the old man's arm and shoulder together, we told him that it might be uncomfortable for a few minutes. He understood and grunted a few times when we had to manipulate the arm. His daughter went berserk and called 911 again, screaming, "What kind of people did you send over here? They're torturing my father!" Gene and I looked at each other, speechless, and continued taking care of our patient. As we were moving him onto the stretcher, a whole team of police arrived, including a sergeant and a lieutenant. The officer in charge asked the old man if everything was all right.

"Yup. These guys are taking good care of me," he said. His daughter was still screaming and ranting as we left. She lodged additional complaints at the hospital, even accusing Gene of driving drunk. We spent a lot of time after work writing incident reports. The patient himself had nothing but praise for us. Complaint unfounded.

After work I headed over to Beekman to meet with my Kenya-bound colleagues. Each person traveling on the tour had filled out a medical form for us, detailing their medical history, medications taken, allergies, anything that might be of interest. We spent a few evenings in Dr. Sixsmith's office at Beekman, reviewing these as we worked out our medical protocols. None of the people were Olympic athletes, but they were all in reasonably good health and the trip wouldn't be too strenuous, so we didn't expect any major medical problems. I was prepared for any emergency scenarios that might arise, and I had had the advanced trauma training, but I still had a lot to learn about family G.P.-type medicine.

On the ambulance, if someone called 911 for a case of diarrhea, I'd be pissed off, and, as in any nonemergency, I'd simply take him to the hospital and drop him there. But in Kenya if someone in my group had minor medical woes, I'd have to know which medication or antibiotic to administer. Most of these decisions are simple, but I had never had any formal training in these areas. It's pretty ironic when you think about it: medics can save your life, but they aren't trained to help you with little problems. If it's not life-and-death, or at least somewhat serious, you shouldn't be calling an ambulance or dealing with a paramedic.

Dr. Sixsmith, who kept trying unsuccessfully to get me to call her Diane, wrote out indications and dosages for all of our medications. Although she tried to go over everything fully, she never talked down to us or implied any lack of confidence in us. We all knew that, however complete the protocols, the ultimate decisions would be ours. There would be no medical control physician to contact, no second opinions. Diane knew we'd be using her medical license to administer this stuff, or to decide not to administer it in some cases, and I appreciated the faith she showed in us.

Slowly, now that the trip was a sure thing, I started telling people about it. Of course, all my medic friends wanted to know if we needed anyone else, and I was glad to be able to pass the buck. I could honestly say, "I'm sorry. I'm just the hired help." Moffett was the administrator. I helped him do a lot of the scut work associated with pulling this together, but it was his show.

Pete and I received a call for a Jumper Down. No surprise there; you get a lot of Jumpers. Of course, not all "Jumpers" do it on purpose—a lot of people simply fall from high places. Scaffoldings collapse, window washers lose their grip, construction workers fall. Anything over six or seven stories is usually pronounceable. The injuries are obviously so extensive that there's nothing to be done except to document the time and place and describe the injuries in great detail so no one will haul you into court and sue you for not having tried to save the victim.

A lot of them do literally jump, though. This is something that makes city medics wish they were working somewhere out in the countryside. I don't know what it is about tall buildings that makes people want to jump from them. I guess they want to show the world something. It's the most inconsiderate form of suicide I can imagine. They almost always splash down on a public street, traumatizing all sorts of innocent passersby. And there's always the chance of one of them landing on someone. Kids stand by and wonder what the body looks like under the sheet. If a Jumper goes from very high, his brain matter may fly down the block. Why subject people to that type of abuse? The street also has to be closed, diverting traffic. The strangest crowd reactions I've ever seen followed Jumpers, such as the episode at the Trump Tower I had witnessed earlier as an EMT, and this was no exception.

On this job the dispatcher advised us that they were getting multiple calls, a sign that it's for real. As we approached the scene we saw the "positive by-stander response." Crowds are usually only a problem at the minor emergencies. For the really big events—huge fires, collapsing buildings, or bad multivehicle accidents—there are usually enough police to keep them back. In this case, Pete and I got there before the cops did.

The victim had jumped or fallen thirty-two stories into a driveway that led into an underground parking lot on West End Avenue. Every joint was fractured and turned the wrong way. His legs bent the wrong way at the knee. His head was completely flat, and his brains were about fifteen feet away from his body.

We pronounced the body dead from inside the ambulance, but we climbed out to keep people away. Not only is it a very ugly sight, it is also a crime scene until proven otherwise. The police and crime-scene unit soon arrived. While we did our paperwork, the cops went up to the victim's apartment and found a suicide note.

The crowd, meanwhile, was outraged and practically violent. Not because this person had decided to end his life. Not because of the horror of witnessing such a thing. No, these crazy New Yorkers were furious because they were not able to park. Those who had their cars in the lot were hysterical because they couldn't get them out.

It was definitely time to get out of the city for a while.

Steve and I spent hours trying to pack the backpacks we would carry. Easier said than done. We had EKG monitors, IV fluids, cardiac drugs, oral medications, antishock pants, intubation supplies, two oxygen tanks, you name it. It was worse than a jigsaw puzzle, keeping the airway supplies readily accessible, squeezing the MAST pants into their compartment, fitting in the dextrose and the sodium bicarb, which are particularly bulky. The packs ended up weighing about seventy pounds apiece. Luckily, this would be a first-class operation, with porters all the way.

We had gotten permission from the Kenyan consulate to bring our supplies and equipment into the country to be used exclusively on the members of our group. It would have been awkward if a Kenyan national had a stroke right in front of me. I probably would have treated him anyway, but it might have caused some legal problems. What we hadn't reckoned on was the layover in London. The extremely conscientious Heathrow security officials were interested in our equipment, especially the EKG monitors/defibrillators, which don't present a clear X ray and could conceivably be used for storing bombs. Unfortunately you can't open the monitors up without busting them. We had a few uneasy minutes before we got the bright idea of turning the machines on and giving the security people a demonstration of how they're used. That was good enough; they let us through.

I had been assigned the blue group, and except for one person, they were not a lot of work. We were only a few hours into the flight when the one whiner started. "I'm not feeling well. I'm nauseous. My feet are swelling." She was a constant pain for me, but that was what we were paid for.

It was by far the most exciting, incredible trip I'd ever been on. My photography training finally came in handy. I took dozens of rolls of film and got some great pictures. The daily itinerary was basically the same, mostly gawking at animals. They were well worth it: lions, giraffes, elephants . . . not your standard New York City vermin.

Part of me felt guilty about having such a good time on the Africa trip. I knew all about survivor's syndromes, and I told myself there was no reason to feel guilty, but I couldn't help it. It was only a year and a half since Jo-Ann had died, and part of me was actually glad that she was gone, glad to be able to go to far, exotic lands and do exciting things. I could never have done any of this if she were still in the hospital or still paralyzed at home. It also crossed my mind a few times that your average paramedic would never be able to pay for a trip like this. Are stockbrokers really so much more important to society than we are that they should be rewarded this way? Maybe instead of meaningless awards and pins, EMS should start giving us incentive trips. Twenty documented saves and you go to Kenya. I have an active fantasy life.

I had never given much thought to preventive medicine before; in the 911 business, you never see the patients before their crisis, so it's always too late for prevention. Here, I was with these people all day long, and I could try to nip things in the bud. I wasn't sure how much I ought to nag people, and I was unprepared for the amount of worrying I did about when they wandered off alone. I begged people to drink more nonalcoholic fluids. I felt like an overprotective den mother, which was ironic since I was probably the youngest person in the group. I didn't nag much, though, partly because I was uncomfortable in that role, but also because I realized that if there were no medical problems at all, the company might regret having hired us.

The two big problems were Nairobi Tummy—all sorts of stomach-related disorders—and dehydration. The altitude was higher than most people were used to, and though the sun was very strong, there was a pleasant breeze, so you didn't realize you were sweating and getting dehydrated until you suddenly wanted to fall over. Most of the dehydrated people could be rehydrated with regular fluids; I only had to start one IV line while I was with my subgroup.

On our return to the States, customs officials at Kennedy Airport opened one of my bags. They found five hats, five safari shirts, and a dozen carved wooden animals. They sent me right through. A big-time smuggler I'm not.

• • •

Everyone wanted to hear about the trip, which was convenient considering how desperately I wanted to talk about it. My photo album was passed around for weeks. My nonmedical friends were fascinated with the game runs and the sights. What were the people like? How was the jungle? My coworkers wanted to know what we had to do medically. I felt almost guilty admitting that the closest thing we had to an emergency was at dinner our last night in Nairobi, when all four subgroups were gathered together. One of the guests passed out and struck his head. I started an IV and Dr. Sixsmith stitched him up. Not too tough.

A month or so later, I was working one lovely spring day while there was a 10K run in Central Park. Anyone who knows me knows that running is not my thing. I can understand running to catch a bus, but running long distance is ridiculous. I don't care about the alleged physical benefits. Forcing yourself to continue running when your heart is pounding, you can barely breathe, your head is splitting, your legs are rubber, and you have to go to the bathroom, vomit, and collapse at the same time, is crazy. The way I look at it, you only have so many heartbeats in a lifetime: why waste them running through all five boroughs? I'll drive instead, thanks.

Medics see a lot of running injuries, especially during the summer in Central Park, which is right in the middle of Roosevelt's area. Most aren't serious. You see pulled muscles, dehydration, and often, pedestrians versus bikers, which is almost a fair confrontation. The person on foot gets hit harder, but the biker usually goes flying and gets pretty banged up, too.

I was trying to stay away from the park the day of the 10K run just on general principles. I figured Central Park Medical, a nonprofit volunteer organization, could handle it. They're a good group of people, EMTs who carry a police department radio in their ambulance and respond to calls for people hurt in the park. They work every weekend year-round and whenever there's a special event in the park, such as a race or a concert.

I have a lot of respect for volunteer ambulance groups. ("Volunteer" corps are unpaid. Calling a hospital "voluntary" just means that it is not city-owned.) There's a new volunteer squad in Bedford-Stuyvesant. You have to admire people who volunteer in such a tough neighborhood—they have to work hard. There are a lot of volunteer ambulance corps in New York City, mostly in Brooklyn and Queens, and the only one which bothers me is Hatzoloh, the "Matzoh Box" ambulance. I deal with the upper West Side division and, as people, I like most of them. But I don't like their organization because, although they claim to respond to anybody in their area, they don't make their number available. Everybody knows 911, but you only know the Matzoh Box number if you go to the right synagogue. I also think professionals should allow women, or anyone else qualified, to work on their ambulances. Hatzoloh doesn't for religious reasons.

Anyway, I don't know where Central Park Medical was when a good samaritan came running over to us and told us about a guy who had collapsed inside the park at about Sixty-third Street and the southbound park drive. We drove in and found the patient, a twentyish white guy in considerable distress, extremely dehydrated and disoriented. He obviously hadn't been drinking during this run and it was pretty humid out. He was having muscle spasms and couldn't control himself. He needed IV fluids and electrolyte replacement. Under normal circumstances we would put him on the stretcher, administer some oxygen, start an IV, and drive over to the hospital. Unfortunately, just as we were about to move him to the ambulance, a N.Y. Road Runner doctor came onto the scene. The doc told us to move the patient over to the medical tent they had set up by the finish line. I refused. The patient needed IVs and an E.R. visit. The physician announced that he was one of the official EMS-recognized race doctors and was taking over scene control. He demanded that we transport the patient to the medical tent.

I was delighted when an EMS supervisor assigned to the special event responded, but he turned out to be only an EMT and there was no way he would contradict the doctor. I was upset about it but it was out of my hands. I demanded and received all sorts of signatures from the doctor and the EMS supervisor, I even went on the radio to announce to the borough that I felt this was not in the patient's best interest.

I felt vindicated and, in a warped way, almost glad when an EMS ambulance rolled into the Rosy E.R. about forty-five minutes later with the same patient, now having seizures that did not seem to stop. According to the EMTs who brought him in, the patient was in the medical tent with no IVs, just one of those funky outer-space blankets—very strong aluminum blankets designed to keep the heat in—trying to drink some fluids, when he started seizing. The staff at the tent wasn't able to start an IV, so they had to transport to the hospital.

I was shaken because I *knew* that this guy should have been taken to Rosy first. Down in my bones I felt that I shouldn't have given up the fight so easily. But I was getting tired of always having to argue with on-scene docs. I was at the point in my career when I knew I could trust my instinct, but any bozo with an M.D. could come along and nearly kill my patient just because he had the two letters after his name. The runner did eventually walk out of the hospital, but it took a few days longer than it should have. He's probably back out there running again.

Soon after I got stuck working a night shift with Ted Dunn. Amazingly, we managed to get through almost an entire shift without any major confrontations. I had been on the job for a while now, so Teddy no longer seemed so impossible to understand. He was trapped in a job he hated. There was nothing else he knew how to do, nothing that paid as well. He had a high level of training, but it was very specific and only applicable to this job. At times, when he wasn't being too obnoxious, I could even feel sorry for him.

It was a quiet, uneventful tour. Then, ten minutes before we were scheduled to get off, the EMS dispatcher called us.

"Don't answer it," Ted ordered. "Let them call someone else."

"Fourteen Young for the Cardiac Seventy-seven and Columbus," the EMS dispatcher repeated. It sounded like he wouldn't take no for an answer.

"Yeah, Fourteen Young with overtime personnel,"

Ted said, grabbing the radio. "You got anyone else available for this?" Neither of us were on overtime.

"Sorry, Young. Take it over to Seventy-seven and Columbus for the male, sixty-three, Cardiac. Time now . . . ID number . . . Dispatch . . ."

Ted drove faster than I had ever seen him go. He didn't want to be on this job, but he had no choice. I knew what he had in mind: a classic "scoop and run." You find the patient, toss him in the back, and run like hell to the hospital. Unfortunately, the patient had other plans. He seemed to be having a heart attack.

It was another jogger; this one had been out for an early morning run. He was standing on the corner, clutching his chest, his eyes wide with pain and fear. He stumbled to the back of the bus when we pulled in, lights and siren. I put him on the stretcher and started to check him out.

"Am I having a heart attack?" he asked, obviously terrified by the thought. His gray hair was matted with sweat.

"You might be," I said matter-of-factly. "Don't worry. We'll take care of you." Medics don't need the kind of bedside manner that doctors do, but some patients do need emotional support. People having real medical emergencies are often scared and embarrassed. Some people hyperventilate, some apologize over and over again as if repeating a mantra. They need to be reassured, sometimes to have their hand held. I exercise a lot of tact and patience on the job. This may surprise people who know me, as I don't usually bring it home from work with me. Sometimes it's a sincere response on my part, sometimes just reflex, but it's an important skill to develop. If Ted had ever learned it, he had lost it along with his patience. He managed to control himself just long enough to get me a set of vital signs.

"Okay," he said then, chewing on his mustache, "let's get the hell out of here."

"Wait one minute," I said. "I just want to put him on the monitor and drop a line."

"What, are you nuts?" Ted snapped. "We're down the block from the hospital. Slap some oxygen on him and we'll be there in two minutes. Let them do that shit."

"Ted"—I tried to lower my voice so it didn't seem that we were arguing in front of the patient—"this guy is a rule-out M.I." Heart attack. "I've got to *at least* run a strip and start an IV."

"We'd have been inside the E.R. by now," Ted growled. He didn't seem to care if the patient could hear or not.

"That's bullshit patient care," I said quietly, while attempting to stick on the EKG electrodes. "And we're twenty blocks from the hospital."

"Fuck patient care," he whispered angrily. "It's close to change of tour, and I'm not getting stuck here late. I've got things to do."

"I think we should also give him a Nitro," I said.

"Fine!" Ted said sarcastically. "I'll be in the front. Let me know when you're ready to go." He slammed the door as he got out of the back of the ambulance. I heard him cursing me as he got in front. I really didn't need this shit. After we got the patient to the hospital, as I was fuming about Ted's attitude, it occurred to me that I had come a long way. Working with Ted, or with anyone as burned-out as he is, would never be fun or easy, but at least now we were doing things my way. I was calling some of the shots.

I felt pretty proud of myself until I got home. Lying in bed, trying to fall asleep with the bright daylight seeping through my curtains, I realized that I didn't feel angry at Ted. The first few times I had worked with him, I came away from the shifts so riled up, so disgusted, that I wanted to hit somebody. Where had all that passion gone? Did I care less now?

Ted was wrong, but part of me almost understood why he had acted that way. I would never not treat someone who needed treatment, but I could imagine myself being as rude as he had been. It was the end of our tour; we were tired. So what if Ted was unsympathetic? Medics see a lot more death and suffering than most people. They get jaded. Compassion is tough to muster day after day or even hour to hour. Most medics will take an extra two minutes with the little old lady who isn't really sick but who called 911 because she's scared and lonely. Most medics will be nice to a patient's family or bystanders on the street, especially if they want help carrying stuff up five flights. But you can get tired and cranky and not want to be nice anymore.

There was still a wide gap between Ted and myself, but, as much as I hated to admit it, the gap had somehow gotten narrower. I wasn't burning out, but I realized that maybe I could someday, and the idea did disturb me.

Most medics go into this job because they want to save lives. They had a certain vision of medics helping people directly and simply. They never pictured the squabbles within hospital ambulance departments, between the hospital departments and EMS, between EMS and the fire and police departments, and the political pressures put on the EMS. For people who are so streetwise, medics can be awfully naive.

In June, 1987, I was temporarily and wrongfully suspended from EMS for about a day. I did absolutely nothing wrong medically. I was a victim of politics. As an employee of St. Luke's/Roosevelt Hospital Center, I am not technically a member of New York City's Emergency Medical Service, although the hospital subcontracts us out to the city. Both the hospital medics and the EMS medics work in ambulances on the streets of New York City, responding to 911 calls. We operate under the same rules and are dispatched by the same EMS Central in Queens. Ninety-nine percent of the time the only difference between city and hospital medics is the color of our pants. (City medics wear green, most hospital crews wear blue.) But the last thing I need is to be accused of posing as an EMS employee. I have an EMS shield number, but my paycheck says St. Luke's/Roosevelt.

On rare occasions the disjunction of services does come into play. There have been some doozies of arguments between the hospital ambulance supervisors and the EMS supervisors. In the hospital, I'm supposed to take my orders from my hospital supervisors. Out on the streets, while subcontracted to EMS, I'm supposed to take orders from their lieutenants or supervisors. It doesn't always happen that way. EMS medics have to be respectful to their bosses or they could find themselves transferred to Staten Island in a hurry. Not me. If I mouth off to the city supervisors, I still show up to work at Roosevelt. Even if EMS suspends me from working 911, I'm still employed by the hospital, and my supervisors there will probably fight the decision.

At this particular time, the EMS had been getting a lot of bad press so the hierarchy decided to maximize their media coverage by only assigning EMS ambulances to high-profile calls, such as building collapses or bomb threats. The dispatchers wouldn't give a hospital unit a call in the middle of its own area if they knew there were going to be television cameras; they'd assign it to a city EMS unit that was farther away.

The Bolshoi Ballet was in town for a week, and the NYC police department was worried about something happening due to some anti-Soviet feeling at that time. They requested that EMS keep an ambulance available. So Ten Adam, a city BLS unit, stood in front of Lincoln Center from five P.M. to one A.M. every night.

Unfortunately, the EMS system got backlogged and Ten Adam was needed to cover a call elsewhere. My partner and I had just gotten some takeout Chinese food when we were assigned to a possible bomb threat in Lincoln Center. We were right across the street at the time, so we advised EMS that we were already on the scene.

There must have been a quick panic in the communications office when they realized that they had sent a hospital unit by mistake, because they immediately ordered us to leave. They said a different unit was responding and that we should leave the scene and go back to our available status.

No way. We had already been greeted by an Emergency Services Unit cop who had told us that this was a real bomb and sent us into the command post they'd set up. We couldn't leave the scene of a confirmed bomb when the other ambulance hadn't even arrived yet. We called the dispatcher to tell him so, but the lieutenant on the Manhattan board told us to leave anyway.

We are supposed to take orders from those guys, but this was ridiculous. We started to quote EMS directives and operating procedures to the communications department over the radio. All these communications were taped. EMS rules state that in the absence of an EMS supervisor on the scene, all units are to take their orders from the highest ranking police officer present. The highest ranking police officer had told us to stay, so we were staying.

When the city unit arrived, the dispatcher again ordered us to leave the call. We quoted another EMS guideline: in the absence of EMS field supervisors during a special operation or event, administrative as well as medical control of the scene will be under paramedic control. The city unit was an EMT unit and we were the paramedics. We weren't leaving.

The Manhattan borough commander threatened to put us "off service," purging us from the computer and sending us back to the hospital. I told him to do as he liked, but we weren't leaving. I was still trying to finish my dinner, which was getting cold. He put us off service, but we stayed.

I called my boss, Dan Mathisen, on the hospital radio to advise him of the situation. He was baffled but told us to stay on the scene if we thought it necessary.

A strange voice came on the radio. "Car Two to Central. Place Fourteen Young off service and have them return to their facility immediately." Dispatch advised Car Two that we had already been placed off service but were refusing to leave the scene.

The bomb guys had been in there for quite a while when an EMS lieutenant finally showed up. The only supervisor available, he had driven like mad from somewhere far away just to order us off the scene and put us back on service for other calls. Now we had no choice.

We left, technically. We got in the ambulance, drove down the block, stopped, turned the vehicle around and parked. Lincoln Center was in the middle of our area. If the bomb went off, we would still be there to respond.

A few minutes later we were assigned a call way out of our area. As we started to respond, the dispatcher canceled the call, placed us off service again and ordered us to return to our hospital.

Dan was waiting for us at the hospital. I asked him who Car Two was.

"The number two guy in the entire EMS system. Above the chiefs. Above everyone except the director. . . . I want incident reports. Very detailed incident reports." I wrote half a volume on this call.

While I was writing, Dan got a call advising him that my partner and I had been suspended for gross insubordination and were no longer allowed to work in the 911 system. Dan backed us up, calling EMS, arguing with them, quoting EMS rules and guidelines.

"EMS says you guys were never assigned the call and you jumped on it. Since you had no right to be out on it, they felt justified in ordering you off it." I was dumbfounded.

"Not assigned. . . . Bullshit! I had hot food! I wouldn't have jumped on a call with hot food."

"Danny, we were assigned. They called us. Tape search," my partner prodded him.

"Tape search," I agreed. "Go out there and listen to the tapes."

To his complete credit, Dan drove out to Maspeth, Queens, that night at ten P.M. to listen to the tapes of the EMS radio. Not surprisingly, the machine that plays back the tapes "went out of order." They couldn't prove that we had jumped the call, but we couldn't prove that we hadn't.

We would have liked an immediate reinstatement and an apology, but that's not EMS's style. They said they would "allow Mr. Negron and Mr. Shapiro to continue working pending a full and thorough investigation." This must be one of the most thorough investigations in EMS history, because it's been going on for almost three years now. I wonder if I'm in the clear yet.

A few months later I was written up for refusing to do a mandatory overtime. The fact that the voluntary hospitals may support their medics in disputes with EMS doesn't mean that they are necessarily better employers than EMS. If the hospitals can't actually make a profit, they're determined to at least not lose money. They do this by skimping on their employees' salaries or forcing people to work overtime so they won't have to hire anyone new.

Roosevelt had a hiring freeze and wouldn't hire anyone to fill the slots we had open. If a per diem wasn't available, the hospital would force full-timers to fill in. You'd work eight hours, come in at the end of the tour, and find out that you had to work another eight hours. Too bad if you had plans or a class to take or just didn't feel well. I was working the day shift, eight A.M. to four P.M. When I got stuck working overtime until midnight, that didn't give me a whole lot of time to myself before I was scheduled to be back at work at eight A.M. This was happening at least once a week to everyone in the department.

In this case, I had informed the supervisors two weeks in advance that I would be unable to work at that time no matter what—my great-aunt and -uncle were coming in from Ann Arbor—but they slated me for it anyway.

It was becoming clear to me that it all came down to money. You start out in this business because you want to help people, but you come to realize that it *is* a business. Ambulance rides aren't free. Medics don't care about billing, about finding patients who will pay their bills, because their salaries don't depend directly on the patient's check—they got their paychecks whether or not an individual patient has paid his bill.

If a city EMS ambulance responds to a 911 call, the patient or his family will eventually receive the bill—$150 to $175 for a basic life support ambulance, or $250 to $275 for a medic ambulance. Voluntary hospital ambulances charge more. Rosy currently charges $225 for basic, $350 for advanced life support. Each hospital has a different fee scale. Insurance and Medicaid usually pick up a lot of it. The homeless get a free ambulance ride but the medical center tries to pick up some of their costs from state funds. If a hospital crew and an EMS crew work together on a call, the one that transports the patient will receive the payment. There's never any argument about who will transport because the medics on the street aren't concerned with the financial aspect. No bill is generated for a DOA, just for patients who are transported, or in certain cases, who are treated but not transported. If medics show up to a cardiac arrest, do CPR, put tubes down his throat, start IVs, administer meds, work on him for a half hour or so, but he doesn't make it, the family will get a bill. If a diabetic with very low blood sugar goes into insulin shock, medics show up and start IVs, put him on oxygen and give him the proper meds. Often he will wake up, alert and oriented, and won't want to go to the hospital. The medics take out the IVs and leave, but that person will get a bill because he received an advanced level of care.

Personally, I couldn't care less if bills are sent or not. You can't stop to ask about insurance. If you have an unknown patient in cardiac arrest, you don't care who he is. You do what's got to be done and transport, putting John or Jane Doe, unknown address, on the paperwork. If they ever find out who he is, they can bill him then. If someone were to die because you delayed treatment to get his address and Social Security number, the hospital would lose a multi-million-dollar lawsuit, so it's really not worth it. Much better to give a few free rides than to worry about the billing.

But if there were never any paying patients, I'd probably be out of a job. The hospital has a budget and has to worry about the bottom line. The infuriating thing about the mandatory overtime rule was that it was penny wise and pound foolish anyway, because it would have been cheaper to hire more full-timers than to pay all the overtime.

• • •

I began to wonder why I put up with all this nonsense. So much bureaucracy, so many people telling me what to do, so little respect . . . was it worth it? The trip to Kenya had been more than just a great travel opportunity: it had been a refreshingly positive work experience. The excitement involved in traveling had made up for the missed thrills of treating trauma on the streets.

I started to think about trying to do something like that for a living. Steve agreed that it was worth a try: getting paid good money to accompany groups throughout the world, all expenses paid. A great idea, especially if we could find large groups that would look at it as a tax write-off, or a way to lessen their insurance payments. As far as we could tell, it had never been done before, and there had to be a market for it. We hired an attorney who helped us draw up all the papers you need to become a legal corporation. Steve became the president of American Medics International; I took the roles of vice-president and treasurer. Dr. Sixsmith was the medical director, and Steve's wife Arlene our corporation secretary. We had stationery printed, business cards, the works. We sent off hundreds of letters, interviewed with some very large companies, and made a few presentations at local business clubs. The incorporation process took a few months, during which time we were hired for another trip, this time to Bermuda. Unfortunately, it was a small group and they only needed one medic, so Steve got to go. I would have loved it, but I didn't have any more vacation time coming to me from Rosy anyway. I couldn't argue. I was happy, in any case, that the company had some business. Maybe we were on the right track. Perhaps this could really work.

Steve and I flew out to Chicago for a long weekend to scout out the International Travel Convention. We didn't drum up any business, but we had a good time pretending to be businessmen. About all that came out of it was that I let myself get talked into plunking down seventy-five bucks for a new toy, a light/music/computer gadget that spins and flashes in time to music being played on a stereo. The sales rep said it was great for relaxation, meditation, and whatever else ails you.

When I got back to New York, it was raining nonstop. Working in the rain sucks. You get wet. Over and over again. You walk out to the ambulance and get wet. As you climb into the bus, you shake off the water and get sticky. You sit in the bus, feeling damp and uncomfortable. As soon as you get dry, you're assigned a call. You pull up in front of the building, climb out of the bus and get wet as you pull the stretcher and equipment out of the back. Inside the apartment you start to dry off. Back outside, wet again. Damp, sticky, and uncomfortable again on route to the hospital. Inside the E.R. you get dry, but you just have to go back out into the rain again. Roosevelt gave its people raincoats, which was a nice thought but didn't work too well. They didn't have pockets for the equipment and were way too hot, so people rarely used them. There's no noticeable decrease in the call volume, because there are lots of fender-benders and lots of little old ladies slip and fall.

So this day, I was wondering again why I put myself through all of this. In Chicago, in businessman mode, there was the *Wall Street Journal* with breakfast and networking at cocktail parties. In New York, in medic mode, there was boredom, discomfort, and frustration.

We got a call for an Uncon and started to respond, then EMS dispatch pulled us off that assignment and sent us to a report of a pedestrian struck at Broadway and Sixty-fifth Street. It was highly unusual to be called off a priority assignment; I decided the pedestrian struck must be in particularly bad shape. Apparently there were a lot of 911 calls reporting the accident.

We went lights and sirens, but not too fast, because the roads were slippery with the rain. I noticed three things right away that told me how serious this call was.

1. The police officers were not sitting in their car. They were standing outside in the rain.

2. The cops weren't wearing their raincoats. They were using them to cover the victim, an elderly lady lying in the street.

3. They were frantically waving at us to hurry.

"She got hit by that truck," a cop told us. "I think her arm is really bad."

My partner that day was pulling equipment off the ambulance as I approached the patient. She was conscious and alert. I tried to keep the rain off her face and mine as I spoke to her. She was in psychological and physical shock, and denied any pain whatsoever. But she said she couldn't move her right arm.

"I think her arm is really bad," the officer repeated.

As I lifted the police raincoat away, I saw that the patient's own raincoat underneath was saturated in blood. I began cutting the woman's sleeve away without asking her permission. Copious amounts of blood poured out onto the street, mixing with the dirty rainwater in the gutter.

"Oh shit!" I said aloud. "Her arm is really bad." The old lady didn't react. Not a good sign.

I was crouching in a puddle, trying to hold what was left of her arm in place. Besides two different open fractures, and perhaps a busted shoulder, there was a complete degloving of the arm. You could look inside her arm and see each bone, each muscle, ripped vein, and artery. A very nasty injury.

The force of the hit implied possible neck or back injuries, so we had to immobilize her. We didn't have time to worry about a little water, so plop, the trauma bag went into the puddle; the longboard went into a puddle; when we rolled the patient onto her side to get the board under her, *she* rolled into a puddle. I was wet. My partner was wet. The patient was wet. Everything was wet and dirty and slippery. My uniform was trashed. I could barely see through my glasses. God, I hate rain.

We started an IV on the patient's good arm on route to Bellevue, but the arm was so wet that the tape wouldn't stick. The tape we used to secure her head to the longboard wouldn't stick either. She was slipping further into shock and it was impossible to keep her warm. I was happy to finally turn her over to the E.R. staff and to shake the water out of my hair. But only a minute later, I was back in service and cursing about it.

Back home later I waited until it got dark outside, shut out the lights, and hooked my new toy up to the stereo. Green and red LED lights flashed and spun around at tremendous speeds, creating patterns out of the music. The salesman was right. It was very relaxing. I experimented with all sorts of different music. Pink Floyd was perfect.

I spent hours that way, kicking back on the couch with a cold beer, staring into the center of the light, listening to the music. I knew it was bullshit, but it was cheaper and safer than drugs.

I wasn't the only one in the department getting frustrated and angry. I was working Christmas, a double shift in fact, but I didn't really mind. My family was spread all over the world and my apartment still felt very empty without Jo. Christmas Day is usually okay workwise, just kind of slow except for a few dead people under the tree. ("Gee, golly, look, I got a Nintendo . . . and Grandpa's dead!") Someone dropping dead on Christmas tends to bum out the whole family.

I was in the hospital between the two tours, talking with Gene. He had just finished the Christmas Day shift, which he had agreed to do simply because he's a good guy. He was about to head home for Christmas dinner when a supervisor came in and told him he had to do four hours' mandatory overtime. Merry Christmas, Gene. He was as mad as I'd ever seen him. I knew something had to give way with this system. I didn't know what we could do that we hadn't already done; we had been complaining and writing letters about it for months. I remembered the psuedo strike the ambulance department at St. Clare's had staged when they asked everyone not to bring patients there for two days. That had proved effective, but I didn't know if something like that would work at

Rosy, where the department was a lot larger and a lot less unified. But we had to do something!

I was finishing up my double shift, so I wasn't too human anymore when we got a call for a cardiac arrest. We showed up, as did Thirteen Charlie, the St. Clare's BLS bus. This old lady had dropped dead about ten minutes earlier. Her whole family pleaded with us to "Help her, help her, try to help Grandma!"

Grandma had terminal lung cancer, but because it was Christmas and they all wanted us to help her, we decided to try to resuscitate. It was ugly. One of her lungs had exploded inside her body. Blood was coming out of the tubes, pink and frothy. Normally when you squeeze the AMBU bag when it's attached to the endotracheal tube, air goes straight into the lungs and they expand like balloons. But Grandma's lungs were so fibrosed, sclerosed, and scarred from the disease that it was like trying to get lead bags to expand. After about twenty minutes of this futile attempt, I called the medical control doctor to request permission to terminate the arrest as the patient was clearly dead. There was no reason to continue to run the code with bits of her lungs coming up the tube. We were just beating up on a dead person at this point.

Unfortunately, the control doctor was brand new. He had gotten stuck working Christmas Day because he didn't have any seniority. He was hesitant to give us orders to terminate because it was Christmas Day and the patient's whole family was there. He told us to start dopamine, which was absurd since we had already given five milligrams of epinephrine, two of atropine, some calcium, etc. After five or six minutes without results on dopamine, we called back and he finally said okay to terminate.

I broke the news to the family and they took it well. But I felt bad because we had made a complete mess of the bedroom, needles and syringes and bloody stuff everywhere. I'm always dropping things as I work, used alcohol, pads, bloody compresses, the packages of whatever supplies I use, the latex gloves. I try not to leave too much of a mess and always take away the "sharps"—anything with a needle on it. I asked if they had a garbage bag, but all they could find was a fancy A&S bag that still had some presents in it. It was gut-wrenching to see them dump their kids' gifts out of this festive red and green bag so we could fill it with gore. It was all wrong.

As if I didn't have enough to bother me, my certification was about to expire. Time for a refresher class. I was less than thrilled. I've got a bad attitude about recertification, but if EMS took attitudes into account, they wouldn't be able to keep any employees more than a year or so.

There were about twenty medics in the refresher class given at St. Vincent's, most of whom I knew at least to say hi to. The world of emergency medicine is a relatively small one. I cross paths over and over again with the same people. One EMT I worked with at Empire State became a medic for St. Clare's and I'd run into her from time to time. Another became a flight medic in Suffolk County; I ran into him on a rescue call with my volunteer fire department. People I trained with at Beekman would turn up on calls, at other hospitals, at our continuing medical education classes. I expected to see more of my former class-mates from Beekman—their medic cards had to expire the same time as mine—but most of them were taking the course somewhere else. Moffett was there. We sat in the back of the class and griped together.

Paramedics are "certified professionals," as opposed to nurses and doctors who are "licensed professionals." Once M.D.s and R.N.s have their licenses they never have to prove anything again. A ninety-two-year-old R.N. licensed in 1915 who helped the WWI guys and hasn't done any nursing since, can walk into a hospital today and her license is valid. A medic may do his job full-time and use his skills every day, but if his card expires before he's scheduled to take his next test, he won't be allowed to work because his certification has lapsed. An M.D. who took his national boards in Idaho can present his license, pay a fee, and be allowed to practice in New York, but if I wanted to move to Pennsylvania, I would no longer be able to work. I'm certified nationally as well as in New York State, but some states, including New York, don't recognize national certification. I'd still be fully capable of doing the job, my knowledge would not have evaporated overnight, but my skills would no longer be accepted.

Steve and I had been full-time medics for three years. Some of the others had been medics for six or nine years. We all thought it was absurd to have to keep proving that we still knew bleeding and bandage control. I understood the logic behind the regulations: an awful lot of volunteers handle very few real calls and need to take refresher classes. But still.

Recertification is a drag. In addition to taking the state refresher courses and passing the test, to work as a medic in New York City, on the 911 system, you also have to take Continuing Medical Education (CME). This involves thirty-six hours a year: twelve hours of call review, twelve of lecture time on various subjects, and twelve of emergency room observation time.

The State of New York requires a state-approved refresher class every three years. Some of these involve 120 hours of classes. The Vinny's course was a "challenger" refresher. For this I just showed up for an hour or two the first two nights and then took tests for each field of knowledge—obstetrics, medical emergencies, cardiac emergencies, etc. I did well enough to be exempted from having to sit through the lectures again, although I had to attend a few mandatory classes to prove that I still knew CPR skills, bandaging skills, etc. The whole thing only took about twenty hours, including the testing time, but it was my free time, nights and Saturdays, and it put me into a lousy mood.

"Hmmm, let's see." I scribbled down some notes. "Sixty-five miles an hour, not faster—I don't want to draw attention to myself. Seven hours of traveling time. Hmmm. That would get me 455 miles from the city." I double-checked my math.

"Yup. They'd never find us." I chuckled quietly. It was just after one A.M. on a slow, boring night. My partner was sound asleep in the back and I was plotting to steal the ambulance. No reason in particular; I was just bored.

Ohio, I figured. Not that I really wanted to go to Ohio, but no one would ever think of looking for us that far west. By the following day we could be in Michigan. I have family there. Maybe even Chicago. I know lots of people there.

By morning, when we didn't return, the hospital would be sure something was up. Even if they elected to call the police, which I wasn't sure they'd do right away, they'd probably start with the local NYPD. They might think we were ambushed and lying dead in some alley. After a while they might contact the State Police. When they finally got around to calling the Tri-State Highway Patrol people, we'd be far past them. There was no way they'd find us.

It was a fun thought, but not too realistic. As disgusted as I could get with the job, I really did want to keep it. I had to assume that I'd be fired if I took the ambulance across time zones.

On the other hand—my evil mind would not be discouraged—I *could* make it to Atlantic City and back without getting caught.

It would be risky, no doubt about that; but it could be done. It would depend on my partner, too. We'd both have to be willing to risk it, and to suffer the consequences if caught.

I wrote some more notes. "Okay, figure 125 miles to A.C. Two hours down and two hours back. If we leave at twelve-thirty A.M., we'd get there by two-thirty. Stay until four A.M. if it's a weeknight, five it it's a weekend. Then drive back and be in the city by seven A.M. We could even have breakfast before returning to the hospital. Piece of cake."

We'd have to be careful. I didn't want to get nailed to a wall for it. But there were ways we could cover ourselves to give us the best chance of succeeding.

First: both me and my partner in crime would show up promptly for the midnight shift, in uniform, all ready to go.

Second: we'd sign out the narcotics, radios, blood pressure cuff and anything else that we needed for a normal midnight-to-eight shift. We'd pick up the keys and head out to check out the ambulance.

Third: we'd get on the radio and advise the EMS dispatcher that we were in the bus and ready for assignments, hoping like hell we don't get banged with one right away. The supervisor on duty would probably be listening to the radio in his office, so we'd have to give him the in-service signal.

Fourth: we'd drive down Ninth Avenue and head for the Lincoln Tunnel, stopping only long enough to make a phone call to the Manhattan EMS dispatcher.

"Manhattan board," the dispatcher would answer the phone.

"Hi, Manhattan, this is Fourteen Young," I'd say, sounding dejected. "I hate to tell you this, but we just blew our radiator. Yup. Sorry. We're out of service, mechanical, until the morning. Yeah. We're right in front of the hospital. The mechanic is going to come in first thing and replace it. Our supervisor is already on the phone making calls. I'll let you know if we get fixed sooner. Okay, thanks. See you later."

The dispatcher would have no reason not to believe us. He'd also assume that our supervisor was aware of it. Why would we lie?

Our supervisor would have no idea that we called the dispatcher by phone, putting us off service. Why would we? After a few hours he might wonder why he hadn't heard or seen us. But frequently no news is good news.

Now we'd be cruising south. Two hours to get there, three hours there, two hours to get back, and the shift would be over. We'd make up a few calls, put the fake ACRs in the envelope, stagger back at a quarter to eight, drop our stuff on the desk and split for the day.

At two in the morning it seems so easy. Hell, we could even park in front of Atlantic City Medical Center. It's across the street from Bally's!

Gas money! I suddenly thought. We could fill up at our service station before crossing state lines—is that a felony?—but we'd probably have to put a few bucks into the tank to make it back safely. We could swing that.

For a really long trip, we could get a large white Styrofoam cooler, fill it with beer, seal it and label it "human liver for transplant." Who would have the balls to stop us and search it?

My boss called me off the streets to inform me that I had to go downtown to the Assistant District Attorney's office to give a deposition. It's not unusual for medics, witnesses to crimes or to the results of crime, to be called to testify in court or to make depositions for the D.A. Full-time medics don't mind receiving these subpoenas because they get paid for the day. I've been down to the D.A.'s office a number of times to make depositions in criminal cases where I treated the victim or, sometimes, the perpetrator. If someone is injured during an arrest and wants to charge police brutality, the medics might be called in to make a deposition about the extent of the injury. Most of the complaints are bogus and most of the cases never go to court.

This time, my boss told me the name of the patient in question, but I drew a blank. I had no idea who he was talking about. I didn't remember the address or even the call. But when I saw the ACR I had written over a year before, it all came back to me. I always try to do reasonably thorough call reports, especially when the cases might pop up in a court-room some day. You never know. A case might take two or three years to come to trial, and if I'm going to be subpoenaed and put on the stand to either defend my treatment or justify my actions, I want to have everything documented.

This one was the stabbing Gene and I had handled over a year before, the one in an elevator on West End Avenue, with internal bleeding. We had rushed the victim to St. Luke's for immediate trauma sur-gery. He must have survived, because the charge was attempted murder.

I had never testified in court, so I was quite interested to see the whole process from start to finish. Before the trial, I had to meet with the Assistant D.A. to go over the events. When I arrived on time for my eleven A.M. appointment, the people in his office said he had just stepped out for lunch and would be right back. I immediately developed an attitude problem: I figured he was out having a three-martini lunch with hotshots while I sat there cooling my heels. My attitude did a 180-degree turn two minutes later when he bopped in carrying a McDonald's bag, fries sticking out of his mouth. He shook my hand and asked if I wanted some fries. My type of D.A.

As I went over the events with him, he pointed out that most of my medical jargon would be inappro-priate in court and would give rise to all sorts of objections. He didn't coach me, or tell me what he wanted me to say; on the contrary, he told me to answer everything as simply and truthfully as I could.

But, for instance, I described the wound by pointing to where it had been inflicted. You can't do that in court. I said the guy had been "stabbed," but the ADA told me I couldn't use that word until it had been shown that a stabbing had occurred. I had to stop and think about how to describe the wound specifically, without pointing, without coming out and saying that it was a stabbing. I finally settled for something like, "He was bleeding from an approximately five-inch-long laceration that appeared penetrating in nature, similar to stabbing wounds I had seen in the past." I couldn't say that the patient complained of shortness of breath because that was hearsay. I had to say that it became apparent that he was having shortness of breath with obvious increased accessory muscle use.

The actual court appearance was kind of intimidating. They kept me in a cell-like witness room before I testified, and then when I took the stand, the defense attorney tried to trip me up in cross-examination. I was the first witness, and my testimony was very simple since I hadn't seen who stabbed the victim, had no idea why he was stabbed, and hadn't asked him anything about it. All I could say was that the wounds were life-threatening. The defense was claiming that it was self-defense, not attempted murder, that the assailant just wanted to scare the victim. But we had found the patient in shock with a lacerated spleen. It was not just a little slashing to scare someone.

Had the defense attorney wanted to impeach me as a witness, he could simply have asked me to identify my patient. If he had been in the courtroom, dressed in a suit, not bleeding, I wouldn't have recognized him. In a case like this, you're so focused on the wound that you barely notice what the patient's face looks like. I guess I was credible enough, though, because they didn't bother calling Gene to back up what I was saying. The defendant was convicted.

This is a job of extremes. You go from treating the richest people in the world to the poorest; from the most beautiful apartments to the most sleazy skell holes; from the most crucial life-and-death cases to hypochondriacs; from horrific crimes and senseless violence to cuts and bruises. Some cases are so absurd and trivial that they'd make you laugh if they weren't so infuriating. And, often as not, the cases are legitimate, but the patients are infuriating.

An old woman fell down and broke her hip crossing Seventh Avenue. When Gene and I arrived, she was sitting on the corner of Fifty-fourth Street in a comfortable chair a kind store owner had brought out for her. A businessman with a portable phone had called her relatives to say that she had had an accident and would be late.

"I want to go to Lenox Hill," the blue-haired lady told us.

"We can't go to Lenox Hill," I said simply.

"I won't go anywhere else!" Gene and I shook our heads. Why did this always seem to happen to us? People often try to treat the ambulance as a glorified taxi service, demanding to go to *their* hospital, no matter how far it is. It drives me crazy. There is a small section on the ambulance call report where you list which hospital you go to and why. Ninety-five percent of the patients get taken to the closest facility. The rest either go to a specialty facility—microsurgery, burn center—or are taken farther because the nearest hospital is full up and has requested a diversion. When the call is relatively close to more than one hospital, I don't mind taking the patient to the one she's used to, where her doctor is, or whatever. Unfortunately, you get the occasional patient who is convinced that she has the God-given right to be transported to Lenox Hill. She doesn't. Yellow taxis are wonderful. You wave your arm, they stop, you tell them where you want to go and they take you there. That's not my job. I don't have time to drive across the city.

"We can't take you to Lenox Hill," Gene tried to explain. "We're down the block from St. Clare's and we're right by Roosevelt. We can't just bypass both hospitals."

"I don't care," she yelled. "I'll just stay right here until someone takes me to Lenox Hill."

"You have a fractured hip," I yelled back. "You can't stay *right here*."

"Oh yes I can!"

"Oh no you can't!" Gene chimed in.

"Oh yes I can!"

I turned to the police officer on the scene. Maybe he could help.

"Ma'am," he said, stepping forward, "you have to go with them. You can't stay here. You have a broken hip."

"Why can't they take me to *my* hospital?" It was beginning to sound like she owned it.

"Because they work for EMS," he explained. "EMS is only allowed to go to the nearest hospital."

"That would be St. Clare's or Roosevelt," I jumped

in. "We'll give you your choice." I tried to sound like
we were doing her a favor."

"Neither."

Give me a polite AIDS patient or a cooperative
skell any day, I thought. The crowd around us had
grown and it was getting closer and closer to four P.M.,
quitting time. This blue-haired lady was like some
elderly relative who comes to visit and won't go home,
just sits and criticizes everything about you.

"You're not being rational," I said to her.

"And you're not being reasonable," she countered.

"What do you think?" I asked Gene, away from the
patient.

"I don't know. What do you?"

"I don't think we can just toss her on the stretcher
and take off."

"No, she'll raise holy hell."

"I don't need another complaint this week. . . ."

"Okay, ma'am," I said to the patient, "here's what
we're going to do. We're going to immobilize your
hip. That will protect it from further damage and
hopefully reduce some of the discomfort." She didn't
argue.

"Then we are going to take you to Roosevelt
Hospital. *Listen to me*," I shouted as she tried to
interrupt. "Once you're there you can transfer to
Lenox Hill."

"Will you be taking me to my hospital?" she asked.

"No," Gene answered. "We're the 911 ambulance.
We can only take you to the nearest facility. But you
can get a private ambulance to take you anywhere you
want."

"I won't let them touch me there," she sniffed.

"That's okay," I assured her. "You don't have to let

anyone inside the hospital touch you. That's your right."

"Fine," the old lady said finally.

When we arrived at Roosevelt, a nurse came over to our patient.

"Hello, ma'am," she said. "I'm going to be your nurse."

"Oh no you're not," the old lady snapped. "I'm transfering the hell out of here right now."

"Oh really?" the nurse asked.

"Yes, really! Call my son. Call my doctor. Call Lenox Hill."

Gene and I watched, amused, as the E.R. staff tried to reason with her.

"At least let us take an X ray and see if it really is broken."

"No. I want to go Lenox Hill."

"Maybe it's not serious and you can just go home. Why don't you let us take a look at it?"

"No. I want to go to Lenox Hill." Over the normal mayhem, we could hear the old lady from across the E.R.

"They don't have a chance," I said to Gene.

"None whatsoever," he agreed.

Gary Pollino and I responded to a confirmed bomb on Fifty-first Street off of Sixth Avenue. A bomb is a hurry-up-and-wait call. You've got to get there in a hell of a hurry in case it goes off, then you've got to wait and wait and wait while the bomb squad tries to make sure that it doesn't.

The first thing to do is to set up a staging area. For simple emergencies, someone sick at home or hit by a car in the street, you can go straight to the scene and treat the patient immediately. In more chaotic situations, like an occupied high-rise fire (a 10-26), or a structural collapse (a 10-33), you can't drive straight to the call and park in front of the building. You don't want to block the other emergency vehicles and you have to make sure that you're going to be able to get away from the scene quickly. Traffic in New York City is crazy to begin with, but when the police and fire department block off two or three streets and bring in dozens of emergency vehicles for a call, it's impossible. The first ambulance on the scene has to set up a staging area that is close enough to the call for you to be effective, but not close enough to put you in danger or for you to get in the way, and allows for a quick getaway.

An aircraft incident/crash would also call for a staging area somewhat removed from the actual incident, but the only 10-40s I've responded to about crashes in the Hudson River all turned out to be prank calls. EMS has even "prepared" for a 10-47, a nuclear substance spill, or a 10-49, an earthquake or hurricane. I don't know what EMS expects the first unit on the scene to decide, but in the event of a nuclear accident or a hurricane striking New York City, I would place the staging area somewhere near Cleveland.

Gary and I set up our staging area on the southeast corner of Sixth and Fifty-first—when it's a real bomb, I don't want to be too close. We got our stretcher out of the bus and loaded all the equipment onto it. After a few minutes an EMS lieutenant arrived on the scene.

"Are you guys Fourteen Young?" the lieutenant

asked, sounding nervous. I checked around. We were the only ambulance on the scene.

"Yessir," I responded. It never hurts to give the EMS supervisors a little respect.

"I want you to move your bus across the street." He paused for a second looking toward the corner. "To the northeast corner."

"Okay, lieutenant." I didn't ask what was wrong with the southeast corner. Whatever he wanted.

"I'm getting hungry," I said to Gary when I returned from repositioning the bus.

"Yeah, me too." He looked at his watch. "It's getting to be about that time."

The confirmed bomb had brought out the best in the emergency services. ESU cops were all over the place. Bomb squad detectives in explosive-proof suits ran the show. The fire department was on the scene in case it went off. Gary and I sat waiting. The bomb squad stays alive by doing everything very slowly and cautiously, so these calls can take forever. Another EMS supervisor arrived, a Special Operations captain. He came over to us.

"Okay, Fourteen Young!" he barked. "I need you to move your unit over to the southeast corner." Gary and I exchanged glances.

"It used to be on that corner," I said, as respectfully as I could.

"Well, put it back there." He returned to his "command post."

"This is stupid," I said to Gary, who nodded. It was a classic case of too many chiefs and not enough Indians. Wouldn't it be nice, I thought again, to be my own boss instead? As Gary moved our bus back to its original position, I saw another EMS boss arriving, this time a deputy chief.

"We've got to get out of here," I said when Gary returned. I had had enough of mindlessly obeying mindless orders. If these guys had nothing better to do than argue about which side of the street made a better staging area, let them fight it out between themselves.

"I'm still hungry," he said.

"Look across the avenue."

"Hot dog vendor! I could go for that."

"Me too." I smiled. "I'll go tell the brass."

"Excuse me, Chief," I said interrupting the pow-wow. "We're going across the street for a bite to eat. Would anyone like anything?"

They were too shocked to speak. Had I asked for permission to leave the scene, they would undoubtedly have refused, but my asking if they wanted anything threw them for a loop. They just stood there silently, shaking their heads no.

"Okay. We'll be right over there." I pointed to the Sabrette's stand. "If it goes off, we'll know it." No danger of anyone stealing our equipment with all the cops standing around.

Gary and I sat down by the hot-dog stand with our food. We had a great view of the proceedings. Everyone was running around, talking into radios, looking busy and concerned.

"Another soda?" I offered.

"No, thanks." Gary stretched his legs out on the sidewalk. "Not a bad way to handle a call," he commented.

"Not bad at all."

The bomb never went off. Gary and I finished our picnic and took off.

Enough was enough. Everyone in the department was sick to death of being stuck with mandatory overtimes, of never being able to make plans because you could never be sure that you'd really be getting off work when scheduled to. We had put up with it for about a year, but no more. The hospital had reduced the amount of mandatory overtime to four hours per shift, but it was still happening to somebody nearly every day and was unacceptable.

Then, in the week of Thanksgiving, 1988, there was a Great Coincidence. My phone rang Sunday night at midnight. I wondered which Roosevelt supervisor it was.

"Hello," I answered cheerily.

"Hello, Paul." It was Sal Gonzalez. "Are you interested in coming in and working tonight?"

"Uh . . . no," I answered, trying not to sound too amused. "Are there a lot of openings tonight?"

"Uh, yeah. . . . So far just about everyone is sick for tomorrow," Sal admitted. "Since you're scheduled to be off tomorrow anyway, I was wondering if you'd like to come in and give us a hand."

I had to laugh. Every single full-timer sick at the same time—it must have been some strange contagious illness. Our department had never managed to agree about anything before, but we all agreed about how sick we were those two days.

"No. Sorry. I can't," I said. Even if I had wanted to work, which I didn't, crossing our little protest line would have meant instant departmental death.

"What about getting a few per diems in?" I asked.

I knew damn well that every per diem employee had been called and advised that working this Monday or Tuesday would be detrimental to their health.

"Uh, so far not one of them has been able to come in," Sal admitted. No kidding. Even the two per diems who had been prescheduled to work had mysteriously canceled out of their tours.

Everyone on the four-to-midnight shift was held over for four hours of mandatory overtime, but as of four A.M., St. Luke's/Roosevelt Hospital couldn't run any ambulances. No 911 units, no transfer units, no FastCare units. Even with all the supervisors working, they were only able to run one ambulance to try and cover the private service and do emergency transfers.

Sean Faughnan called me on Monday night.

"Hello, Paul," he said. "How are you feeling?"

"I'm fine," I answered without thinking. "How are you?"

"Oh, I'm fine. I was just calling to find out if I was going to see your happy, smiling face in the morning."

Hell. I had been thinking of Sean as a friend, not as management. I had forgotten that I was going to have to call in sick.

"Um . . . Cough, cough," I said feebly. "Actually, I'm not really feeling very well. I was about to call in sick."

"I thought you were fine."

"I was wrong."

"You'll need a doctor's note if you expect to be paid for the shift," Sean said, very much the supervisor.

"Now wait a minute," I said indignantly. "I've only called in sick one or two times in the past year." I didn't actually have any idea how many times it had been, but I knew it wasn't a lot. "How dare the department not believe me if I say I'm sick?"

"I don't know," Sean said quickly. "Dan says everyone needs a note or they don't get paid for the days."

That was okay by me. We had anticipated this, and if I dropped a day's salary, it would still be worth it in the long run.

People weren't actually left in distress without ambulances for those two days. Ambulances from the other areas covered our calls, but arrival times were slightly longer and those units tended to bring the patients to their own hospitals. The supervisors went out of their minds. They didn't know how long this would last; they had to call upstairs and explain to the administration why we weren't running any ambulances, why there were no patients being admitted to the E.R.

Everyone felt better two days later and came back to work. We had a meeting with the administrators, told them what needed to change, and it happened. They still try to run three ambulances a day, but if they can run at least one, they won't hit people up for mandatory overtime. If they have to knock one out of service for a while, they will. They hired more people and gave us all a raise.

Very recently the pay scale has been improving, but the changes are slow in coming. A lot of good people want to do this job and can't afford it. Every year when the police or fire department hold their open written tests for recruitment, a substantial number of EMS employees take the test. For each new officer class in the P.D. or F.D., EMS loses a large percent of its work force. Not because the work is better, but because the support is there. Medics still have virtually no retirement platform. Police officers retire with half pay after twenty years or three-quarter pay after thirty years. If a cop or a fireman is injured on the job and becomes disabled, he retires on three-quarter pay with medical benefits for himself and his family for life. A medic gets disability and that's it. Even if medics don't lay their lives on the line every day, there are occupational hazards. Back injuries are common from all the lifting we do, carrying patients and equipment. Medics have had stairways collapse as they carried down a patient. Some have slipped on or down the steps while carrying. There are motor vehicle accidents and freak accidents. There's currently some concern over the new radios we've been issued. There have been reports that the microwave frequencies cause medical problems, particularly related to glandular malfunction.

Gene and I were assigned a call in a very sleazy skell hole of an SRO. We found a patient sitting up in obvious respiratory distress. She looked thin, pale, weak, dehydrated, and had sunken eyes. A social worker who had been following the patient's case for the past few months was on the scene. Gene and I were both sure the woman had AIDS—after a while on the job, you get to know the look—but she denied it. She admitted to having pneumonia, intravenous drug use, and a questionable sexual history, but not AIDS. Fine. We didn't really care if she had it or not.

As we talked to her, I noticed a pronounced Adam's apple. I glanced at Gene to see if he had detected anything wrong with this picture. He obviously had. Looking more carefully at the patient, I

saw facial and chest hair. This was either a woman
with very serious physical problems or a man with
very serious mental ones. The social worker always
referred to him as "she" and so did "her" neighbors.
Gene and I shrugged at each other; it was none of our
business. We put "her" on the stretcher and carried
her into the hallway. Suddenly she had a seizure,
clamped her mouth closed and died. If she had done
this two minutes prior to our arrival we could have
pronounced her and left her there. But now she was
on our stretcher, in front of witnesses.

Gene and I were a good team. We had one of the
best save records at the hospital. Partners who work
together regularly become "married" professionally. I
loved working with either Pete or Gene because I
would know without asking, without looking, what
they were doing and what they would do. I never had
to ask for a second set of vitals; it was understood. I
never had to worry about them doing something
wrong. Most of the time we didn't need to speak. If
we had a difficult decision, we would just have to
glance at each other to know what the other was
thinking. But here, suddenly, we bordered on the
incompetent.

"Oh, shit. What do we do?" I asked.

"*Gloves!*" we both shouted. We slid them on.

"I guess we have to start CPR," Gene said. I
tossed him the AMBU bag and did compressions
while hooking up the EKG monitor. We switched
positions while I intubated her (him?) and Gene
started an IV. We looked around for help, but there
wasn't any. Everyone had disappeared, the neighbors
as well as the social worker. The police arrived a few
minutes after the fiasco started and were reluctant

helpers. One of them did compressions while the other squeezed the AMBU bag. Gene and I were then able to decide which drugs to administer.

As "good fortune" would have it, after a few moments of aggressive intervention, this person came back with pulses. She/he still wasn't breathing, but at least the heart was beating. We hightailed it out of there as fast as we could, notifying St. Luke's that we were coming in with a forty-year-old postcardiac arrest. They were all waiting for us when we arrived. Gene gave the story.

"Approximately forty-year-old male who thinks he's a female, found in obvious respiratory distress. Be advised we think he has AIDS."

"Then what the hell did you resuscitate him for?" the nurse in charge whispered to us.

"Because he died on our stretcher," I told her.

I think everyone felt bad about it. Normally bringing someone back from the dead is a good thing. But only if there's some hope for the future. Inside a private house, behind closed doors, you might report that there was dependent lividity and pronounce him dead, even if you were a little premature about the lividity. An hour later no one would be able to say it wasn't there. But in public view, with witnesses, you have to watch your ass legally.

I don't know why the calls seemed weirder than usual that winter, but it seemed all the laws of nature were being broken. So it shouldn't have surprised me when Pete and I heard a BLS unit calling for a paramedic backup to pronounce a DOA. This is not kosher. The BLS crew can either pronounce or they can call the medics to assist them in running a cardiac arrest, but they aren't supposed to need help deciding if the person is dead. The EMS dispatcher informed them of this, and after a short pause the BLS crew replied that although lividity was present and there was no pulse, they were going to start CPR because the patient was still moving! Pete and I looked at each other, eyebrows raised. It was way out of our area, but we had to see this. We flew over to the upper East Side to find out what the hell was going on.

When we arrived, the EMTs were carrying a fortyish female out of the building on a stretcher, still continuing CPR. The patient looked dead, very dead, with significant dependent lividity. I was not about to work up a dead person who met the criteria for pronouncing.

According to the EMTs, when they entered the apartment the cops were already there. The patient, a thin Hispanic woman, had no pulse and was not breathing. The family said she had been like that for forty-five minutes. The lividity was already present. The EMTs told the cops they were going to pronounce. The cops said, "Okay, but if you look closely at her feet, you'll see she's still moving."

As we put her in the back of the EMT ambulance we stopped CPR for a moment. No pulse, no breathing, a flat line on the electrocardiogram—no electrical activity whatsoever. Nevertheless, her feet were still rotating inward and outward, slowly and rhythmically. None of us had ever seen anything like this before.

We ran the code. I started an intravenous line and Pete passed an endotracheal tube. We pushed a few drugs, a milligram of epinephrine and another of atropine, and sure enough, our very dead patient came back with a pulse and blood pressure. We arrived at Harlem Hospital moments later with the patient still alive. We spent at least fifteen minutes trying to explain the dancing feet to the emergency room doctors because once her heart was started she stopped dancing.

"Now what the hell caused that to happen?" one of the EMTs asked us as we cleaned up our equipment.

"Well, it could have been some involuntary reflex action," Pete ventured. "Maybe there was enough agonal respirations to give her some brain function."

"How about an endorphin response?" the other EMT guessed.

"Maybe. What do *you* think?" the first EMT asked me. I shrugged my shoulders.

"God or Mickey Mouse," I said, quoting Dr. Zweil. "I have no idea."

Another aspect of that weird winter was the war between the city services. In a real emergency, cops, fire fighters, and medics work together as a team. Supposedly. That was one of the aspects I enjoyed most about my job. But when the NYC Fire Department and the NYC Police Department started feuding, EMS got caught right in the middle.

Traditionally, firemen handled fires, gas leaks, and some hazardous material problems. The police, and particularly their Emergency Services Unit, would handle all other emergencies, such as building collapses, automobile crashes, water rescues, and the like.

When medics need special help, we call on the ESU cops. We respect them and they don't get in our way when patient care is involved. Most of them are

EMTs, and some used to be EMS paramedics, so they understand how we operate.

Over the past ten years, however, the number of fires in New York City has been decreasing. That's wonderful, except that the resulting cuts in the fire department's budget were forcing firehouses to close and threatening the jobs of the very people who had improved the fire safety of the city. The fire department, trying to increase their call volume, decided to start responding to calls that had always been the property of the ESU. All of a sudden if someone was pinned in his car, a fire truck would come with the hydraulics, the Jaws of Life, to free him. The fire department started training personnel in scuba diving to respond to water emergencies.

The police, who are fiercely protective of their status, began complaining. There were almost violent altercations when both departments showed up on calls.

In response to Mayor Koch's traditional support of the police, the fire department launched a media blitz to gain popular support. "Shouldn't the police be stopping crime? With all the crack and violence, shouldn't that be their first priority? The fire department has always been here. Let us pick up the slack." It was an effective campaign.

While the city's administrators were hashing out guidelines, it was getting ugly on the streets. Cops were writing tickets to firemen who had always parked "illegally" next door to the firehouse. Firemen were going to civilian complaint boards and criticizing the police for parking next to fire hydrants.

The worst came when someone called 911 to report a man in a building with a gun. Someone also called 911 to report a fire in the same building. The police arrived first as usual, since they are already in cars and out on the street. They only knew of the report of the man with the gun, so the first car to arrive pulled up in front of the building and parked next to a fire hydrant. Another squad car parked next to the fire hydrant on the other side of the street.

The fire trucks showed up, but couldn't get access to a hydrant or put the ladder truck near the building because the cop cars were in the way.

Luckily both calls were false alarms, but the cops and the firemen were incensed. Words were spoken, insults exchanged. One of the firemen demanded to know the shield number of one of the police officers driving. The cops refused and got in their cars to leave. A fireman stood behind a patrol car to write down the license number. The driver didn't see him and backed into him. The fire lieutenant saw his guy get hit by the police and smashed the back window of the patrol car with an axe.

It became standard procedure to send supervisors on every call where both agencies were responding. Both groups would respond as swiftly as possible—not necessarily to help the victims, but to ensure that *they* would be in charge. EMS was left in the middle. As a medic, I don't care who comes along and cuts the car open so I can reach the patient. I just want it done quickly. At this point both agencies seemed more interested in arguing about *who* was going to do it than in actually getting it done. Personally, I do think it's easier to work with two ESU cops than with a whole group of fire fighters. It's easier to keep control of the medical emergency for which *we* are supposed to give the orders.

Eventually the jurisdictional dispute seemed to get ironed out. Both agencies respond to building collapses, but the fire department is in charge. Water rescues and auto extrications are handled by whoever is there, but the P.D. has scene command. Haz Mat (hazardous materials) is Fire's responsibility. Bomb scares and actual devices belong to the cops unless the bomb goes off, at which point Fire takes over.

The fire department recently started a pilot program, sending a fire truck with EMTs to some of the more critical medical calls. Any cardiac arrest or choking call that was dispatched to EMS in certain areas also had a fire truck respond. This doesn't work out too well. The firemen can't believe how many calls for "someone not breathing" turn out to be garbage. Even if the victim is fine, however, the rescuers can't leave the scene until the ambulance shows up. That would constitute abandonment and could result in massive lawsuits. If a fire breaks out, it's just too bad that the truck is tied up with a bullshit call. I could have told the F.D. that they'd have a problem responding to EMS calls. The ESU tried it a while back and gave it up after two weeks. The F.D. and P.D. may try to steal each other's calls, but nobody wants my job.

I wasn't even sure that I still wanted it after Pete and I responded to a call for a thirteen-year-old boy who dropped dead in gym class while jogging around the track. He was a perfectly healthy kid with no history of trouble, no drugs. He just died. We thought it was a spontaneous brain hemorrhage but we had no idea what caused it.

The constant sight of death since I started this job has changed the way I think about life and the way I lead my own. I am inured to death in most forms, but sudden accidental deaths and the deaths of young people can still throw me. I don't like to get philosophical about life and death—in a job like this, you have to take each case as it comes and try not to let the bad ones grind you down—but when I see freak deaths like this, it really makes me stop and think. Mostly it makes me want to live life now and forget about tomorrow. My attitude borders on the irresponsible because you should plan for your retirement, your future, for all the things down the road. But shit happens so fast, and tomorrow you may be dead. I say, if you want to take a year off to go to Europe or to not go to Europe, do it.

A lot of things about this job lead naturally to a bad attitude. No one could enjoy getting bled or puked on. None of us like being treated like dirt by the people we're trying to help. I don't like the bullshit politics that can get in the way of doing the job the way it should be done. I don't like being stuck in traffic when trying to respond to a good call or hearing a good call assigned to someone else because I'm tied up with a garbage call. I don't like getting wet in the rain or carrying fat people up and down several flights of stairs. Sometimes it's hard to find things not to hate about this job.

One friend of mine recognized the symptoms of burnout in herself. She was very crispy, to the point where she was potentially dangerous on the streets. She took a year off, tended bar, and was able to come back per diem with a much better attitude.

I was not burned out, but I began to worry about the future, to plan for the day when I might be. What would I do? What was I trained for? Should I even wait around to get burned out?

Burnout isn't the only reason medics quit. Up until this year the pay scale for the EMTs and medics was so poor it was almost impossible to raise a family. A single guy could pay the rent and put food on the table, but anyone planning a future knew he had to get "a real job."

Almost every medic I know sooner or later starts wondering about his or her job future. We talk about it late at night, debating pros and cons, encouraging and discouraging each other, sometimes dreaming, sometimes just blowing off steam.

Nursing has some advantages. So does being a physician's assistant. How hard is respiratory therapy? Medical school? Maybe I should just get out of medicine altogether, I thought. Some start doing less hairy street work like driving for private ambulance companies, or they switch to desk work. A lot disappear off the streets altogether.

American Medics International would have been ideal for me, but it seemed to have stalled. Our services were tailored for large groups, particularly incentive outings, but with the financial crisis in America, companies that used to send hundreds of their sales staff on incentive trips were laying them off instead.

The blame was partly ours. Steve and I are paramedics, and good ones, but we're not executives and certainly not publicists. Neither of us had a flair for marketing our services and neither of us wanted to devote the time and energy it would have required. When business didn't come our way, we let it slide.

The company is still salvageable and our services still available. If anyone is interested, call me.

Nursing is perhaps the most realistic and tempting alternative. It's only a two-year program. Recently they've been offering some pretty sweet deals with tuition reimbursement and time off from work, with pay. Once you get your license, you're set for life. The money is good and you have a lot of options: working in the E.R., critical care nursing, flight nursing.

I needed to get away at this point, to travel, to decide what I wanted to do. All my vacation time was used up by the Kenya trip, so I requested a six-month leave of absence. As with everything at Roosevelt, I put it in writing. Again the scheduling gods were smiling. No one in the department was on leave or extended disability. Staffing was adequate. I don't remember exactly what psychobabble I wrote in my request, but I got the point across that if I was refused the leave, I would quit. To my surprise, it worked. I got the leave, and I was flattered that they actually cared.

CHAPTER 8

I took a great trip to Hong Kong and China, where I visited my folks. It was summertime when I got back to New York, so I figured I'd just hang out at the beach and play volunteer fireman. But I couldn't stay off the streets. I needed the money and I wanted to keep my skills sharp; but more than that, I missed the job more than I had expected. I couldn't work part-time at Rosy because of the leave of absence, so I started picking up per diem shifts on Thirteen Willie, the medic unit for St. Clare's Health and Hospital Center. I went back to being a "paramedic prostitute," passed around from partner to partner, shift to shift.

Medics at Clare's work twelve-hour shifts as opposed to the eight-hour shifts at Roosevelt, so I only had to work two or three shifts a week to get by. Some people think the twelve-hour shifts are too long, but I don't. Once you're actually at work the extra four hours is a piece of cake, and a three-day work week is sweet.

I was impressed with some of the doctors at St. Clare's. There are fewer doctors, fewer nurses, assistants, aides; fewer everybody and everything; but some of them are exceptionally competent, caring, and qualified. Where Roosevelt might have two Attending physicians and a handful of interns in the E.R., Clare's might have just the two doctors, one medical, one surgical. In some ways this might even be better for you, unless the E.R. is very busy. On a quiet night as a Clare's patient, you don't have to worry about brand new interns or medical students working on you. You get an Attending physician to yourself.

I don't mean to criticize Roosevelt or the docs there, some of whom were also excellent. But it was clear that despite its rep as a dumping ground for skells and AIDs patients, Clare's could be a good place. They didn't have pediatric facilities, obstetric facilities, psychiatric facilities, or any of the "extras," but they had a competent E.R.

I had really been looking forward to my first shift at St. Clare's, and I wasn't disappointed. I was working seven P.M. to seven A.M. on Thirteen Willie with Seth Greene, a great guy who used to work occasional shifts with his wife Patty before she gave up medicking to join the Yonkers police force.

As soon as I walked into the Clare's E.R. I could feel that the atmosphere was more relaxed than I was used to. There was a sign above the crew room door with the department slogan, "Do the strange thing," along with the phrases "home of 13W & 13C" and "home of Midtown Madness—Hell's Kitchen, NYC." The medics coming off duty were pretty scruffy-looking. One of the guys had long hair in a ponytail. Another was wearing a pin that said, "You've obviously mistaken me for someone who gives a shit." Rosy and Clare's are close enough that we overlapped on a lot of calls, so I had known most of the medics at Clare's for years. These guys greeted me warmly and seemed pleased that I was joining their department. I felt right at home.

Clare's was famous for its constant money problems. They never had great equipment, the vehicles were serviceable at best, and they could never pay as much as other hospitals. But everyone from Clare's I had met over the years seemed to enjoy it there, and I was beginning to understand why. The atmosphere and people made a wonderful place to work.

For most of the people who worked at Clare's, the more relaxed atmosphere made up for the lower salary. But it began to get ridiculous when Clare's was giving $12 or $12.50 an hour and other places were paying $15 or $16. That difference really added up. Clare's medics were being paid thousands less a year to do the exact same job, or maybe an even more difficult job because the area was so bad. Some good people felt they had to leave even though they didn't want to. Some of them have come back since Clare's raised the pay scale. It's still a little less than I get at Roosevelt, but it's an acceptable difference.

I had a busy first night with Seth, full of good, life-threatening calls. He showed me "the Batcave," a dark, quiet spot off the Central Park South loop where Clare's medics pull in on a slow night. It has since become a very popular spot, and you sometimes have to fight with Lenox Hill and New York Hospital units to get it. We didn't have a chance to "Batcave" that night.

"We're really cooking," I said as Seth drove up Tenth Avenue.

"Yeah, we're on fire!" he agreed.

"Yeah," I said. "We're really busy."

"No!" he shouted. "Look at the engine! *We're on fire!!*"

Shit. Smoke and flames were coming from under the hood. Seth slammed on the brakes, shut off the engine, and we dove out of the vehicle. The flames soon died down. I stood there on the street thinking, Isn't this why I left Empire State?

We were right around the corner from St. Clare's so we walked over to the hospital and called the boss, waking him up. Marc Hartog, the department director and one of the reasons why Clare's is a great place to work, asked if we could drive the bus back to Clare's instead of waiting hours for a tow truck. Seth and I conferred on the safety and wisdom of doing this. No one at Roosevelt would ever have attempted something as stupid as getting back into that ambulance and trying to start it up. But at St. Clare's, as I was learning, we played by a different set of rules. We knew that Marc wouldn't really want us to jeopardize our lives, but what the hell, we were game.

We got back in, both of us armed with a fire extinguisher. We kept the windows down, the doors slightly ajar in case we needed a quick exit, the hood propped up with a piece of wood. There was a puff of smoke when Seth started it up, but no flames. With the lights flashing and the siren blaring, we drove the fifty feet to Fifty-second Street and down the block to the hospital. There, once we felt the risk of fire and/or explosion was small, we switched the equipment into another bus and continued with the shift. The night was relatively uneventful from then on.

The ambulances at Clare's broke down a lot. Private ambulance companies are usually the worst about maintenance. They slack off because they're more concerned about profits. St. Clare's was always concerned about the state of the buses; they just didn't have the money to get things fixed promptly. They sometimes had to send vehicles all over the tri-state area to find a place they didn't already owe money to. But the Clare's people were more dedicated and they wanted to keep the ambulances in service, even if they had slight problems. At Clare's, if they had air-conditioning in the back for the patient but not in front, it was good enough. A Roosevelt crew would never work under those conditions. At Roosevelt, if the low or the high beams didn't work, they would pull the ambulance out of service, but at Clare's they figured that if they had one or the other they were doing fine. The built-in clock in the back of Thirteen Willie, the Clare's medic unit, was permanently stuck at ten o'clock, although it continued to tick.

Breaking down on the way to a call is as bad as being stuck in traffic. Sometimes you get there, treat the patient, put him in the back, and then the ambulance won't start. You have to call for another unit to come get him. But face it, if you drive anything twenty-four hours a day in New York City, you're going to have problems. And with all the drains on the power from the lights, sirens, radios, suction units, etc., the ambulances blow a lot of fuses.

St. Clare's recently acquired two new diesel buses, so they may not have as many mechanical problems for a while. The buses have a sign on the gas tank reminding the gas station attendant to fill them with diesel. Of course every now and then some idiot fills them with regular instead, which doesn't help.

Being a per diem, you don't have the stability of a full-timer; you can't fall into a regular rhythm. When I was first taken on as a per diem at Rosy, I was desperate to get a full-time slot so the work would be guaranteed and I'd get the health benefits that went with it. After working full-time for years now, I could appreciate the freedom of being a per diem again. I could pick and choose my shifts, working only when I wanted to. I usually accepted whatever shift they offered me, but it was wonderful to have the option of saying, "No thanks, I can't make it Saturday night, or at all this weekend. But thanks for calling." I tried to work Tuesdays, Wednesdays, or Thursdays and take a very long weekend at the beach.

I almost never turned down a shift with Lucy Winton or Maggie Staiger. "The Frisky Sluts," as they named themselves, were among the first female paramedic teams in the city. They've been working at Clare's for more than ten years, the last six as regular partners on Thirteen Willie.

Maggie is barely over five feet, but she is a definite presence, a funny, bright woman who considers herself a poet and a musician as well as a medic. She used to change her hair color every few months. Not just regular colors, but stripes, polka dots, woodchuck hair, really weird stuff. She has somewhat mellowed and has stayed with more traditional tones for a couple of years now.

"Juicy" Lucy—which, believe it or not, is not a derogatory term: no one speaks of either of the Friskies without respect, at least not around me—is lovely, tall and thin, with long brown hair. She is a self-proclaimed "fashion designer, hairdresser, and bogus astrologer" who will belch like a sailor and then say in the sweetest voice, "My, that wasn't attractive, was it?" She is studying at the Fashion Institute of Technology, but I hate to think of her leaving Clare's when she graduates.

There aren't many women medics, although there's no reason why there shouldn't be. The job requires some physical strength to carry patients down stairs and to lift them into the ambulance, but two average women working together shouldn't have a problem doing that. The Friskies are not particularly big women and they manage to do the job very well. They have no credibility problem with the police or fire departments: when they walk into a crazy scene with multiple casualties, they have no trouble taking charge and ordering the cops and fire fighters around.

I tend to think of each of them as one of the guys. Seeing Lucy do her nails in the crew room before a tour, watching them come off a shift loaded down with shopping bags from a twenty-four-hour Love Store, or hearing them complain that an overweight male Clare's medic has bigger tits than they do, doesn't change that impression. When I told them recently that I was writing a book, they asked me to tell the world that they have really big tits which are a problem on the job and that they dress on and off the job like models in the French edition of *Elle*. I didn't know that models in *Elle* wore jean jackets and roller-skated into work.

I'd rather work with either Maggie or Lucy than with three quarters of the male medics out there. They do the job the way it should be done and they're more fun to hang out with between calls. I don't do much hooker scoping when I work with them, but they're good sports.

Perhaps the best thing about being a per diem again was not having to worry about department politics or administration. It was very simple. They'd call me to work a shift. I'd show up. I'd do the best job I could. I'd walk out at the end of the day. That's it. No bickering, no politics—just work.

But there were things I had to to get used to, such as Thirteen Willie's primary area of response. Uptown at Roosevelt we had our share of projects and skell hotels; but we also had the fashionable upper West Side of Manhattan with the resident rich people and yuppies. The 13 region, Clare's area, covers midtown Manhattan between Thirty-fourth and Fifty-seventh streets. In Willie world, we not only had the skell hotels, we also had the Port Authority, Penn Station, Times Square, Grand Central Station, Hell's Kitchen, and some of the gamiest shelters in the city. A significantly different clientele.

As I mentioned earlier, a lot of medics think of St. Clare's as a dumping ground for indigent patients. Given a choice between Roosevelt and Clare's for a smelly, homeless, bug-infested, noncritical patient, Rosy crews usually brought the patient to St. Clare's.

Working now for Clare's, I was tempted to play the same game and drop these folks off at Roosevelt, but surprisingly enough, the administrators at Clare's actually wanted us to bring as many people as possible to the their E.R., even the skelly people. So we did.

Working Clare's also provided me with a welcome increase in comic relief thanks to the numerous calls in the Times Square area in peep shows, live sex shows, and porn theaters. Places that advertise deals like "$3.99 for 45 straight movies over a three-day period. Porno yourself into oblivion!" These calls were usually for intoxes or people who had seizures. Very rarely was it anything serious; just sad and sordid.

If a call came in at a live sex show, ambulances would volunteer for the call to break up a boring day. If it came in as something like "twenty-seven-year-old nude female, impaled on a rock," you would hear a burst of radio traffic: "Thirteen David, we'll back Willie," "Thirteen Charlie, *we'll* back Willie," "Thirteen Henry, we're down the block, we'll respond."

It would get funny when there were a couple of cops, two medics, maybe two EMTs as well, all wandering up and down the dark aisles (the floors in these places were always slippery and sticky—I'd like to think it was from people spilling their soda), trying to find the patient and commenting on the show:

"Hey, is that girl up there double-jointed?"

"I don't know but I think it's disgusting."

"Really, you think that's disgusting?"

"I don't know. But don't they have sheep laws in this state?" etc.

I had been a medic for five years already, so

nothing much disgusted me anymore. I think I'm immune to disgusting. But I couldn't help taking an occasional glance at the show while interviewing the patient.

"Do you take any medicine? . . . Oh, look at that! . . . Phenobarb, okay. Are you allergic to any medication? . . . Oh, wow! . . . Okay, you're not allergic, do you have any other medical problems? . . . How does she *do* that? . . . Do you want to go to the hospital? . . . You want to stay and watch *this*? . . . Come on, let's get the hell out of here. You really should see a doctor. So should she, for that matter."

There was the occasional middle-aged heart attack in these places, but most of the victims would wander out of the theater before getting up the nerve to call 911. It wouldn't go over well with their wives for them to say, "Well, honey, I split early from work, went into Hell's Show World and had a heart attack watching the babe on the screen." Much better to say, "I was walking down the block when all of a sudden I had this terrible pain in my chest."

As much as I liked Clare's, I have to admit that I also had my worst shift ever there. It wasn't even a holiday, just an ordinary summer day I worked with Gary Pollino, the guy I picnicked with during the confirmed bomb call. He had since left Rosy to work at Clare's full-time.

It was a weekend and I had hoped to have a nice, quiet day, but it was too damn hot. I'd always hated New York City in hot weather, and being stuck in an ambulance just made it that much worse. The streets, the ambulances, tempers . . . everything was hot. Everything normally unpleasant about this city seemed magnified: traffic, crowds, gridlock, noise, the heat, the smells. Especially the smells.

Before we even had a cup of coffee, we were hit with a call for a "female unconscious, said she's unable to get up." You know a call is going to be a pain in the ass when the description doesn't even make sense. If she's unconscious, how does she say anything? And if she's truly unconscious, of course she can't get up! Some of the calls I would get were so absurd that I had to wonder if the Call-Receiving Officer had gone out of his mind, if he even listened to what the caller was saying. I've gotten calls like, "Cardiac arrest at Eighty-sixth and Lexington, patient states he's going into cardiac arrest." Sorry, but that is *not* a cardiac arrest. Heart attack, maybe, but I doubt it.

In this case we found the patient—female, white, about sixty—lying naked on a bed without sheets or blankets, obviously incontinent. Not the way I like to start my day. She was fully conscious and didn't appear to be in any distress. The closer we got to her, the more pungent she became.

"What's the problem here?" Gary asked her.

"Nothing," she said. "I just can't get up." She had no trouble breathing, wasn't in pain; her vital signs and neurologic exams were fine. "I can move around on the bed but I just don't have the energy to get up."

Gary and I tried to decide what to do. We could have goofed around and tried to get her up on her feet by arguing, cajoling, whining or whatever, but was it worth it? I nodded at him and he understood: we'd just put her in the chair, carry her to the ambulance, dump her at the hospital and be rid of her. The morning was young and we could probably still enjoy the day. After a few minutes of pushing naked, flabby flesh around, we got her into the stair chair, out the door, down the stairs, and onto the street.

As we opened the back door of the ambulance to get the stretcher out, the patient peed and defecated in our chair, vomited all over herself and then died. We couldn't work on her in the chair, so we tossed her onto the stretcher and lifted her into the ambulance.

Gary called for a backup on the portable radio and we were greeted with the EMS theme song: "Sorry, Thirteen Willie, nobody available to back you up." There were no police on the scene and no bystanders to recruit into helping us.

I was suctioning the lady's airway and attempting to artificially ventilate her with an AMBU bag, but with every squeeze of the bag, more vomitus sprayed out. Gary was doing CPR compressions and trying to get the EKG monitor on her. She was drenched in sweat, vomit, and urine, so the EKG electrodes wouldn't stick to her. I wasn't able to intubate her because more garbage would come out of her throat with every chest compression. A foot cop wandered by a few minutes later and asked if he could do anything to help. With the cop doing compressions and me ventilating, Gary drove us to St. Clare's. The patient didn't make it.

By the time we finished with the paperwork and cleaning up the ambulance, it was close to ten A.M. We decided to seek sanctuary on the end of the pier at Forty-fifth Street, a calm spot.

After a short rest there spent watching people playing Frisbee, a lady walking a little dog, and a few sunbathers, I began to feel more human. The sun was out and hot. Gary was catching a few minutes of shut-eye. I read the papers.

Then EMS called us.

"Thirteen Willie, take it over to 724 Madison, fifth floor, for a male, fifty-nine years old, chest pains. Your ID is 0904, time now 11:16, I'm Disp. 801."

Gary woke at the sound of our call sign. I wrote the call information down. We shut the doors of the ambulance and Gary started it up. We rolled only a foot or two before we heard a high-pitched squeak, the sort of sound you hear when the tire rubs up against the curb. We weren't near a curb and couldn't imagine what it was. So Gary put the bus in reverse, rotated the wheels the other way to avoid whatever we were up against and ran over the little dog for the second time.

All hell broke loose. The dog's owner ran over, hysterical beyond any reaction I'd ever seen before.

"*Aaahhh!!!* What have you done? Are you crazy? Help! Help! Murderers!"

I felt terrible and so did Gary. But what could we do? The lady had obviously let the dog off the leash and he had sought refuge from the sun under our front wheel. We hadn't known he was there and we had certainly made enough noise slamming the doors and starting the engine to warn him. Unfortunately the lady did not see our side of the story. We apologized profusely, begged forgiveness and tried to explain, but there was nothing we could do and we had a fifty-nine-year-old male, possibly having a heart attack, waiting for us on the other side of town.

I felt worse than I had during our previous call as we drove away and left this poor woman crying on the end of the pier.

The Madison Avenue fellow was only having angina pains. We treated him and transported him to the hospital. For the rest of the day we had an assortment of injuries and illnesses. We barely spoke about the dead lady or the dog.

We were parked in front of the hospital with only about twenty minutes to go on our shift when a very big, tall, mean-looking man knocked on my window. I lowered it and he growled, "Are you the guys that killed my dog?"

I almost wet my pants. The temptation was overwhelming to say no, but I wanted to be an adult about it. I apologized to Paul Bunyon and tried to remain calm.

"Well, why didn't you stop?" he asked. I must have looked confused then. I explained that we had stopped, gotten out of the ambulance and talked with the hysterical lady. The man took a deep breath and a step backward and then apologized to us.

"I'm sorry, guys. I didn't get the full story." He paused before explaining. "My wife is an alcoholic. But she'd been sober for four years. She joined AA. When she dried out, we bought this dog. It was a symbol. And when I came home today she was crying in bed with a bottle of vodka half empty and all she would say is that the paramedics from St. Clare's killed our dog and drove off." I assured him that this was not the case—well, not exactly. He apologized. We apologized. He went back into the hospital and withdrew the complaint he had already lodged with the administrator on duty.

To recap: a fat, ugly, naked lady peed, shat, vomited and died; we handled lots of garbage calls; we killed a dog; a nice lady blew four years of staying clean because we killed her symbol of sobriety. It was the kind of day that made me wonder if I'd go back in the next day; if I should go into some other kind of work; if I should ever get out of bed. But I did, I didn't, and I do, in that order.

CHAPTER 9

When my leave of absence from Roosevelt expired, I
had to go back there. The summer months were over
so I was ready for steady, full-time work. If a slot had
opened up at Clare's I would have been tempted to
stay, but no such luck. Clare's only had eight full-time
medics, and they all seemed happy there. I needed
the security and benefits of the full-time position, so I
went back to Rosy. I would still take per diem shifts at
Clare's when I could. As long as I fulfilled my duties
at Rosy, they wouldn't care what other jobs I had on
my own time. A lot of full-time medics are on the per
diem lists at other hospitals.

I'd have to start paying more attention to my
appearance again. I had gotten lazy at Clare's, showing up with a five-to-ten-day shadow. (I don't like to
shave much.) Both hospitals require their medics to
wear dark shoes (I wear black sneakers), dark work

pants, belts, and a white shirt with identifying patches. But Clare's, typically, was much more laid-back about it. Roosevelt provided us with uniforms and laundry service, so they expected us to look pretty good. The most extravagant-looking medic at Rosy—the department's one full-time woman medic, who wears multiple earrings, layers of black eye makeup, and has smurf heads and other weird stuff hanging from her belt—would look commonplace at Clare's.

I would have been happy to go back to my previous time slot with Pete and Gene, but that slot had been taken over by that same woman medic. There was only one shift open for me: the one left by Mike Gebhardt, who had recently been promoted to supervisor. Another medic I liked to work with, now out of circulation. I congratulated him half-heartedly on his promotion. If it was what he wanted, I was happy for him, but I was sorry for myself and the other street medics who wouldn't get to work with him anymore. The loss wasn't just personal. With all this turnover, the department was losing good street medics. New guys were being hired, of course, but they weren't nearly as competent or enthusiastic about the job as the veterans who were going.

Mike Gebhardt and Mike Roth had been partners. When Gebhardt became management, Roth was left alone on steady days. I thought of the shifts I had worked with Mike Roth, the teasing, the dumb jokes. . . . Could I stand it full-time? Not likely. Did I have a choice? Not really.

Working with Mike was always an adventure. I never knew what he would do, I just knew that I would be able to laugh about it, whether with him, at him, or for him. We could laugh about screwing up on the job when it didn't leave somebody dead. Actually, we sometimes laughed about it even when it did leave somebody dead, but I shouldn't admit that. Mike laughs all the time. Even when he's telling tales of how some of his ex-wives try to make his life miserable, he laughs it off. His humor is childish, if not moronic. I've seen him sit next to the bathroom on an airplane and tell people that it's out of order.

For a big guy he gets around pretty well. He doesn't do anything fast, but he always treats patients with compassion and never fails to do the right thing. Of course, you'd never know it to see his belt explode, as it does once or twice a year, sending his radio and gear shooting down the street and his pants hurtling to the ground. It's not a pretty sight.

One of Mike's favorite pastimes is instigating arguments. If you put him in a room with Mother Theresa and Mahatma Gandhi, he'd walk out five minutes later, chuckling and leaving them at each other's throats.

For no particular reason, just the lack of anything better to do, Mike decided to cause trouble between the St. Luke's obstetrical delivery department and the Roosevelt obstetrical delivery department, who usually worked well together. Both hospitals were more than competent at delivering babies, but St. Luke's also had a wonderful neonatal intensive care unit. If a baby was born at Roosevelt with severe medical problems, say he was premature or had heart disease, our department would transport the kid, in an incubator with a doctor standing by, to Luke's. If a woman came into Roosevelt preparing to deliver and they suspected that there would be problems—if she was a crack mother, for instance—we would transport the mother to Luke's before she delivered.

When we went to the Roosevelt site that day to pick up an expectant mother to transport, Mike went up to the nursing staff and said, "Boy, St. Luke's is really mad at you guys. They say you don't know how to deliver babies down here. For every little problem, you just hit the panic button and send the mother away. They say you people don't earn your money and really shouldn't be in business." This, naturally, completely enraged the Roosevelt staff.

When we arrived with the patient at Luke's, Mike shuffled over to the nurses there and said, "Boy, is the Roosevelt staff laughing at you guys! They're happy because they just got rid of their last pregnant woman and don't have to do any work. They say that anytime anything comes up that requires real work, hey, fuck St. Luke's, we'll just send the mother there. Let them deal with it." So the St. Luke's nurses became equally irate.

The two staffs began sending each other obscene messages and faxing images of someone giving the finger. Mike loved it, and I have to admit that it was pretty funny. The feud went on for months.

The Pre-Hospital Care Department took over a nurses' room to use as a dispatcher office. It was just a hole in the wall and didn't even have a window. You wouldn't think it was worth fighting over, but the nurses were pissed off and supposedly put a curse on the room. It seemed pretty funny until people started being hospitalized. One of the supervisors started developing chest pain every few days.

If they had known about some of the less heroic

stunts Mike and I pulled, *all* the supervisors would
have had chest pain. Mike and I were once assigned
to a cardiac arrest in a very chic East Side apartment.
We were met by an elegant lady of sixty who was
struggling to keep her self-control. "It's my sister,"
she said. "I came home and found her like this."
Dead, that is. The sister had either had a heart attack
or a stroke, had urinated and defecated on herself,
fallen off the bed and died. There was no chance of
resuscitation.

Mike and I led the lady into the living room to get
some information from her and provide some level of
psychological support. The police arrived and, because of the death, called their sergeant. The living
sister, Ann, told us that the dead sister, Jane, was
sixty-three. We were about to leave when Ann asked
us, "Do you think I should tell my mother what has
happened to Jane?"

"Where is your mother?" I asked.

"In one of the other bedrooms," she replied.
"She's very hard of hearing and bedridden. She's
ninety-four."

I said she would have to tell her mother. The old
lady would probably notice that something was wrong
if she didn't see Jane for a few days, and it could be
quite a shock if she saw the funeral or morgue people
come for the body.

Ann feared that this horrible surprise would kill
her mother. We went with her to break the news, just
in case the old lady did have such a reaction. The old
lady cried and tried to get out of bed.

"My baby. I must see Jane, my baby," she yelled.
But Jane was not in a pleasant way to be seen. Mike
took over and was wonderful. He held her and talked

to her, and managed to calm her down. It was a side of Mike I had rarely seen before, nothing like his usual drooling, wisecracking, lecherous, infuriating self.

When the police sergeant arrived, we left the mother's room. Soon one of the cops called to us that the mother was trying to get out of bed again. Mike rushed back, caught her and put her back to bed. He was sympathetic but firm, saying, "It isn't going to help anything. You should remember her as she was. You just have to be strong now." To emphasize the point, he continued, "You have to be strong. Face facts. Ann is dead and you have to accept that. Ann is dead!"

The mother let out a horrible wail and fell back onto her pillow, screaming, "Ann's dead too?!" Yes, Mike had announced that the wrong daughter had died. I thought the mother was going to die right then. Trying to go above and beyond the call of duty, to show sympathy and caring, Mike had really screwed up. He realized his mistake and started to babble.

"No! It's just Jane. Just one daughter. Just one's dead. It's okay." I fetched the living daughter from the living room to reassure her mother. We were lucky. The mother didn't drop dead, and Ann forgave us.

Mike and I were face-to-face with a particularly unlovely skell lying in the street. It was mid-fall, still pre–skellcicle season, so he wasn't in any danger of freezing to death, but he was sick. He had had a seizure, had urinated on himself, and had bugs. Not a pretty sight or odor. The patient was awake when we arrived and wanted to go to the hospital.

The nearest one was an "upscale" East Side hospital that likes to call itself the finest medical facility in the city. It isn't, of course. They don't like it when we bring any patients there, but when we bring someone with bugs, they go bonkers.

As of a couple of years ago, this hospital had the only Manhattan hospital E.R. without a shower room. They had a good burn center, a helicopter, high-risk neonatal transport vehicles, and all sorts of other high-tech toys, but no washroom. When a homeless person or someone with bugs (usually lice) comes into an E.R., he gets a shower. At this place, he had to be washed by hand.

I had already gotten into a huge fight with a nurse there who didn't want to accept a patient because he had bugs. That wasn't my problem. He was sick. He needed an emergency room and this was the closest facility. End of argument.

"*Our* paramedics would never have brought him here," she had said. I glanced down at my St. Luke's/Roosevelt ID card and looked back at her.

"Well, I'm not one of *your* paramedics," I told her, and I was glad it was true.

So in this case Mike and I were more than happy to take our skell there. Before we put him on our stretcher, we opened up two sheets and crisscrossed them. We then put our patient in the middle and wrapped the sheets around him, sort of mummifying him. We didn't want the little creepy-crawlies to get off him and into our nice, clean ambulance.

We kept the patient mummified when we moved him onto the E.R. stretcher. A nurse, about five feet five with shoulder-length sandy-blond hair, came over to us for the report. She would have been pretty if she ever smiled. When I reached the part about the bugs, I thought she was going to go out of her mind.

"Do you want to be here?" she asked the patient. He looked around and mumbled to himself. I handed the nurse my ambulance call report and asked her to sign it. The patient is legally our responsibility until a nurse signs our paperwork.

"He doesn't want to be here," she said haughtily, refusing to sign. She was trying to get him up and have him walk out.

"I think he should be evaluated first," I said. She didn't seem to care what I thought, and continued to refuse to sign. It was at this point that I realized the nurse was a dead ringer for a young Eva Braun. I got angry. I walked out of the hospital and called the dispatcher on the EMS radio.

"Fourteen Young to Manhattan Dispatcher, with a problem."

"Fourteen Young, what's your problem?"

I responded slowly and clearly over the taped radio for the entire borough to hear, "I'm delayed at [this East Side Hospital]'s emergency room because the nurse refuses to sign my ACR for a patient with bugs who needs emergency treatment. I will be here for a while, while I call the New York State Department of Health and report the hospital for violating state law." A few seconds of dead air followed.

"Ten-four, Young," the dispatcher said, sounding confused. "I'll make a note of it."

A moment later I heard a siren. A medic unit from that hospital came screeching around the corner. They pulled up to me.

"Which nurse?" one of the medics gasped, out of breath. I took him inside. There were two other staff people trying to get the patient to stand up now. We went up to the original nurse. The medic, holding my ACR book, demanded that she sign. She did.

I used to carry around a newspaper article about a male nurse in Nassau County who was arrested, tried, and convicted for refusing to accept a patient who had arrived by ambulance. The nurse said it wasn't an emergency. New York State law is very clear on the question: if he shows up, the staff must see him. Just like if someone calls 911 and says he broke a fingernail, an ambulance must respond. We all have our crosses to bear.

Mike was off, so I was working with a new per diem. We were parked between calls when a man in a suit, eating a hot dog, walked over to the bus and stuck his head in my window.

"Hey," he said abruptly in a New York accent, "why is the word 'ambulance' written backward on the front of the ambulance?" Maybe if he had said "excuse me," or made any attempt to be polite, I'd have given him a straight answer. But maybe not. This had to be the fiftieth time I'd heard the question, and I had been working with Mike for a few months. He'd had his effect on me.

"Huh?" I said with a confused look. "What?" I climbed out of the ambulance, walked around to the front and exclaimed, "Oh my God! I can't believe it! Those idiots! They screwed up. I can't believe they actually printed it backward! Thank you, sir, for pointing this out to me. I'll make sure they fix it right away."

The man walked away, looking proud of himself.

My partner just shook his head and went back to his newspaper.

The dispatcher broke in with a report of an explosion on Columbus Avenue. I drove over there to find that every manhole along the length of two city blocks had exploded. This actually happens more often than you might expect. Natural gas explodes underground and sends the manhole covers, which weigh hundreds of pounds, shooting up into the air. It's the closest thing New Yorkers have to volcanoes. They just go *boom* without any warning. It is usually reported as an "unknown condition" or as an explosion in the street. Amazingly, there aren't usually many injuries from this—just a lot of cuts from broken glass—but it scares the shit out of people.

This time one patient was cut with flying glass when a manhole cover tore into a car. Another lady was injured inside her second-story apartment when a manhole cover flew up and crashed into a street lamp, shooting pieces of metal and glass hurtling through her window.

I was treating a man who had bits of asphalt and concrete in his eyes and multiple facial lacerations. As I irrigated his eyes, my patient asked nervously, "Am I going to be all right?"

"Yeah, relax. You're going to be fine. We'll take care of you," I said.

Suddenly I heard a voice over my shoulder saying, "Don't worry, son. You'll be fine. You've got the best paramedic in the city taking care of you." I looked around, wondering who the hell would say something like that. I didn't recognize him at first because of the police uniform. It was Father Bill, the Luke's E.R. nurse who had had such a terrible orientation shift with me several years before. I didn't take his comment too seriously—it was blatant flattery—but considering that he had only ever seen me handle garbage and dying causes, it was nice of him to say it.

"So you're a cop now?" I asked when I finished treating the patient. A minister-nurse-policeman?

"Police chaplain," he explained. "I wasn't assigned to this call, but I heard it come over the radio and I thought it sounded fun." It wasn't Kilauea, but it was close enough. I didn't have time to ask him why he had left nursing. I could think of enough possible reasons.

I don't want to give the wrong impression about my abilities. I think I'm a pretty good paramedic and most of the people out there are competent. There are some excellent medics riding around the streets, and I've been lucky enough to work with some of them. I don't want to sound incredibly egotistical and only tell stories about saving lives, climbing under a subway to start IVs, or intubating someone in a stairwell without lights or electricity. I have to admit that there are times that we don't perform as well as we could, when it would almost have been better if we hadn't shown up at all.

I may have been the first medic to perform a radical mandible-ectomy in the field, and an inadvertent one at that. Mike and I were backing up a BLS crew assigned to a confirmed Jumper Down. A forty-year-old Hispanic male had jumped from the fourth-floor fire escape in an apparent suicide attempt. He wasn't breathing. The EMTs put him on a longboard and made some attempts at a hasty spinal cord immobilization. As Mike and I arrived on the scene, the patient had just lost his pulse. We started CPR.

The problem was ventilation. Attempting to push air into this guy was almost impossible. He had experienced a facial implosion when he hit the pavement. All the bones in his face were smashed and all his teeth were loose and coming out. His airway was obstructed by blood, vomit, teeth, and God knows what else. I tried to remove the large chunks from the mouth with my (gloved) fingers while Mike used the Magill forceps to pick out some of the smaller pieces. To use the AMBU bag there must be a good seal around the patient's face, otherwise the air leaks out around the sides and doesn't get into the lungs. But this guy didn't have a face to speak of anymore. I decided to try to lift the patient's jaw out of the way so Mike could intubate him.

The jaw came out, right in my hand. I'll never forget the sound of it popping out of his face, like the sucking sound you make when you pull your foot out of a six-inch-deep mud puddle. The jaw had apparently become disconnected in the fall and had been floating in the face. I freaked out, cursing vividly, and dropped the bone on the floor of the ambulance. Mike laughed loudly. The EMTs looked stunned.

"Is this guy going to be all right?" a cop asked. I do worry about the police sometimes.

We headed off to St. Luke's, lights and sirens, but we knew this guy wasn't going to make it. Later, after he had been pronounced, the cop came out with a plastic baggie, saying, "The doctors want whatever pieces of him are still in the back of the bus." Mike made a point of adding "successful intubation following jaw removal" to the call report.

I told Maggie that story when I worked a shift with her for St. Clare's not long after. She laughed, but then she surprised me by saying, "You know, you're one of the few people I'm scared to work with."

I must have looked hurt because she hurried to assure me that it was nothing personal.

"It's just that whenever I work with you, body parts seem to pop off or spill out of patients." I couldn't deny it.

"Yeah, well, shit happens," I said. It's a popular EMS expression because shit does happen, and too often.

That night, she and I treated a man who was gut-shot in the belly on the corner of Fifty-fifth Street and Sixth Avenue at four in the morning. The victim was wearing a fancy white suit and lots of gold chains and jewelry. According to the police, he had been shot by a man who fled in a lime-colored Cadillac.

"Definitely a pimp-related incident, wouldn't you say?" I asked Maggie as we cleaned the back of the bus.

"Gotta be," she agreed. To hell with due process. On the streets it's guilt by color scheme.

"We need a medic backup for an elderly male in Acute Pulmonary Edema," a BLS unit told the EMS dispatcher.

"Feel like taking a ride?" I asked Mike. The call was slightly out of our area, but it had been a slow morning. We decided to go for it.

We pulled up behind the EMT ambulance, got out of the bus and pulled our ALS equipment out of the back. We figured that the BLS crew probably had their stretcher, so we didn't need to bring ours. We walked into the building carrying the drug box, EKG monitor/defibrillator, and oxygen.

Up to that point everything had been fine. We should have just stopped and gone for lunch because from there on, nothing else worked.

The building was a classic upper West Side place with different elevators all going to different parts of the apartment. We took the wrong one; it left us at the back door of the apartment. We knocked loud and one of the EMTs came over and opened the door. It was at the end of a long, narrow, dark hallway lined with books piled high against the walls.

I had to turn sideways, hold my breath, and inch down the hall to squeeze through without knocking things off the walls. I wasn't too successful. Poor Mikey, twice my size even without all the equipment he was carrying, had even more trouble. With every step he took, something fell off the walls. We couldn't help giggling, but our laughter dried up when one of us hooked the oxygen bag on the TV stand and knocked the whole thing over, sending the television crashing to the ground. Still, when Mike and I exchanged "Oh shit, we're in trouble now" looks, we burst out laughing again.

Our patient was not laughing, or doing much of anything except trying to breathe. He was in left-sided heart failure. The part of his heart that was responsible for taking blood from the lungs and circulating it throughout the body was failing. Fluid was building up in his lungs and he was starting to drown in his own fluids. Acute pulmonary edema is a serious condition, but we're usually able to treat it effectively with aggressive therapy. Not this time.

I couldn't start an IV. The patient's chest was so

wet and cool, the EKG leads kept slipping off. We wiped part of his chest dry, and the electrode stuck for a minute and then fell off again. I love to tell funny stories about Mike, but he really is a very good medic with extremely good skills. Even he couldn't get an IV going on this guy. We put an oxygen mask on the patient's face, but the man kept pulling it off.

Just then an elderly lady wearing a nightgown came hobbling into the room on her walker.

"Is he going to be all right?" she asked.

"We're doing everything we can," one of the EMTs said. Which means "No."

"Okay," she said calmly. She turned and left the room. I don't know why, but Mike and I thought that was very funny. Her husband, or maybe it was her brother, was dying. Four medical people were frantically working on him in the middle of her living room, and she wandered in, said a casual "Okay," and split. She didn't even notice the busted TV set.

We had to get that poor guy out of there. He was getting worse and we weren't helping. We had to get him to the hospital. The BLS crew didn't have their stretcher but they did have a stair chair. We tried to open it and it broke. Now we couldn't even get him out of the apartment. One of the EMTs ran down and got their stretcher as we started to carry him out of there by his arms and legs.

When we got into the back of the BLS crew's ambulance, we tried to put an external jugular IV in place. It hurts the patient to put an IV in the large vein right on the outside of the neck so we don't usually put them in patients who have a mental status, but this guy was going down the tubes and desperately needed the IV medication. We blew that line, too.

It was clear that we were not going to get IV access. We couldn't administer any meds. We had made a pincushion out of this poor guy and accomplished nothing. I probably should have just said the hell with it, but there was one last thing we could try. Our patient had almost stopped breathing, so we were ventilating him with the AMBU bag. If I could intubate him, we might force enough air into his lungs and give him a chance.

I moved to his head and took over the bagging. Mike set me up for the tube and got into position to assist. I slid the laryngoscope into the guy's mouth. *Crunch*. He bit down and promptly smashed what was left of his teeth on the metal blade. So much for that idea.

We blew into St. Luke's at warp speed. The patient still had a pulse, but we weren't sure for how much longer. I had no idea what his EKG rhythm was; I had given up trying to get the leads to stick. We were ventilating him and desperately trying to get the attention of someone to give us a hand. Finally, a doctor I never liked very much came wandering over to us and said, "You know we're supposed to be on diversion."

Mike likes to tell people that I punched the doc in the nose and threw him out of the E.R. It's not true. I wanted to, but I didn't.

After the call, when I was finishing up the paperwork and Mike was cleaning up the EKG machine, both of the EMTs came over to us.

"We want to talk with you for a moment," they said seriously.

Mike and I looked at each other. This was not going to be pretty. We stepped out of the E.R. for a little privacy. I hate to be yelled at in public.

"We really want to thank you for backing us up," one of them said, holding out his hand for me to shake.

"That was a bad one. We're glad you showed up," his partner said, shaking Mike's hand.

It took us a minute to realize that they were serious.

"You guys are nuts," Mike said. "If I was you, I would have thrown us the hell out of there."

I had to agree. "I would have called the dispatcher and said 'Send us two more medics. These guys aren't working out.'" Mike and I were in near hysterics.

"We arrived, knocked all their books off the walls, broke the TV, couldn't get the oxygen to stay on his face, couldn't start an IV, couldn't give him any medication, delayed on the scene, broke your stair chair, blew a neck vein, busted his teeth, couldn't intubate him, barely got him to the hospital alive, and you're *thanking* us for backing you up?"

They just stood there, dumbfounded. Nice guys, but new, very new.

Mike and I had a long dry spell of nothing but garbage calls, hours to sit in the ambulance and tell and retell all our stories, to plan future trips to Las Vegas, to think of wild rumors to spread about unsuspecting friends.

Finally, we got a legitimate call for an adult male with difficulty breathing. The door was opened by a home health aide. Our patient was only forty, but he was the largest person I had ever seen. Before I could even ask what the problem was, I had to ask him his weight.

"I don't know," he said. "The last time I weighed in I was over five hundred pounds, but that was a while ago."

Fat people cause us a lot of grief. I'm not talking about chubby or overweight people—I could lose ten pounds myself and Mike could probably lose a lot more—I'm talking about massively obese people over four hundred pounds.

"So what's the problem here?" I asked, as if not being able to stand up wasn't a problem in and of itself. "You said you're having trouble breathing."

"Yeah," he wheezed.

"You smoke?"

"Five packs a day for twenty years," he said, almost proudly. He most definitely had emphysema, and having all that fat resting on his diaphragm didn't help him breathe.

"Anything else wrong?"

"Uh, I have a small foot infection." Actually, both his legs were completely discolored and deformed with massive infections. There was no pulse in one foot and he barely had circulation in the other. He hadn't been out of bed for weeks, but he had to choose my shift to call 911.

"So, you want to go to the hospital, get everything checked out?"

"Yes." Mike and I stared at this guy, wondering what to do.

Fact: We had a patient who wanted to go to the hospital.

Fact: He needed to go to the hospital.

Fact: We wanted to take him to the hospital.

Fact: There was no way we could get him there. At least not without a lot of help.

I called the EMS dispatcher and explained the problem.

"You want me to send a backup BLS unit?" he asked.

"Negative, we're going to need more than that. Like a fire rescue unit with at least five more men and a stokes stretcher."

"Are you sure that's necessary?"

"Absolutely," I said firmly. Mike was still talking to the patient, trying to get a medical history out of him, but also distracting him from this very unflattering conversation.

During the ten minutes it took the ladder truck to arrive, Mike and I attempted to do a physical exam. It was unlike any exam I'd ever conducted. How do you palpate an abdomen that is so fucking big? Our blood pressure cuff didn't come close to fitting around this guy's arm. I wasn't sure if I was hearing his lungs correctly through all the layers of fat.

Even with the fire unit we had trouble. He didn't fit in their basket stretcher and ours had a maximum capacity of 350 pounds. The patient had his own wheelchair, specially built for superfat people, but he couldn't fit in it anymore. The two Midtown North police officers who had been assigned to this job got on their radios and requested that the Emergency Services Unit also respond. ESU didn't sound too enthusiastic about being assigned to "back up EMS and fire and police unit North Adam for an obese patient." An ambulance, a police car, and a fire truck, and we still needed help. We had an emergency services conference on the spot. I wondered how the patient felt about it: two medics, four police officers, five firemen, all to help him get to the hospital. Lucky for him he wasn't in acute distress.

We finally managed to get him out using two body bags—large, extremely strong canvas and rubber bags normally used to carry corpses. We used leather straps to wrap him in the bags, and then the eleven of us dragged him to the ambulance.

But that wasn't the end of the trouble. Our patient wouldn't fit in the back of the ambulance, not with all the stuff we usually have in there. We removed the stretcher and the stretcher mounts from the floor of the ambulance and slid the patient, body bags and all, onto the ambulance floor. We had to ask the fire department to bring our stretcher to the hospital for us. It was funny to see a fire truck with our stretcher on top of their ladder, going lights and siren to the hospital.

Then the hospital couldn't find a stretcher that could support the patient's weight. Someone eventually found a special stretcher for extremely obese people and we could finally turn him over, two hours after we first set foot in his apartment.

As soon as they got him in the hospital, he stopped breathing. I couldn't believe it. He was eventually intubated and taken up to the intensive care unit, but it was chaos: nobody could find a vein to start an IV, and it was almost impossible to intubate him because the fat around his neck made it almost impossible to move his head. Luckily at that point it was no longer our problem; it was the E.R.'s.

"Where do you want to go for lunch?" Mike asked me. We looked at each other and said, "Salads!"

A few weeks later I heard the fat guy was still alive

and had weighed in at close to seven hundred pounds. He was going to be taken up to the metabolic unit at St. Luke's. Our department usually handled the transportation of patients from Rosy to Luke's, but there was no way I was going to handle this guy again. I charged into the supervisor's office ranting, "Not me. No way. I'll call in sick. I'll hurt myself. I'll drive the ambulance into a brick wall first."

"Okay, slide another table over and put it on the end," someone called out as another few people stumbled into the restaurant. There were at least twenty-five people—hospital administrators, Rosy medics and EMTs, a few EMTs and medics from St. Clare's, and a couple of nurses—mostly blasted, and shouting war stories, usually focusing on gruesome ones involving Mike Gebhardt. It was his going-away party.

The nurses' curse on the Pre-Hospital Care Department had struck again, seriously this time. Gebhardt was diagnosed as having marfan syndrome, a condition that causes a weakness between the left ventricle and the ascending aorta, which in turn could lead to an aneurism. He had to retire.

I was very sorry to see him leave the hospital. He was a damn good medic and he had taught me a hell of a lot. And he wasn't just leaving the hospital; he was leaving the city. I was really going to miss him.

The party was held at a bar/restaurant down in Greenwich Village and the turnout was impressive. Mike had been at the hospital for years and was well-liked. The original plan had been for a few friends to take a few tables in the back, but the crowd kept growing bigger and louder.

"No, no . . ." one of the many half-blasted medics shouted out. "It was horrible. There was blood and body parts everywhere." The storyteller still had a huge smile on his face, as did everyone else at the table. Medics have no trouble talking about these things while eating. We're used to grabbing a slice of pizza right after dealing with gore. This is why medics, cops, fire fighters, nurses, and doctors tend to stick together.

"But that didn't stop Mike from doing. . . ." The storyteller continued his tale. A couple of civilians sitting at a nearby table rose to leave. They were hardly done with their meal.

"Was it something we said?" I laughed, pointing them out to the EMT sitting next to me.

"Hey, we drove out another pair!" he announced to the rest of the party.

I wondered how much longer the few remaining nonmedics in the restaurant would hold out. I gave them ten minutes, tops. Lay people almost always ask about the worst thing I've seen or treated, but they don't really want to know. When I start to answer, to describe what the bashed-up, mutilated body looked like with twisted flesh, pus oozing from where the head used to be, mangled bones, etc., the person who asked begins to look distinctly ill and asks me to stop. When I visit my parents, it's a reflex for them to ask me how work is going. I've learned to limit my responses to "I had a good/bad day." They're not really interested in the details, and especially not at dinner. Fair enough. I might ask a businessman how work was going, but it wouldn't thrill me to hear him go on forever about deals, mergers, and projected earnings.

It was Mike Roth's turn to tell a Gebhardt story: "Mike was yelling at this guy, 'Sir, you must relax your arm!' He was being real nice, but firm. 'Sir, you must relax your arm, I need to start an IV.'" I half listened to the story Roth was telling. I had heard most of these stories before, but somehow, they got better each time I heard them. The copious amounts of alcohol didn't hurt either.

"Then, finally, the guy relaxed his arm. And Mike, you know, relieved, says, 'Thank you for relaxing your arm, sir. Now you will feel a little stick." Then he looks up at the guy and shouts over to me, 'Oh shit, he's dead!' This guy just up and dies and all Mike can say is 'Thank you, sir, for relaxing your arm!'"

Not long after Gebhardt left, Jim O'Kelly got his degree in engineering and decided to take a job with the Metropolitan Transit Authority as a "Door Engineer." A door engineer? After being one of the top street medics in the city? I couldn't understand it.

There was another going-away party, this time at a medic's house in Queens, and another good turnout, but I was getting a bit sick of saying good-bye to everyone.

I looked around the department and found myself near the top of the seniority list. I didn't have to worry about getting stuck working holidays or about when I could take my vacation time. I was even functioning as an unofficial union rep, helping people write up their grievances with management. It felt strange. What happened to all the guys who used to run the show? Sean went up to management, Gebhardt and O'Kelly were gone, two other senior medics became bosses at other hospitals. . . . How can you expect to have good people on the streets when rookies are being broken in by other rookies?

The department had changed, and not for the better. Some of the new guys were good, but they lacked the devotion, dedication, and intensity that the old medics had brought to the job. It was definitely an attitude problem more than a simple question of years. Clare's was different, though. Aside from Maggie and Lucy, most of the medics there were also relatively new, with only one or two years of experience, but they were eager and willing to run around the city buffing calls. What they lacked in experience they made up for with enthusiasm.

CHAPTER 10

After about six months with Mikey, I found myself wondering again how long I could continue this way. I hadn't been able to stay away from the streets, I needed to be out there medicking, but now that I was back doing it full-time, I realized that I didn't want to do it five days a week.

I wanted to get away, to travel some more. I asked Roosevelt for another leave of absence, but I didn't really expect them to give it to me. When they refused, I quit. I think the bosses were surprised. With all the people in the department who were just doing the job to make ends meet or until they moved on to something else, I was one of the few who really seemed to thrive on it.

I knew I'd be back. My name was still on the per diem list. My friends and coworkers knew it, too. They threw me a little bon voyage party, but there were no emotional farewell scenes. I got one real gift, a Walkman, and some gag gifts, like a sideview mirror I had ripped off one of the vehicles, and an iron because my uniforms were always wrinkled.

"Yeah, see you," they said. "Have a nice trip."

I think Roth was actually sad to see me go, although it's always hard to tell when he's serious. Even if I came back, I probably wouldn't be working with him anymore.

Since American Medics International wasn't going to send business my way, I wondered if there was another way that I could combine emergency medicine and travel. At that time Saudi Arabia liked to hire American paramedics. There were always classified ads in the back of *JEMS* and *Emergency Services*. The money wasn't as good as it had once been—due to lousy exchange rates, I guess—but the benefits were interesting: lots of time off, free travel, free room and board, tax-free income. But a Shapiro in Saudi Arabia? I didn't think so.

I had been to visit my folks in China during my leave of absence. I went back there this time to stay with my sister, who had moved there after Morocco. My father and sister were both "Foreign Experts" in journalism there. The Chinese government hires "Foreign Experts" in all sorts of different fields. Maybe they could use a paramedic to help them set up their EMS system. I was taken on a tour of their new emergency medical center and entered into a series of discussions about this with various officials. But money was a problem, as were resources, timing, and bureaucracy. The concept went on hold.

I enjoyed my time away, but I didn't come to any

great realizations or decisions. I slid back into New York and right back over to Roosevelt. There were no full-time slots open at Rosy or Clare's, but I didn't want to work full-time anyway, so I figured I'd pick up occasional shifts. Somehow, though, I found myself "promoted" (demoted?) to per diem supervisor at Roosevelt. I still can't figure out how it happened. It certainly wasn't a deliberate career move on my part.

Instead of working an eight-hour shift on the street, I'd work a twelve-hour shift inside the hospital, overseeing shift changes, checking radios and narcotics in and out, keeping track of equipment, dispatching the private ambulance, and doing a lot of paperwork. Not exactly the trauma I thrived on, but I'd give it a try. What the hell. I'd still have lots of time to pick up per diem street shifts at Clare's whenever I wanted.

I did a two-day orientation to learn the job; it was about a day and three-quarters too long. The worst thing about the job, aside from the absolute boredom, was the cramped, windowless cell of an office. I didn't see the humor in the nurses' curse anymore, now that I had to work in there. I got along with most of the nurses, though, and they told me they had taken the curse off. I didn't fall mysteriously ill. I just got seriously bored.

Being management was less nerve-wracking than working the streets, but infinitely less interesting. In the Roosevelt Pre-Hospital Care Department office, I spent most of my time shuffling papers and answering phones. Definitely not exciting. It paid more, but that wasn't as important. I like the streets. I need the streets. As I had found during my leave of absence, I couldn't stay away from the "real" work. I began picking up more and more shifts at Clare's, and an occasional street shift at Roosevelt, too.

I was riding for St. Clare's with a young new medic named Peter "Skippy" Dworsky. He was wearing a pin on his collar that said, "I'm hungry for your blood." I'd seen a number of medics wearing pins showing a happy face with a bullet hole in the forehead and blood trickling down, but this one was a bit more original.

A craggy seventy-year-old lady got hit by a bus in front of the Port Authority. She insisted that she was okay, but she couldn't get up to walk away. If someone wants to refuse treatment, that's fine with me, but she has to get up and walk away. That's my criterion. But this lady, lying in the street, said she "didn't feel like it."

She jumped with pain when I felt her right leg, but she still said she was fine. She tried to stand but couldn't, and it looked like part of her leg was moving in the wrong direction. I told her we'd have to cut her pants to look at the leg, and she started screaming that we didn't have the right, that she'd report us to the police.

"Okay, report it to me," a police officer on the scene said.

I cut the seam of her pants to mid-thigh and there was another pair of blue jeans underneath. I cut those. Thermal underwear. Then knickers, then tube socks up to the knee. When I finally cut the socks, the blood poured out. She had an open tib-fib fracture. The tibia and fibia were shattered and sticking out, but she still insisted that she was fine.

"You're not fine. You broke your leg," we told her. She started screaming again.

"I didn't break my leg! That *bus* broke my leg!"

Skippy and I also got a call for a "woman who won't wake up." The call was only a few blocks from the Port Authority, which is definitely a magnet for lunatic behavior. This was a Hispanic household. At the risk of offending lots of people, I'll mention the condition known in EMS as "the hysterical Puerto Rican syndrome," usually involving a hyperventilating female screeching "AyAyAyAyAy."

The woman in question was around thirty years old and was not really unconscious. She failed all the standard tests. A truly unconscious person will let her hand, if held over her face, fall and strike her face. She let it slide off. Brushing a finger lightly over the person's eyelashes will provoke a small fluttering response if she's conscious at all. She fluttered, but she refused to respond. A number of people feign illness, but this was Academy Award–style acting.

There was lots of family about, but the only ones who spoke English were our supposedly unconscious patient and an eight-year-old boy. A lot of New York City medics speak Spanish, but I don't, and a lot of my partners don't. If we can find a competent translator, great. Otherwise, with no information from the patient, you can't do as much invasive care because of the risk of misdiagnosing. You have to stick to basic life support. Of course, when the patient is unconscious it doesn't matter if he can speak English or not.

We began to apply painful stimuli. I tried a sternal rub. No reaction. Skippy tried a neck pinch. No reaction. It began to seem funny—at least to us. Because of the language barrier, we couldn't explain to her family why we appeared to be beating her up. We started competing to see which one of us could do something worse to her without getting a reaction. Finally Skippy said, "Well, if she won't wake up, we'll have to draw some fluid out of her eyeball." I brushed an alcohol pad over her eyelids as if to prepare the area. That did the trick. She sat up and started screaming, "What are you, crazy? Get the fuck out of my house!"

A lot of the fakers have psychosomatic illnesses. They tend to be repeat callers, so you get to know them after a while. This usually saves a lot of trouble, but can occasionally screw you up, because one day a faker who always complains of chest pain may actually have a heart attack and you'll think he's still faking. It's the "boy who cried wolf" syndrome. Losing patience could mean losing patients.

Some people blatantly lie about their history. A patient may give you a realistic, credible story, but when you repeat it to the doctor in the E.R., he says, "Really? He's had two heart attacks? Since he was here last week?" That sort of thing drives me crazy.

Knowing that I was scheduled to work a street shift with Lucy for St. Clare's helped me get through a deadly dull week in the Roosevelt Pre-Hospital Care Department office. I was a full-time supervisor at Rosy now, mostly because they had offered me a shift that was too good to refuse: Sunday, Monday, and Tuesday nights. A four-day weekend.

When I put my street medic uniform back on, I felt like I had stepped back into my own skin. I seemed to fit in Thirteen Willie infinitely better than I fit in the tiny Pre-Hospital Care office.

Our first call that night was for a cardiac arrest at the Roseland dance center. That fit, too. Lucy and I had a history of always starting off the night with a cardiac arrest. I don't know why, but it always happened, and we always blamed each other for it.

Roseland is the only remaining old-style big band dance hall in the city. It's a little goofy in this day and age, but rather charming. When we got there, a small crowd was in the corner of the dance floor. Two people were doing CPR on an eighty-two-year-old man who had collapsed without warning while dancing.

The bystanders in this case were, at first, a great help. When a patient is in real trouble, you may need someone to hold up an IV bag. A cardiac arrest on the street without a backup unit is pretty tough to run without the help of people doing CPR. Over the years, I've become an expert CPR instructor, teaching people how to do it in ten seconds.

The whole crowd knew him and apparently loved him; he had been going there regularly for years. They shouted to him while we worked: "Come on, Charlie. You're going to make it. It's not your time yet. Don't give up, Charlie. We're here for you." It was impressive. Everyone wanted to help. We had two lines of people, one doing the compressions, the other squeezing the AMBU bag. When one person got tired, another would take over, and the verbal encouragement never stopped. Unfortunately, the arrest was not going well. All these people were shouting "You're going to make it!" and Lucy and I would look at each other and our eyes were saying "I don't think so."

When the BLS unit finally arrived, they tried to

take over the CPR and were met by hostile resistance.

"No, that's our job. He's our friend and we're going to do this." It took the police to get the bystanders back and let the professionals work.

There was still no hope for Charlie, but I don't think this is a sad story. An elderly man died without suffering, doing what he loved to do—dancing—surrounded by his friends.

The following night, my batteries recharged from working with Lucy, I signed up to work an extra shift on Fourteen Adam, Rosy's BLS bus. Working on the basic life support ambulance can be like a vacation. You're assigned to more calls and probably see more patients than the paramedics do, but most of the calls are lower priorities, most of the patients can walk, and you don't have to carry nearly as much equipment. I may sign up for an occasional BLS shift if someone I like will be working with me. This night I was working with Ann-Marie Connors, a pretty, blond EMT who recently married a Midtown North Cop.

We got a call for an Emotionally Disturbed Patient in the Midtown North Precinct. EDPs can be quite scary to deal with, even with police backup. There's a police-type stick behind the driver's seat in some ambulances. If a patient gets violent and out of control in the back of the ambulance, the driver might want to go to his partner's rescue. I've never had to use the stick, but it makes a good visual aid to warn someone off. The big flashlights medics carry can do the job too.

With an EDP, like a skell, it's easy to overlook medical problems, especially since you can't always trust what they tell you. You often shrug off their complaints as psychological.

Frequently people under arrest or acting crazy will be taken from the police station to a hospital for psychiatric evaluation. The police need this clearance before taking the suspects to central booking for arrest processing. It's usually very simple. The patient walks out to the ambulance, handcuffed. The arresting officer and one of the EMTs ride in back with the suspect, and you have a leisurely ride to the hospital. Not this time.

When we arrived, a police officer said, "I didn't call EMS, I wanted ESU. But hang out, we'll probably need you, too." You know you're in trouble when a whole precinctful of police is requesting an Emergency Services Unit to help them handle a suspect who's already locked up.

The suspect in question was about six feet, five inches, maybe 350 pounds, and he had a look that seemed to say, "I could pull your head clean off your neck if I wanted to." A convicted child molester with a long history of violent outbursts, he had violated a court order prohibiting him from visiting his mother, and she had turned him in. Even the guy's mother wanted him off the streets.

Incredibly, the cops who arrested him had no trouble taking him into custody. It wasn't until they got to the station and told him that he would be taken down to central booking that he went completely berserk. The inside story is that on one of his previous trips to central booking he supposedly got the shit beaten out of him by the cops, so the mention of central booking set him off.

When the ESU unit showed up with their large

handheld Tasser stun guns, I told the patient we were going to take him to the hospital.

"I want to go to St. Clare's," he bellowed. Ann-Marie and I looked at each other, both thinking, He *must* be crazy! No one ever *wants* to go to Clare's.

One ESU cop was telling him, "Sure, no problem," while I explained to the other that we couldn't do that because Clare's doesn't have psychiatric facilities.

"Once he's in the bus we can take him wherever we want," he said. And we did, but this guy knew the city too well.

"Why are we going downtown?" he screamed. He kept pulling at his restraints and scaring us all shitless.

"Uhhh . . . we're not," I lied nervously. "We're heading up to St. Clare's."

"Then why did we just pass the Thirty-fourth Street Y?" he roared. I looked over at the officer with us for an answer. Silently, he unbuckled his gun for easy access to it, and I figured I'd either be bludgeoned to death in the back of my own ambulance or be shot by the cop trying to save me.

Even with the EDP cuffed, it took eight people to get him on a stretcher at Bellevue. Even when he was finally tied down in six-point restraints—each arm and leg tied down, another strap across his knees, and one more across his chest—no one wanted to get near him or sign the ambulance call report to take official/legal responsibility for him.

The medics and EMTs on staff at Roosevelt were coming in late too often, and as a result, the in-service times of the hospital's ambulances had fallen. Something had to be done. The worst offender, predictably, was Ted Dunn. He had been late five times in the last two months. The next time he was late, the supervisor on duty would have to write up a disciplinary action form.

I was hoping like hell that someone else would get stuck with that mess. You could be nice to Ted, flatter him, make jokes, and he'd still give you a hard time. I didn't want to think about how nasty he could get about being written up, especially by someone who was still in high school when Ted was first certified as a medic. I never liked playing the heavy. I had so far avoided writing anybody up—I had never enjoyed getting the disciplinary forms, and I didn't think I'd enjoy giving them, not even when they were deserved.

Of course, the next shift I worked as a supervisor, Ted called around eleven-thirty P.M. to say he had gotten stuck somewhere and would be an hour late for his midnight shift. Damn.

I consulted the files and basically copied verbatim a written warning for chronic lateness that had been issued to someone else, inserting Teddy's particulars. I decided to pull Ted off service a half hour early to give him the write-up. I would be getting off duty then, and Sal, the day supervisor, would have already gotten in, so he could witness the action form.

It was common practice to have the union rep present to make sure a union member's rights weren't being trampled on. Mike Roth was acting as union rep that week, and I did not want him there. He might make a joke and piss Teddy off even more. Or I might crack up just looking at Mike. Ted didn't have much respect for me to begin with; it would be terrible if I went into hysterics when I was supposed to be disciplining him. I reluctantly sent a bus to Roth's house to pick him up.

"I can't believe you actually wrote up Teddy Dunn," Sal said. The tone of his voice could have been interpreted as meaning, "You've got balls," or "Boy, you're screwed."

"I know," I said nervously. "It's just a wimpy one, though. Chronic lateness." I waved the disciplinary action form in the air.

Mike waddled in, smiling. I kept thinking of all the times he and I had done something wrong and had been called on the carpet by a supervisor. Before going into the office, Mike would always give me a pep talk. "Remember," he'd say, "just deny everything. Deny, deny, deny. If they catch you lying, deny you're lying. If they have pictures of you doing it, deny it's you in the picture." We'd go in, the supervisor would ask, "Did you guys . . ." and Mike would immediately burst out, "Yeah, we did it! Hee-heehee!" and the two of us would laugh hysterically. This felt all wrong. I was on the wrong side of the desk.

With the three of us, the tiny office was already crammed full. Ted's tall thin frame appeared in the doorway, but there was no room for him to come in. His mouth was bent in a frown, outlined by his thick mustache.

"All right," he growled. "Let's get this over with."

"Okay, Ted," I said, trying desperately to ignore Mikey, which was impossible in such close quarters. "This is a written warning issued because of your chronic lateness." I could feel laughter bubbling up inside me, but I fought it down. "Technically, the rules say that you have to be on the premises, in uniform and ready to accept assignment by six minutes after the designated start of the tour. You have been late six times in the past sixty days." I went on to document each case.

"Sorry about that," I finished lamely. I handed Ted the form, and he looked at it without much interest. He didn't dispute the alleged incidents.

"Why isn't this a verbal warning?" he demanded. Verbal warnings disappear in ninety days; written warnings stay in your file forever.

"According to the books, chronic lateness, which you qualified for, warrants a written," I explained.

"Oh," he said, sounding dejected. "Hey!" he exclaimed suddenly, his eyes lighting up, "I called you before being late this time! Doesn't that count for anything?"

"Of course it does. I mentioned it in the write-up. See, right here: 'While it is appreciated that—'"

"So you're kissing me while you're fucking me," he said in more typical Dunn style.

"But I'm wearing a condom. With lubrication." I couldn't resist making the crack, and to my surprise, Ted started to laugh. I was so relieved that I burst into the laughter I had been suppressing. Mike exploded, too.

When the commotion died down, I asked Ted to sign the form.

"You know I don't sign those things," I nodded at Sal, who signed the form as a witness.

"You want a copy of this?" I asked Ted, separating the carbons.

"Uh, sure, why not? I'll just add it to the rest of them." He sauntered out the door.

"Well, that was fun," Sal said.

"Yeah. Not too bad," I agreed, relieved.

I decided to quit the supervisor job. I had my resignation letter typed out and was waiting for the right time to hand it in. I couldn't bear to sit in a four-foot-by-five-foot dispatch room anymore. A few more nights of being stuck in that paper-filled coffin and I'd be completely crazed. I was not alone in that feeling, and my boss knew it. All the supervisors were complaining. So the powers that be finally decided that our dispatch office was too small. No kidding.

The ambulance crew room, which was much larger and had two big windows looking out on the ambulance bay, was turned into a new dispatch office. Unfortunately, this left the EMTs and medics without a place to hang out before and after shifts and between calls. I still tended to think of medics as "us" and supervisors as "them," so I understood how the medics felt. I sympathized, but I really could not have stood working in the tiny, cursed room any longer.

With this change of office, however, the complaints I had outlined in my letter of resignation were shot to hell. They were making it very difficult to quit. More money, the perfect shift, and a much better office. I almost felt like I was selling my soul for a window. Actually, for two windows.

I was very apprehensive when I was scheduled to work another shift for St. Clare's with Gary Pollino. He had left Clare's to become a supervisor at Rosy, but like me, still did some per diem work on the streets. I hadn't worked with him since that terrible shift, the worst ever, when we ran over the poor alcoholic lady's dog.

I was pleasantly surprised. It was a great day. We handled thirteen calls, six of which were serious and required ALS skills, and maybe saved some lives. It was the kind of day that makes me glad to be a medic.

Except for one call, which came in as a Cardiac.

"Hey, this looks legit," I said quietly to Gary.

"I agree," he said, looking at the patient's arm for a place to start the IV. I turned back to the middle-aged man huffing and puffing in front of us.

"How long have you had the chest pains?"

"About two hours," he answered.

"And the difficulty breathing?"

"About four hours. But it got worse an hour ago."

He was pale, cool, and moist. When I listened to his lungs I heard some fine crackling sounds, rales. The EKG was slightly irregular.

"How many packs of cigarettes do you smoke?" I asked.

"One, one and a half."

"Tell me about your medical history again," I said, writing down his answers this time.

"I have heart failure. I had a heart attack two years ago. High blood pressure."

"Okay, let me recap," I said. "You woke up with slight difficulty breathing. You had that for a couple hours. Then you developed chest pains two hours ago. You said the chest pain feels like what?"

"Like . . . tight."

"Okay. Is it like the pain you had when you had your first heart attack?" He had told us that he had only had one heart attack. I was double-checking to make sure that he didn't change his story.

"Only one heart attack," he puffed out. "I have heart failure a lot."

"Compare the pain now to the pain you had when you had the heart attack."

"Similar. But not as bad."

"Okay, just try and relax." To Gary I said, "Grab me another set of vitals. I'm going to do a call-back."

Gary had started the IV and was drawing blood as I wandered into the patient's kitchen to use the phone. When I got the medical control doctor on the phone I presented the case.

"Doctor, Thirteen Willie, on the scene with a fifty-five-year-old male complaining of shortness of breath times four hours getting progressively worse with substernal tightness chest pain times two hours. Patient relates this chest pain to being similar to previous M.I. he had two years ago. Patient also states history of heart failure, high blood pressure, and smoking. He takes nitro and Lasix.

"Physical exam reveals skin that's pale, moist, and cool. Slight venous jugular distention. Lungs have bilateral rales at the bases. Abdomen soft, nontender, slight pedal edema. Vital signs are . . ." I looked to Gary for the answers and he called them out across the room.

"168/88 . . . 104 and slightly irregular . . . twenty-four labored . . . sinus tack with an occasional PVC." I repeated the numbers to the doc.

"Patient states he took two of his nitros a little while ago. I'd like to give him one of ours, give him sixty of Lasix IV, and start titrating the morphine up, start at three mg. and repeat every five minutes or so depending on his condition and vital signs."

"Okay, sounds good," the doc said.

"I'd also like to have Lidocaine on standby if the PVCs increase or become multifocal."

"Sure," he agreed. "Seventy-five mg. IV bolus with a three milligram a minute drip if they increase."

"Thank you, Doc."

"Where are you transporting to?"

"St. Clare's Hospital. It's just down the street."

"Fine. Do you want us to notify them?"

"No thanks. We'll do it."

"What'd we get?" Gary asked when I went back to the patient.

"Anything we want."

"Lidocaine?"

"On standby if those funny little beats start playing games."

We moved the stretcher out into the hall. Luckily the elevator was working; the patient was a big guy. By the time we got to Clare's, he was starting to feel relief. The nitro hadn't helped much, but the morphine had. His lungs didn't seem to clear much, but the chest pain was almost gone. I was feeling good, proud of having done good work.

We walked into the E.R., the nurse took one look at our comfortable, relaxed patient and rolled her eyes back.

"How's Mr. X today?" she asked tiredly. "Please don't tell me you gave him morphine." I felt like an ass. I looked angrily at the patient.

"Don't you know this guy?" she asked, amazed. "He's a junkie. He comes in here every month or so." I threw my hands up.

"Sorry," I said weakly. "He had a good story. Even had basal rales."

"Chronic pneumonias," an E.R. doctor said as he passed by. "He always has some rales." We had been conned. The man had lied about his history, invented the history of heart failure. He knew exactly what to say to get the drugs he wanted.

"Did you see any track marks?" I asked Gary.

"No. Did you?"

"No." I looked for them now and still couldn't find any. He had learned to shoot in other places. He was just a junkie, and we had worked our asses off for him.

It's unfortunate that junkies can sometimes score in the E.R. if their story is good enough. Some of them are really cagey and will read entire books on the subject to prepare. Recently, there was a note on the wall at St. Clare's warning medics that a Clare's regular who had signed out of the E.R. against medical advice had shown up in the Roosevelt E.R. requesting morphine for chest pain complaints. When it was refused, he pulled a knife on the E.R. nurses. They called the cops, but he got away before they came. They expect him to keep trying.

Some people do succeed, unless you can positively ID them as belonging to the category of "the scum that lie." Most of them look presentable, respectable, and have very complete, specific stories to tell.

"Last time I was in the hospital in New Jersey, they gave me that little pill under my tongue, but it didn't help. They gave me a shot of something called M.S.?" He *knows* that the pill under the tongue is called nitroglycerin. He *knows* that M.S. is morphine sulfate, but if his act is good and his timing is right, he'll score.

There are E.R. regulars who try different shifts and different days. Every July when there's a new batch of interns there are renewed opportunities to succeed with this kind of con.

After a while it begins to seem like everybody in this city is hooked on something. I don't see as many heroin ODs as I did when I first started, but crack is everywhere, and now there's ice. I occasionally see an icehead in Room 14, Rosy's psych room, completely strung out, paranoid, stomping on imaginary spiders and smacking imaginary bugs on the wall. It's gotten much more popular lately, God knows why. Its technical name is crystal methamphetamine, but it's basically just ground-up speed mixed with some other stuff and smoked like crack. I saw an article on it recently in *Rolling Stone*. Just what we needed, another trendy drug.

Maggie called to ask me to take a shift for her. As always, I took that as a compliment. Out of consideration for each other, neither of the Friskies took days off at the last minute unless they could find a partner whom the other considered acceptable. I started off the night with a good attitude. I liked working for Clare's, I liked working with Lucy, and I liked working nights. This one was a clear, mild October night, which turned into one of the most memorable shifts I ever had.

Our first call came at 19:53 hours as a "difficulty breather" on the top floor of a walk-up on West Forty-eighth Street. We arrived in four minutes and found a Hispanic woman wearing a housedress waiting for us in front of the building. There was also an older man yelling at us to hurry from the fifth-floor window. We pulled out the stair chair, oxygen, EKG monitor, drug box, airway bag, and charged up the stairs. You never actually run, no matter how serious the call. The few seconds you would save would be wasted as recovery time. You can't treat someone if you're out of breath. Still, by the time we reached the fifth floor, I was seriously thinking about using some of the oxygen myself. When you have a call on the street or in a building with an elevator, you can load everything onto the stretcher and wheel it painlessly. But a call in a walk-up involves carrying bulky, heavy bags. The oxygen tanks are only slightly smaller than the ones scuba divers use and weigh about fifteen pounds. The EKG monitor isn't any lighter. It's also a very expensive piece of equipment, so you don't want to drop or bash it on the handrail as you climb the stairs.

The patient was a seventy-year-old woman lying on her bed. It was obvious that this wasn't exactly a "difficulty breather," since she wasn't breathing at all and had no pulse. We should have known; Lucy and I *always* start the night with a cardiac arrest. We pulled her onto the floor and started CPR. As I called for a backup on the EMS radio, Lucy said, "This is your fault."

"Yours," I corrected her. We didn't have time to argue it out. As arrests go, this one was a bitch. It was a small apartment, too hot, not enough room to work, and it was full of crazed family members. One of the neighbors was helping us with the CPR since our backup hadn't arrived yet. The patient had been down for a while and, after twenty minutes of aggressive resuscitation attempts, we realized that there was really no way she would come back. She was just plain dead. We should have pronounced her then and left her there. There was nothing anyone or any hospital could do for her, but her husband and children were there and they weren't handling this very well, and there were reportedly other relatives already waiting for us to arrive at St. Clare's. We decided to transport her. It was purely a cosmetic move. She would either be declared dead by us or by the hospital. Either way, she's dead, but sometimes the family feels better if they hear it from a doctor in an emergency room.

Unfortunately, we now had to haul this dead lady down five flights of stairs and continue CPR. She was at least two hundred pounds and the stairway was small, creaky, and dark. It would have been okay if all four of us—Lucy, me, the two backups—could have each taken a corner of the scoop stretcher and carried her down, but only two people could fit on the stairway at a time. We kept switching off, stopping at each landing to put her down and continue CPR. The IV lines kept getting tangled. The AMBU bag got disconnected from the endotracheal tube we had placed in her lungs. We were working very hard to move a very dead person around.

When we finally got to the hospital, the staff looked at her for a few minutes, administered one more medication—epinephrine, which we had already given her five times in the field—and pronounced her dead. We knew it, but it made the family happy to think that everything possible had been attempted.

About an hour later we were cleaned up, the oxygen tanks changed, the drug box restocked, laryngoscopes cleaned, EKG monitor put back together, the ambulance straightened up. We were back on the road by 21:39. Thirty-six minutes later we were assigned to, yes, another cardiac arrest.

As I drove up Amsterdam Avenue, lights and siren, I said, "You know this is really your fault." It was time to finish the argument we'd started earlier.

"My fault?" Lucy moaned. "This *never* happens when I work with someone else."

"Oh, sure," I said condescendingly. "Well, this *never* happens when I work with anyone else either."

"Well, I'm full-time here so I can blame you."

"Well, since you're full-time I consider you more responsible for things than me. So this is really *your* fault." I had the last word because we were already at the scene, Amsterdam and Seventy-sixth Street.

The St. Clare's EMT unit, Thirteen Charlie, arrived a minute before we did. As we climbed up the stairs again with all our equipment, I was thinking that this was getting to be a real drag and that maybe I wouldn't sign up to work too many more shifts with Lucy. Luckily or unluckily, depending on your point of view, this guy was already dead. At least a few days dead. We had to push hard against his door to push the body back to get in. He was stiff as a board, blue and discolored, and smelling mighty ripe. It was an easy call for us: a few minutes of paperwork and we were out of there. The cops could babysit the body until the morgue guys came.

We drove over to Mrs. Field's Cookies for a snack but they were out of the type of cookie Lucy likes, so we said the hell with it and went back to the ambulance. As I was about to pull away from the curb, I heard rustling in the back of the bus. I hopped out and yelled at whoever was there to get out. It was a thirty-year-old black male, obviously homeless, carrying a somewhat lifelike doll under his arm. He was smoking a cigarette and taking a sponge bath with our Wetnaps. We had forgotten to lock the doors when we threw the equipment back in the bus after the last call, and he had gotten in when we went out for cookies. He didn't take anything; he just wanted to have a bath with his doll. I doubt this would happen to an ambulance crew in Idaho. I gave him a few Wetnaps for the road and kicked him out.

At approximately 23:46 hours we saw two guys beating the hell out of a third. The beatee was lying on the sidewalk getting kicked. Lucy requested a cop car over the police radio and I put on the lights and siren and pulled over to where the assault was taking place. The assailants jumped back into their car and drove away. The victim was shaken up and bleeding from his nose, which might have been broken. This was not a robbery or a mob rub-out type of thing. It was a simple case of idiocy versus real nastiness. The idiot was a twenty-seven-year-old who had moved from California to New Jersey three days previously. This was his first trip to New York City. He was crossing Forty-second Street and Seventh Avenue, right in the middle of Times Square, when the guys in the car started to run the light and cut him off. Whereupon the pedestrian gave the driver the finger and called him an asshole. Proving the pedestrian's point, the guys in the car got out, right in the middle of the intersection, chased him onto the sidewalk and started to pummel him. What they did was inarguably wrong, but this is New York. It's not smart or healthy to go around calling strangers names in Times Square at midnight. Our victim didn't want to go to the hospital, so we checked him out, cleaned him up a bit, and sent him on his merry way. The cops were nice enough to give him a lift over to the Port Authority so he could catch a bus back to Secaucus.

Three minutes after we finished with him, we were assigned to a simple call on Fifth Avenue and Sixty-ninth Street. An elderly lady had probably had a stroke, not her first, and we took her to Lenox Hill.

At one A.M. we were out of the Hill and returning to our area when we were assigned to a call in the Port Authority bus terminal for an elderly male cardiac/chest pain. Any call that comes in from the Port Authority or Penn Station is cause for apprehension— it's almost always one of the resident homeless, drunk and perhaps abusive, certainly smelly. Amazingly, this was not a street person with bugs but a sixty-seven-year-old gentleman with a suit, tie, briefcase, and an actual heart attack. More surprising yet, he was even more stupid than the kid from New Jersey.

He had already had a heart attack a few years before, had frequent angina and took an entire drugstore of cardiac medications. He had been in New Jersey on business that day when he started to have chest pains. He took his nitroglycerin, but got no relief. N.J. paramedics rushed him to a hospital where the doctors wanted to admit him to the intensive care unit. He wouldn't stay because he wanted to be home for the Jewish holidays. He signed himself out of the emergency room against medical advice and took a bus back to New York. Surprise, surprise: on the bus, in the tunnel, he had another full-blown heart attack. He arrived in NYC with no blood pressure. Had he stayed in N.J. for the usual three-day admit, he'd have gotten out of there with only an angina attack. Now he'd have to spend a few weeks in St. Clare's, and a large part of his heart would never work properly again. Is there something in the New Jersey water that makes people do stupid things and have to be rescued by NYC paramedics?

We were cleared from that call by 02:15 hours and it was quiet until 02:43, when we were assigned to back up a basic unit for a report of a person shot on the corner of Eleventh Avenue and Twenty-third Street. Lucy and I welcomed the call because things had gotten kind of slow, and I guess we weren't the only ones because several ambulances responded. Too many, considering that there wasn't anyone shot. False alarm.

At 03:25 we were sent up to Sixty-ninth and Broadway for an injury. Some wacko went berserk and started to break up one of New York's many all-night Korean delis, smashing glass and throwing things around. The owner had gotten a few deep cuts on his face from flying glass while trying to stop the madman. This should have been simple enough: stop the bleeding, wrap it up, take him to the hospital for some stitches. But he refused to leave the store because his only assistant had just arrived in the States and didn't speak English. After about fifteen minutes of insisting, he finally agreed to go with us to Roosevelt. Our conversation was limited and comical.

"It's not too bad," he said.

"No, it *is* bad," we corrected him.

"It's not okay?" he countered.

"Yes, it's not okay," we agreed. And then we started all over again.

When we got to Rosy, I asked them to try to stitch

him up really fast to let him get back to his store before he went nuts. I don't normally push for someone to be treated faster than the others, but I felt sorry for him. Some crazy broke up his place and I'd hate for him to get ripped off while getting stitches.

As we wandered out to our ambulance, we heard EMS dispatching a shooting call on West Seventy-fifth Street to New York Hospital medics Fifteen Victor. Normally that area would be covered by Fourteen Young. I didn't know where the Rosy medics were, but I was sure Lucy and I were closer to the call than Fifteen Victor. I grabbed the EMS radio and advised Dispatch that we were coming out of Roosevelt and would pick up the job. As Lucy was driving there with lights flashing and siren blaring, EMS advised us that it was possible that there were two people shot and that the gunman was still on the scene, possibly on the roof, shooting at pedestrians. Dispatch advised us to "use caution."

"No shit," I said to Lucy.

"You think we can give this one back to Victor?" she asked.

We arrived in front of the building at 04:03 hours. There was only one police car. There were a number of bystanders screaming that there were people shot on the fourth floor of this house and someone else shot down the block. The person shot down the block was supposedly walking around, so I wasn't too worried about him. We pulled the scoop stretcher out of the ambulance, immobilization supplies, trauma stuff, antishock pants, oxygen, and airway equipment. More steps, of course.

On the fourth-floor landing we found a white male, about twenty-five years old, about 225 pounds, facedown in a large pool of blood and brains. He had been shot in the head, the abdomen, and the pelvis. If he had been in arrest we wouldn't have done anything for him, just declared him dead. Brain matter on the floor is a good reason not to resuscitate. But this guy was still breathing and had a pulse. He was going to die, we knew that, and was probably brain dead already—organ donor material—but his body didn't know enough to die, so we had to go to work.

We applied a cervical collar and rolled him onto his back as best we could. We tried, with many bandages and multitrauma pads, to keep what was left in his head from leaking out. There was a lot of blood and other matter in his mouth, but he was clenching down and we were unable to open his mouth to clear his airway. I cut off his shirt, also cutting through three gold chains now caked in blood on his chest, and discovered the other bullet holes. To tell you the truth, I didn't really care. Just something else to note on the ambulance call report. The head wound was going to kill him.

After immobilizing him and giving him high-concentration oxygen, we started the difficult task of carrying him down the steps. Brownstones have small stairwells with tight turns, steep steps, and creaky guardrails, not ideal for carrying down a huge guy who's gushing blood from everywhere. I have to give Fifteen Victor credit for showing up even though we jumped their call. They helped us carry the guy down and even rode with us to the hospital.

Inside the ambulance we attempted to place either endotracheal or an esophageal tube into his throat, but it was still impossible. When a body is oxygen-starved, it often has spasms that cause muscle contractions. The jaw is one of the body's strongest joints, so it is sometimes impossible to pry the patient's mouth open to control his airway. You have to be careful when trying to force the mouth open not to get bitten when the jaw clamps shut.

As Lucy drove to St. Luke's, the nearest trauma center, I started an IV in the back. The patient always had a strong radial pulse so we never did put the antishock pants on him, which was a relief. Since Clare's doesn't have a laundry service, I try not to muck up the MAST pants when I work there. If you get blood and gook on them while working for Rosy, you can just drop the pants liner into the laundry, pick up a new one and be on your way, but at Clare's you have to hose them off yourself in the shower room. It's not very pleasant. Ironically, Clare's uses Gladiator brand MAST pants. I don't think the patients who need them would like to think of themselves as "engaging in a fight to the death for public entertainment," as Webster's defines the word.

We arrived at Luke's eighteen minutes from the time we arrived on the scene, including the time it took to carry the patient down the steps. When the emergency room guys eventually managed to intubate him, what was left of his brains leaked out of his mouth. Pretty gruesome stuff.

We had a chance to talk with the police after the call. They think this guy was an enforcer type sent into the building to hurt someone. This someone was either waiting for him or had someone else waiting for him and popped him first. Another case of life in the big city.

We didn't get another call for the last hour and ten

minutes of our shift. We relaxed down in midtown. After we were all cleaned up, Lucy went back to St. Clare's and had noodle soup for breakfast. I settled for a doughnut and a soda.

It was a great night, or a horrible one, depending on how you feel about it. I loved it. We worked our asses off. A lot of sweat and effort went into mainly dying causes. It was bloody and disgusting, but it was also challenging, unusual, and surprising. And yes, fun. It was good to know that after all this time, I still got excited by good calls, that I didn't mind running all over the city, that I still felt more comfortable inside the ambulance than almost anywhere else. I could go back to my office now and play supervisor at Roosevelt. I had had my fix. I was still trying to find some balance between my work inside and out on the bus. I wondered how long this fix would last.

"Thirteen Willie, you've got an unconscious female at the Hilton Hotel." The fix hadn't lasted very long. Had my shift with Lucy been a dud, I might not have wanted to get back to the streets so soon. Instead I was awake, psyched, and looking for another fun tour.

"God, I hate the Hilton," Maggie said as she drove over there.

"Why?" I asked, amazed. In an area full of skell holes, you would normally be happy to get a call somewhere upscale, where the patient was almost guaranteed to be a citizen.

"They're always so snooty there."

I knew what she meant. The fancy hotels don't like it when medics are called; they always want you to keep a very low profile. Sure enough, when we arrived, there was some momentary confusion over which set of elevators we were supposed to take up to the fourteenth floor. They didn't want us to take the regular guest elevators. Finally, we got upstairs. The security officer waiting for us at the room didn't seem too concerned and neither did the patient's husband, who was standing outside the bathroom door.

The husband, a soft-spoken, sixty-year-old British gent, told us that he and his wife had been doing the tourist thing, going to this building, that museum, all the restaurants. This evening, a lovely evening, they saw *Cats*, stopped for a cappuccino, and headed back to the hotel. His wife said she felt tired and had a headache. She decided to lie down and rest. Twenty minutes later she leaned over and threw up on the wall. Which was not pretty. She went into the bathroom, threw up again, and had a bad case of diarrhea.

No sweat. It sounded like a simple case of tourist tummy, food poisoning, or something equally benign. Happens all the time. By the time we got there, she was feeling better and didn't even want to see us. We weren't going to leave without checking her out, but if she felt better and didn't want to go to the hospital, fine.

The husband tapped on the bathroom door and slowly pushed it open. An elegant, sixty-year-old lady, who didn't look a day over forty, was sitting on the toilet, naked aside from the panty hose around her ankles.

One of us had to interview the patient and one of us had to continue talking with the husband. It would have made sense for us to go boy-boy, girl-girl, but, predictably, Maggie took the husband by the arm and led him away from the bathroom. I silently cursed

Mags as I entered the john and perched on the edge of the tub. Our patient was understandably embarrassed, but not feeling spunky enough to throw me out.

Her skin was a bit pale, slightly cool and moist, but that's only to be expected when you're puking and having the runs. Her blood pressure was a bit high, but not excessively. She had a history of high blood pressure and was supposed to take medication, but she didn't. Pulse and respiration rates were within normal limits. Pupils were equal and reactive, no photophobic reactions. No neurologic deficits.

We had a nice conversation. She told me she was Swedish. She and her husband lived in Italy. Her headache was just about gone, her stomach wasn't hurting anymore, and she wasn't nearly as nauseous. She didn't want to come with us to the hospital. Grēat. The ideal patient.

I nevertheless gave her the standard patter: "Why don't you come with us? I'm not a doctor, I can't tell you exactly why you're sick. It's not a big deal—I'm sure you'll be seen and sent back to the hotel in a few hours. Let's play it safe and take a ride over to St. Clare's Hospital."

Her husband was playing along. "Come on," he said, "let's take a ride with these folks. It'll be another New York experience."

She reluctantly agreed, but not without a bargaining session. She wanted to get completely dressed. I thought we had already spent too much time on the scene. And Maggie had whispered to me that she desperately needed to pee. We compromised: our patient pulled up her panty hose, put on a shirt, and we took the rest of her clothes with us.

She walked over to the stretcher, which she did not want to ride on. As Maggie was picking up the equipment, I checked the patient's vital signs again. Just routine. I felt for the pulse in her right arm . . . and couldn't find it. At first I was pissed at myself for not being able to find the pulse point, but after a few seconds I became concerned. I glanced at her face and immediately knew she was in deep trouble.

There's a medical expression, almost cliché now, that if you're on a bridle trail in Central Park and you hear hoofbeats, you can assume that the animal coming up behind you is a horse and not a zebra. Ninety-nine times out of a hundred, the obvious answer is the correct one.

When we first heard the symptoms—headache, nausea, vomiting—Maggie and I did discuss the possibility of our patient having a cerebral bleed. For about a split second. Then common sense prevailed. Both of us had seen hundreds of patients who complained of headaches and nausea and who did not have a life-threatening bleed. Incredibly, this lady did. Her eyes were wide open and scared.

I called to Maggie just as our lovely patient let out a loud exhale and started to seize. Maggie and I said "shit" simultaneously.

Things happened very fast. I forced an oral airway into the woman's mouth as she clamped down. She started to vomit, still seizing. I tried to clean out her airway as best I could without a suction unit. I pulled out an oxygen mask as Maggie hooked up the EKG monitor. The patient had a pulse and was breathing a bit but she was still actively seizing.

The patient's husband started screaming, "What's happening? What's happening? Darling, what's happening?" How do you tell a man his wife has just been trampled by zebras?

We felt terrible for him, but there was no time to explain anything. I worried about breaking the patient's arm as I forced it to unbend so I could start an IV. Maggie had her hands full pulling medications from the drug box and tossing them to me, so I handed the patient's husband the IV bag to hold up. Maggie ran to the phone and called St. Clare's for permission to administer IV Valium to break the seizures. She knows all the doctors at Clare's, so she got the okay within two minutes, during which time I had established the IV and stuck the IV tubing into the catheter sticking out of the patient's arm.

I reached behind me without looking to turn on the flow regulator on the IV bag, but my hand met only air. I looked around and saw why: the IV bag was being pulled farther and farther away as the patient's husband fell slowly backward in the act of passing out. Maggie caught him just before he hit the floor.

Things were getting out of control. Now we had two patients, one just hysterical, the other having her brain compressed and quickly losing any chance of living. We couldn't, wouldn't stop to treat the husband. We told him we were taking his wife to Roosevelt Hospital and opened the door to leave. We had planned to take her to Clare's before her brain started to become guacamole dip, but Clare's doesn't have a neurosurgeon on site twenty-four hours a day. Roosevelt is much better equipped for immediate action. The police from the Midtown North Precinct were in the hall.

"Hey, guys . . . this is a 10-55, right?" one of the officers asked. The police are required to notify someone when a patient goes to the hospital. They fill out an "aided card" and make phone calls. A 10-55 is when family members are present, so the cops don't have to make the notifications.

We pushed past them, pulling the stretcher toward the elevator, and shouted our answer down the hallway.

"Yeah, family present. He's lying on the bed. If he can't get up in two minutes, call another ambulance and get him to Roosevelt Hospital. That's where we'll be."

"Roosevelt. You got it," they said. They could see there was no time for questions.

"Hey," Maggie said on our way down in the elevator, "I don't have to pee anymore." We rushed through the busy lobby, shouting for people to get out of the way. So much for low profile. The EKG monitor was beeping, I had the IV bag in my mouth because my hands were busy forcing air into the woman's lungs with the AMBU bag. You'd think people would get the hell out of the way, but we had to physically push some morons out of our path. Inside the bus Maggie tried to place an endotracheal tube, but the patient was still clamping down too much.

Maggie gave the standby over the EMS radio as she drove toward the hospital. As I continued to ventilate our patient, I opened her eyes. Her right pupil got larger and larger until it was fully fixed and dilated. Then both eyes deviated upward and to the right. Her brain was dying.

They were waiting for us at Rosy and really busted their asses working on her. They controlled her airway, finally got her intubated, regulated her vital signs, stopped the occasional seizure and placed her on a respirator.

Her husband was brought in by the MTN cops a few minutes later. They were supposed to leave New York in two days. Now if she survived, and that was too close to call, she wouldn't be leaving for weeks, maybe months. Maybe she'd never be taken off the respirator at all.

The CAT scan taken that night revealed a huge cerebral bleed, way too deep for the neurosurgeons to go after, considering her unstable condition.

At first I went every day to the surgical intensive care unit to check on her. Then every other day. After a while, once a week. And then finally not at all. It got too depressing.

It's one thing to walk into a call scene and find an unconscious patient seizing or otherwise equally fucked up. But we talked to this lady. We liked her. She had a sense of humor and a personality. Now she had breathing tubes and a machine, EKG monitors, five different IV lines, catheters to remove body wastes, a distraught husband, an overseas family in ruin. And she might never even know it.

I stopped by Rosy on my night off to get my paycheck and to hang out with Sean for a while. Since he and I split the night shifts between us, I only got to see him at supervisors' meetings, and those aren't really good for socializing. Sean and I were outside while he took a cigarette break around two-thirty A.M. when Fourteen Adam came backing into the ambulance bay. They had a patient sitting on the padded bench, totally covered with sheets.

Bill, the department's newest EMT and my own

recruit from the Saltaire Fire Department, kicked open the back door and stumbled out, gasping for breath. Glenn, a more experienced medic, climbed nonchalantly out of the driver's seat.

"I don't know what all the fuss is about," Glenn said. "I didn't smell anything."

"You'll love this guy," Bill told me and Sean.

"Yeah," Glenn confirmed. "We made him a real swami."

J.J., who was just upgraded to medic status and was working on Fourteen Young that night, wandered over to lend a hand. We walked over to the back of the bus. The skell had fallen over, facedown onto the bench, his makeshift turban all crooked.

"Hey, wake up!" J.J. prodded him. The mystery man rolled slowly over. I had to laugh. It was Donald, my old regular. I had been wondering whatever became of him. I hadn't seen him around Columbus Circle in ages. I stepped closer to the bus and kicked him lightly on the bottom of his foot. Not hard enough to hurt him, just enough to get his attention.

"Donald!" I yelled. "Get up!"

Donald was not in a state to recognize anybody, but I didn't care. I was happy just to see him, in a warped way, happy to know he was still alive.

Bill was fumbling with the ACR, checking the name.

"Oh, Donald and I go way back," I told him.

"Yeah, I know Donald," Sean said. "You can cut it in half, you can chop it, you can burn it, and you can throw it away, but bottom line is. . . ."

I finished the thought for him: "You can't kill shit." Donald wasn't as shitty as most, he wasn't abusive, he just smelled really bad. But he was a survivor.

"All he says is 'I'm sorry, I'm sorry, I know I smell bad, I'm sorry.'" Bill sounded like he didn't know whether to be amused or sad. I knew the feeling. It was funny to see Bill not only starting to learn the same system in the same area, but actually treating the same exact patients.

I was having a typically slow night in the supervisor's office. Seth Greene and Joe Connelly, working Thirteen Willie, brought a patient into the hospital and stopped by the office to visit for a few minutes. When they got a call and went running out of the hospital, I stood miserably at the window, watching the ambulance pull out, lights and sirens.

One of the E.R. Attendings walked down the hall and into my office.

"What were they running off to?" He seemed concerned that the quiet early morning would suddenly be shattered by incoming patients.

"Forty-second Street and Seventh Avenue, in the subway, for three persons shot."

"That's got to be bullshit," he said, reassured, sitting in my chair. He picked up one of the radios and started pushing buttons.

"How do you get the downtown channels?" he asked.

"Here," I said, taking the P.D. radio from him and flipping the knobs to the correct division.

"If there *are* people shot . . ."

"They'll go down to Vinny's or over to Bellevue," I said.

"Good." He went back to fiddling with the radio. "I can't believe that you guys still run for reports of people shot."

I'm not running, I thought sadly. I'm stuck in a stupid office wearing a tie. God, I wish I were on the streets.

"Don't you get disgusted with all the garbage calls?" the doc asked. We could hear the first unit on the scene calling for a slowdown. So far they were unable to find anyone shot.

"Sure."

"Then why run?"

"Why not? Could be legit."

"Doubt it."

"Me, too."

"Then why bust your ass for some skell or druggie who gets popped?" He sounded like he really wanted to know.

"We don't really do it for them," I said slowly, thinking it out as I spoke. "We do it for us." The doctor put the radio down and swiveled the chair around to face me.

"Isn't it the same in the E.R.?" I asked. "Most of it's bullshit, but occasionally something interesting comes in, something you can really work on, something that challenges you. It's fun, isn't it? You get to think, to make a few life-and-death decisions. The adrenaline flows. It's fun. Isn't it? Occasionally?"

"Sure." He nodded slightly. "Once in a while. But to run for something at Forty-two and Seven in the subway at four in the morning. . . . You know it has to be garbage, and even if it's real, would three people shot in the subway be fun?"

"Yes," I said, suddenly sure. "Look, people are going to get shot whether we're there or not. They're going to get hit by cars or run over by subways or whatever. You can't change that. And, what the hell, we might as well be there to pick up the pieces. Someone has to be. This is a great job. Where else can you jump into the middle of mayhem and try to sort it out? In the middle of the most crazy, bizarre, violent, scary, disgusting situations, everyone looks to you to help them out . . . and then, no matter what, at the end of the call, you can just walk away. Good, bad, right, wrong, whatever. You just walk away and get ready for another call."

"And you guys like that stuff?" the doc wondered again, turning back to the radios.

"Love it."

I thought a lot about that conversation over the next few months. The supervisor job was supposed to be a promotion, more money, better hours and less stress, but it seemed more like a demotion to me. The excitement of working one busy street shift with unusual and challenging calls could carry me through a few weeks of routine office work, but why should I work a job that had to be gotten through when there was a job I loved doing just waiting outside my window? I may not want to do it every day, but I need to go out and play, to get my dose of trauma and excitement. I decided to quit the supervisor position and go back on the streets.

I still have trouble believing they pay me to do this. I haven't lost my enthusiasm for the job or for the occasional good call, but I no longer wish catastrophes on innocent strangers—well, not often anyway. I know I've mellowed over the years. I used to nearly jump out of my seat when Dispatch called us for an assignment. I didn't used to mind having my meals interrupted, but after gobbling down more than a thousand meals while sitting in the front seat of my ambulance I can honestly say that I'm getting tired of it. I remember being jealous when the previous crew would come back to the hospital for the change of tour relating some exciting situation they had come across. If I had originally been slated to work that shift but changed my hours, I would kick myself for missing that job. No more. I've come to accept, happily, that in a place like New York City, there will always be enough to go around. I even look forward to a peaceful shift now and then, perhaps because I feel that I no longer have anything to prove.

I hope people don't come away from this book thinking that most medics are burned out, that the EMS system is hopelessly screwed up, and that in case of emergency they'd do better not to call an ambulance. On the contrary. Most of the people, both in the administration and on the streets, are dedicated and competent. Problems in administration are only to be expected in such a large system. And ambulances save lives.

I don't have any mystical words of wisdom. The patients need help; the city's health care system needs help; but I don't have any easy answers. Just throwing money at it won't do it, not that New York is prepared to do so anyway. We need people committed to helping people, not struggling to keep their jobs secure. Make the positions of Emergency Medical Technician and Paramedic real professions. Let us retire after twenty years with full benefits, like the police and fire fighters do. Encourage people who have been on the job for seven or eight years to stay on. Most of the great medics who were at Roosevelt when I started working there are gone. The turnover rate is astronomical.

To the people of NYC: Hey! We're out here, overworked and underpaid, so please don't bust our chops. If you don't need an ambulance, DON'T CALL ONE. It's that simple.

I'll see you out there.

ABOUT THE AUTHORS

PAUL D. SHAPIRO graduated from the University of Michigan with a BFA in 1983. He has been an active volunteer fire fighter for more than ten years, and after six years, continues to work as a paramedic in New York City. This is his first book.

His sister, MARY B. SHAPIRO, is now a writer.

We Deliver!
And So Do These Bestsellers.